LEGITIMACY AND THE EUROPEAN UNION

Since the Maastricht ratification debate of the early 1990s, the legitimacy of the European Union has become a subject of controversy. With unprecedented force, Europeans have begun to question the need for deeper integration. Some fear threats to established national identities, while others perceive the emergence of a distant but powerful Brussels, beyond the reach of democratic control.

Legitimacy and the European Union breaks with established approaches to the problem of the legitimacy of the European Union by focusing on the recent trend toward reconceptualization of the EU not as a super-state or an organization of states, but as a multi-level, contested polity without precedent. The book examines the implications of this reconceptualization for the problem of legitimacy.

Individual chapters focus on policy areas, institutions, and identity politics. Taken together, they reach two main conclusions. While Europeans do not strongly identify with the EU, they increasingly recognize it as a framework for politics alongside existing national and subnational structures. And while the EU lacks central democratic institutions, the integration process has spawned significant informal and pluralist forms of representation. Rethinking recognition and representation outside the context of the nation state points to important, if little understood, actual and potential sources of EU legitimacy.

Thomas Banchoff is Assistant Professor of Government at Georgetown University, USA. **Mitchell P. Smith** is Assistant Professor of Political Science at Middlebury College, USA.

LEGITIMACY AND THE EUROPEAN UNION

The contested polity

Edited by Thomas Banchoff and Mitchell P. Smith

London and New York

First published 1999
by Routledge
11 New Fetter Lane, London EC4P 4EE

Simultaneously published in the USA and Canada
by Routledge
29 West 35th Street, New York, NY 10001

© 1999 Selection and editorial matter, Thomas Banchoff
and Mitchell P. Smith; individual chapters, the contributors

Typeset in Baskerville by
M Rules
Printed and bound in Great Britain by
MPG Books Ltd, Bodmin

British Library Cataloguing in Publication Data
A catalogue record for this book is available from the British Library

Library of Congress Cataloging in Publication Data
Legitimacy and the European Union: the contested polity / edited by
Thomas Banchoff and Mitchell P. Smith.
Includes bibliographical references and index.
1. European Union.   2. European federation.   3. Legitimacy of
governments – Europe.   I. Banchoff, Thomas.   II. Smith, Mitchell P.
JN30.L43   1999
341.242′2 – dc21   98–38355

ISBN 0–415–18188–7 (hbk)
ISBN 0–415–18189–5 (pbk)

CONTENTS

PART 3
Legitimacy and identity

ILLUSTRATIONS

Figures

Tables

CONTRIBUTORS

Thomas Banchoff is Assistant Professor of Government and a member of the Executive Committee of the Center for German and European Studies, Georgetown University. His publications include: *The German Problem Transformed: Institutions, Politics, and Foreign Policy, 1945–1995* (forthcoming); and "German Policy Toward the European Union: The Effects of Historical Memory," *German Politics* (April 1997).

Udo Diedrichs is Lecturer in Political Science and a research fellow at the University of Cologne. He is currently working on EU–Latin American relations. His publications include: "The EU and Mercosur: A New Kind of Group-to-Group Dialogue?" in Geoffrey Edwards and Elfriede Regelsberger (eds) *Europe's Global Reach: Group to Group Dialogues* (forthcoming); and "National Views and European Cleavages: From the Single European Act to the Treaty on European Union," in Franco Algieri and Elfriede Regelsberger (eds) *Synergy at Work: Spain and Portugal in European Foreign Policy* (1996).

Lily Gardner Feldman is Senior Scholar in Residence at the Center for German and European Studies, Georgetown University. She was previously Associate Professor of Political Science at Tufts University, and Research Director of the American Institute for Contemporary German Studies/The Johns Hopkins University. Her numerous publications have focused on the EU as an international actor, US–EU relations, and Germany's role in the European Union. She is writing a book on the principle and practice of reconciliation in Germany's relations with Israel, France, the Czech Republic, and Poland.

John Gaffney is Professor of French and European Politics at Keele University, UK. He is the author of *The French Left and the Fifth Republic* (1989), and *The Language of Political Leadership in Contemporary Britain* (1991). He has edited eight books on French and European politics, most recently *Political Parties and the European Union* (1996), and *French Presidentialism and the Election of 1995* (1997) with Lorna Milne. He is currently conducting research for a book on political leadership.

Rey Koslowski is Assistant Professor of Political Science at Rutgers University, Newark. His publications include: "EU Migration Regimes: Established and Emergent," in Christian Joppke (ed.) *Challenges to the Nation-state* (1998);

"Migration and the Demographic Context of European Political Institutions," in Emek Ucarer and Donald J. Puchala (eds) *Immigration into Western Societies* (1997); and "Intra-EU Migration, Citizenship, and Political Union," *Journal of Common Market Studies* (September 1994).

Robert Ladrech is Lecturer in Politics at Keele University, UK. His work focuses on social democratic parties, French politics, and European integration. He has co-authored *Europe since 1945: A Concise History* (1996), and has published widely in books and journals. He is currently preparing a manuscript on the relationship between social democratic parties and the European Union.

Gary Marks is Professor of Political Science and Director of the UNC–CH Center for European Studies. He is currently Chair of the European Community Studies Association (USA). His most recent books are *Governance in the European Union* (1996) with Fritz Scharpf, Philippe Schmitter, and Wolfgang Streeck, and *Continuity and Change in Contemporary Capitalism* (forthcoming) with Herbert Kitschelt, Peter Lange, and John Stephens.

Melissa Pantel is a doctoral candidate in the Department of Government, Georgetown University. She was a university fellow from 1993 to 1996. Her fieldwork explores the impact of European integration on the relationship between French regional language groups and the French state. She held a Davis teaching fellowship at Georgetown University in 1997–98.

Mitchell P. Smith is Assistant Professor of Political Science at Middlebury College. During 1996–97 he was a Fulbright Fellow in European Union Affairs and Visiting Scholar at the Centre for European Policy Studies in Brussels. His most recent publication is "Facing the Market: Institutions, Strategies and the Fate of Organized Labor in Germany and Britain," *Politics and Society* (March 1998). His work has appeared in *Journal of Common Market Studies*, *West European Politics*, and *Journal of Legislative Studies*, and he is currently writing a book on the relationship between political participation and political development, placing the EU in a comparative context.

Wolfgang Wessels is Professor of Political Science at the University of Cologne, Professor at the Department of Administrative and Political Studies at the College of Europe, Bruges, and Chairman of the Trans European Policy Studies Association (TEPSA), Brussels. His recent publications include: "An Ever Closer Fusion? A Dynamic Macropolitical View on Integration Processes," *Journal of Common Market Studies* (Summer 1997); "The Growth and Differentiation of Multi-level Networks: A Corporatist Mega-bureaucracy or an Open City?" in Helen Wallace and Alasdair R. Young (eds) *Participation and Policy-making in the European Union* (1997).

Carole Wilson is a PhD candidate at the University of North Carolina at Chapel Hill. Her current research focuses on political parties in Europe and Latin America.

ACKNOWLEDGMENTS

This project developed over a two-year period, and benefited greatly from lively interaction among the contributors. It is to this group that the editors owe their first debt. We met twice as a group, in Washington and Brussels, to critique one another's work and to develop some shared – and contested – approaches to the problem of legitimacy in the European Union.

The group was constituted as a Research Planning Group funded by the Council for European Studies. Ioannis Sinanoglou of the CES provided helpful comments on an early draft of the project proposal. He also later encouraged us to present the findings of the Research Planning Group at the March 1998 Conference of Europeanists in Baltimore. The panel provided excellent feedback as the volume was nearing completion.

Georgetown's Center for German and European Studies funded and hosted our first contributors' conference in January 1997. We would like to thank Professor Samuel Barnes, the Center Director, and Natalie Cook-Dristas, the Center Administrator, for their active support. Kim Natoli's organizational skills and conference assistance proved invaluable. Desmond Dinan and Carl Lankowski were excellent commentators on the papers.

A second conference took place in May 1997 at the Centre for European Policy Studies in Brussels. We are grateful to Peter Ludlow for generously making available the Centre's conference facilities, and to Catherine Chanut and Anne Marie Boudou for organizational assistance and culinary advice. We also thank the Council for European Studies for its financial support for this meeting.

Finally, we would like to thank our families. Anja Banchoff and Lynn Lewis provided encouragement and vital editorial assistance. Our children were a source of loving support and welcome distraction throughout. We dedicate this volume to all of them: Emma, Luisa, and Sophie Banchoff, and Micah and Megan Smith.

Thomas Banchoff
Mitchell P. Smith

1

INTRODUCTION

Conceptualizing legitimacy in a contested polity

Thomas Banchoff and Mitchell P. Smith

The uncertain state of the European integration project at the close of the twentieth century raises questions about its very legitimacy. The 1992 Maastricht Treaty marked an ambitious effort to deepen the European integration process. Following the launching of the single market program, European Union (EU) leaders embraced the goals of Economic and Monetary Union (EMU) and deeper political integration. During and after the Maastricht ratification debates, however, European integration lost political momentum. In 1992–93, Danish voters initially rejected the Treaty, French voters barely approved it, and a divisive British debate delayed its ratification. With an unanticipated persistence, Europeans began to question the need for, and costs and benefits of, the integration process. They displayed little enthusiasm for elections to the European Parliament, the EU's only directly representative body, and for the activist leadership of the European Commission under Jacques Delors. In this new context, European elites could no longer forge ahead as they had over the previous decade. The restrained ambitions of Delors's successor, Jacques Santer, reflected uncertainty about the future of integration, as did the modest outcome of the Maastricht follow-up conference that ended with the June 1997 Treaty of Amsterdam.

These developments have sparked a debate about a crisis of legitimacy within the EU. The growing scholarly literature focuses on two dimensions of the perceived crisis – a lack of popular identification with the EU and the undemocratic structure of its institutions. On the one hand, scholars have argued that Europeans do not recognize the EU as an appropriate sphere for politics, as they do the nation state. From this perspective, the EU lacks the levels of affective attachment and identification essential for legitimacy. On the other hand, scholars have contended that the European Parliament, unlike its national counterparts, is too weak to provide effective democratic representation. They critique the most powerful European institutions – the Council of Ministers and the Commission – as unaccountable to European citizens. While one set of scholars draws on survey data to confirm low levels of recognition, the other seeks to establish that institutions do not provide sufficiently for representation and accountability. From different directions, both converge around the diagnosis of a legitimacy crisis within the EU.

This book challenges this diagnosis. We define a legitimate polity as a broadly recognized framework for politics with representative institutions. But we argue that a focus on popular attitudes and central institutions reflects categories of analysis derived exclusively from the experience of the nation state, and which therefore do not capture the dynamics of recognition and representation in the EU. Increasingly, scholars of European integration have broken with those categories. They have reconceptualized the EU not as a superstate or an international organization, but as a multi-level polity marked by the coexistence and interaction of European and national institutions. This book examines the implications of this reconceptualization for the problem of legitimacy. It points to patterns of recognition and representation which, while they do not fit established categories, nevertheless constitute actual and potential sources of legitimacy. We argue, first, that while Europeans do not strongly identify with the EU, they increasingly recognize it as a framework for politics alongside existing national and subnational arenas; and, second, that while the EU lacks strong central democratic institutions, the integration process has created significant informal and pluralist forms of representation.

The book's subtitle, "The contested polity," captures both dimensions of legitimacy within the EU. First, it highlights the fact that the EU has emerged as a recognized framework for contestation. Political mobilization around critical issues, from regional development policy and environmental and consumer protection to competitiveness and employment, is increasingly taking place on the European level. A wide range of actors, from consumer and environmental activists through political, business and labor elites, have come to recognize the EU as an appropriate place to contest policies. This recognition is not universal. Some nationalist critics, concerned about threats to established identities, reject integration in principle. In practice, however, European elites and publics have managed to participate in the integration process – to contest a variety of policies – while maintaining established identities, national and subnational. Such patterns of contestation, we argue, suggest not the weakness but the strength of the European polity. They provide evidence not of the absence of legitimacy but of its emergence. For while Europeans bring contrasting interests and identities to the integration process, they have increasingly come to recognize the EU as a productive arena in which to pursue their objectives.

"The contested polity" refers not only to political contestation at the European level, but also to the contested structure of the EU as a whole. European elites and European publics share no uniform sense of what the EU should look like and where it is headed; its competences and institutional make-up have been, and will likely remain, the object of political conflict. The fact that the EU is a contested, evolving, multi-level polity rules out established patterns of democratic representation through a fixed set of central institutions. At the same time, however, its structure allows for new forms of representation at the intersection of European and national institutions. Parties and interest groups – traditional democratic links between society and the state – are forging new patterns of representation at the European level. And key European institutions, the Commission and the

Parliament in particular, are responding by interacting more closely with and becoming more responsive to societal interests. New forms of representation within the EU, less formal and centralized, are not displacing existing national forms, but are interacting with them in new ways. Moreover, these new patterns of representation, like the new patterns of recognition discussed above, do not require the emergence of an overarching European identity. They are compatible with – and indeed help to sustain – a variety of different national and subnational identities within the integration process.

While the book challenges the thesis of a legitimacy crisis, we do not deny that the EU is engaged in a difficult legitimation process. Some Europeans still refuse to acknowledge the EU as an appropriate venue for politics and policy-making. And new forms of democratic representation are not adequately developed; in many respects, the EU remains an elite-dominated enterprise. Moreover, there is no denying the perception of a legitimacy crisis, whether justified or not. In casting the legitimacy problem in a new light, this book is not intended to dismiss perceptions of a crisis or to serve as an apology for the status quo. Instead, it aims to conceptualize the legitimacy issue in terms that better fit the reality of the EU as a contested and evolving polity. In the process, it points to often overlooked sources of legitimacy, actual and potential.

This chapter sets out the analytical approach that informs the entire volume. A first section discusses the treatment of the legitimacy problem in political theory and integration theory. Political theory points to the importance of combining the recognition and representation dimensions of legitimacy – and to possible ways of doing so outside the established context of the nation state. For the most part, however, approaches to legitimacy in the theoretical literature on European integration draw on statist models. A second section then critiques the two established research agendas in EU studies that address the legitimacy problem: work on public opinion, which often casts citizen orientations in static terms that obscure the significant degree of recognition of the EU as a framework for politics; and work on the "democratic deficit," which tends to focus narrowly on formal institutions and to miss other forms of representation. A third section sets out an alternative approach to legitimacy, recognition, and representation, grounded in an understanding of the EU as a multi-level polity. The final section shows how subsequent chapters draw on, illustrate, and extend that approach in a variety of empirical contexts.

Legitimacy in the theoretical literature

Neither political theorists nor theorists of European integration have devoted much attention to the problem of legitimacy in the context of the EU. Classic theories of legitimacy developed in the context of city states, empires and nation states; their assumptions naturally reflect the political environments within which they emerged. Nevertheless, contemporary political theory does provide a starting point for thinking about legitimacy in the context of the EU. By contrast, major theories of European integration, to the extent that they have addressed the legitimacy issue at all, have done so obliquely. Neofunctionalism suggests a valuable approach to legitimacy in terms of recognition by elites of the European polity, but neglects its representation dimension. Intergovernmentalism and federalism, while attentive to both dimensions of the legitimacy problem, approach it within familiar statist categories. As a result, the established theoretical approaches cannot capture the dynamics of EU legitimacy in the 1990s.

Max Weber's conceptualization of legitimate domination provides a backdrop for contemporary discussions of political legitimacy. Weber defined legitimacy in empirical terms as "belief in legitimacy" (Weber, 1978: 213). Where political subjects recognize rule as legitimate, he argued, it can be considered legitimate. Weber set out a threefold typology distinguishing rational-legal, traditional, and charismatic foundations for legitimate authority. Legitimacy, he maintained, could consist of the recognition of efficiency and the rule of law, of continuity with valued past practices, or of the personal qualities of individual leaders. In keeping with his commitment to value-free social science, Weber did not consider some foundations of legitimacy superior to others. His approach to legitimacy as an empirical, not a normative, matter informed much subsequent research. After the Second World War, for example, Gabriel Almond and Sidney Verba used newly developed survey techniques to measure legitimacy in terms of aggregate levels of support for and identification with particular institutions (Almond and Verba, 1963).

While the Weberian tradition approaches legitimacy as an empirical problem, democratic theory considers it a normative one as well (Held, 1984; Connolly, 1984; Beetham, 1991). Whatever their internal differences, democratic theorists insist that legitimacy entails not only recognition but representation. During the early modern period, John Locke and Jean-Jacques Rousseau argued that legitimate rule derived from the will of subjects expressed through representative institutions. The nature of representation in a legitimate polity – the proper relationship between ruler and ruled – remains the object of ongoing controversy. To what degree should leaders be accountable? To what degree should citizens participate in governance? Despite the proliferation of answers to these and other questions, democratic theory remains the dominant normative approach to the problem of legitimacy. Fascist and Marxist–Leninist alternatives have fallen by the wayside over the course of this century. As a result legitimacy has become almost synonymous with democratic legitimacy (Dahl, 1989).

Both dimensions of legitimacy – recognition and representation – are relevant in the context of the EU. Until recently, however, political theorists have explored these dimensions mainly in the context of the nation state. Weber defined the state in unitary terms as a monopoly of legitimate violence within a given territory. His statist orientation is of limited relevance to the European Union, with its divided and overlapping sovereignties. And democratic theorists from Locke and Rousseau onward have tended to focus on legitimate governance within a statist framework. Their emphasis on popular sovereignty and central democratic institutions does not fit the reality of a European Union in which nation states and supranational institutions exist side by side. These analytical categories reflect the political context within which modern empirical and normative theory developed: the rise and consolidation of nation states. The challenge in the EU context is to apply theoretical insights to new circumstances, to rethink recognition and representation in a new kind of polity.

Contemporary political theory suggests some of the directions that such a rethinking might take. Jürgen Habermas, for example, has sought to move democratic theory away from its focus on the "people" conceived as part of a nation. Legitimate rule, he argues, emerges instead where rational discourse, not bonds of ethnicity or culture, informs collective action (Habermas, 1984). Charles Taylor has addressed the implications of national, ethnic and cultural diversity for democracy. He argues that the mutual recognition of difference, both within and across societies, is vital for political legitimacy (Taylor, 1992). David Held has underscored the importance of reconceptualizing politics and democratic theory in an international context. Limits on national sovereignty and the emergence of a global civil society, he argues, challenge established statist approaches to the legitimacy issue (Held, 1995). These and other political theorists have not developed new approaches to recognition and representation explicitly in the context of the European Union. But their efforts to examine the issues outside the context of the nation state provide a starting point for thinking about legitimacy and the EU.

Established theories of integration, while they approach the problem of legitimacy and the EU more directly, do so inadequately (Caporaso and Keeler, 1995). Neofunctionalism goes furthest in addressing the issue (Haas, 1958; Lindberg and Scheingold, 1970). As a theoretical perspective, neofunctionalism views integration as an elite-led self-sustaining process driven by the logic of spillover. Writing in the 1950s, Ernst Haas acknowledged the recognition dimension of legitimacy. He argued that political elites had increasingly come to recognize the relevance and value of supranational policies (Cram, 1997: 16). Further developing the thrust of Haas's argument, Leon Lindberg and Stuart Scheingold contended that those elites with the greatest stake in the economic aspects of the Community – "industrialists, bankers, traders" and government officials responsible for national economic policy – had come to view it as a critical arena in which to pursue their objectives (Lindberg and Scheingold, 1970: 78). They noted that "one of the most striking phenomena of European integration has been the extent to which interest groups, parties, and other elites have come to accept the emerging Community system as a proper and legitimate framework in which to seek to achieve their goals" (Lindberg and Scheingold, 1970: 122).

The neofunctionalist approach to legitimacy has limited relevance in the post-Maastricht context. In some respects, Haas and Lindberg and Scheingold broke with statist categories in their approach to legitimacy as recognition. Haas's original formulation did suggest the possibility of movement beyond the nation state: a broad shift in identification toward a "new centre" and the creation of "a new political community, superimposed over the pre-existing ones" (Haas, 1958: 16). But Lindberg and Scheingold, more cautious about the prospects of a "new centre," anticipated the possibility of multiple, coexistent levels of government, and less centralized patterns of recognition. The greater problem with the neofunctionalist approach to legitimacy is its neglect of the representation dimension. Haas posited that a permissive societal consensus would continue to sustain integration as an elite-driven, technocratic process. By contrast, Lindberg and Scheingold recognized the potential for integration to activate constituencies among broader segments of society. They discerned, for example, the emergence of a "supranational interest group network." At the same time, however, they viewed politicization not as a means toward greater legitimacy, but as a potential danger for the "legitimacy of the technocratic Community system" (Lindberg and Scheingold, 1970: 269).

Two other established approaches to European integration, intergovernmentalism and federalism, are attentive to both the recognition and representation dimensions of the legitimacy problem. But they continue to take the model of the nation state as their analytical point of departure. Intergovernmentalism rests on the assumption that nation states and national interests drive the integration process. The intergovernmental perspective is closely bound up with a realist tradition that conceives of European nation states as both powerful and legitimate, the political expression of popular sovereignty (Hoffmann, 1982; Milward et al., 1993; Taylor, 1996). Because people recognize and identify with nation states, and because state institutions are democratic, they enjoy political legitimacy. As a theoretical approach, then, intergovernmentalism illuminates political concerns about an erosion of national identity and institutions – concerns that have grown more vocal in the wake of Maastricht.

Federalists view the European Union not as an organization of sovereign nation states but as a kind of super-state in the making (Williams, 1991). Legitimacy at the European level, from this perspective, depends both on the emergence of an overarching European identity and on the creation of central European institutions accountable to European citizens. To the extent that Europeans, bound by a common history, culture, and political values, identify with one another and with European institutions, they will foster EU legitimacy (Wallace, 1993: 101). And, to the extent that those institutions represent and are responsive to European citizens – and not simply member-state governments – they will have the same effect (Neunreither, 1994). Like intergovernmentalism, federalism sheds some light on broadly articulated concerns in the wake of Maastricht – concerns about the EU's "democratic deficit." Scholars in this tradition argue that the absence of democratically legitimate central institutions, such as a European Commission more accountable to a stronger European Parliament, threatens to undermine support for the integration project as a whole.

While federalism and intergovernmentalism approach the legitimacy problem from different perspectives, both draw on traditional statist perspectives (Schmitter, 1996: 132). Each conceives of recognition in terms of shared identification and of representation in terms of central democratic institutions. From an intergovernmentalist perspective, identification with national institutions, reinforced by bonds of shared history, culture, or ethnicity, constitutes legitimacy through time. The nation state is legitimate because its central political institutions express popular sovereignty – the consent of the citizenry. From a federalist perspective, the EU is legitimate to the extent that European citizens, bound by a shared sense of history and culture, identify with it, and to the extent that its central institutions represent their will. Federalists do not want to do away with nation states and national identity. But they insist on the importance of more robust institutions and identities at the European level if the EU is to win broader legitimacy. For intergovernmentalists, then, the model of shared identification and central democratic institutions remains valid in the context of its original embodiment: the nation state. For federalists, by contrast, that same model is relevant in the context of an emergent super-state.

These theoretical approaches to European integration, like the broader trends in political theory upon which they draw, do not address the legitimacy problem in terms appropriate to the EU. The drive to deepen integration since the 1980s has fostered the emergence of a complex, multi-level polity in which European, national and subnational institutions exist side by side. Within this new context, the definition of legitimacy in terms of common identities and shared institutions necessarily leads to the diagnosis of a legitimacy crisis. With its multiple and overlapping identities and institutions, the EU is not, and will not likely become, either simply an organization of sovereign, democratic nation states or a kind of supranational democratic state. This book explores ways to rethink the problems of legitimacy, recognition, and representation in terms more appropriate to the evolving nature of the EU polity. Before setting out an alternative research agenda along these lines, we describe and critique existing empirical work grounded in established theoretical categories.

Established research agendas: public opinion and the democratic deficit

Since the Maastricht ratification crisis, increasing numbers of empirically oriented scholars have addressed problems of democracy and legitimacy within the EU (Andersen and Eliassen, 1996; Niedermayer and Sinnott, 1995; Garcia, 1993). Most more recent work falls into two broad categories: public opinion and European institutions. Work on public opinion and the orientation of citizens reflects a concern with legitimacy conceived as recognition. Here, scholars have drawn links between a lack of affective attachment to the EU and the depth of the latter's legitimacy problem. Work with an institutional focus approaches legitimacy from the perspective of representation. Scholars have discerned a "democratic deficit" where central European institutions do not conform to the traditional democratic pattern, or inhibit legitimate democratic institutions at the national level. While both literatures reveal important problems in European construction, neither confronts very directly the meaning of legitimacy in the context of an emerging polity that does not fit the statist pattern. A critique of each will serve as a starting point for the development of an alternative approach.

Public opinion

Since the Maastricht Treaty ratification debates, many scholars have explored patterns of support for and identification with the European Union at the level of public opinion (Niedermayer and Sinnott, 1995; Anderson, 1995; Franklin *et al.*, 1994). The most recent comprehensive survey of opinion data, carried out by a research team under the leadership of Oskar Niedermayer and Richard Sinnott, points to a "renationalization" of public opinion since the early 1990s, reversing the process of "Europeanization" that took place during the 1980s. The process, strong in Britain, Spain, Germany, and France, is striking because the net decline in support appears to be a product of strengthened opposition to the EU rather than indifference (Niedermayer, 1995: 71). Furthermore, the data suggest that aggregate gains in diffuse support during the late 1980s were the result of upward trends in newer member states. According to Niedermayer, member states of long standing "reached an upper limit in the level of public support" which can "only be increased slightly in the long run" (Niedermayer, 1995: 64). This literature suggests an end to the postwar "permissive consensus" that had allowed integration to proceed over the heads of the citizens of member states.

Scholars have sought to explain this renationalization of public opinion with reference to both European and national political processes. The surveys indicate confusion about the competences and activities of European institutions, and anger at the lack of transparency in the EU decision-making and implementation process. The high-profile role of Delors and Commission policy entrepreneurship under his guidance apparently raised fears of an EU behemoth (Lodge, 1994). At the same time, proposed transfers of sovereignty in sensitive areas like monetary and foreign policy raised for many a threat to national identity, a theme that figured prominently in the 1992 Danish and French referendum debates. Other scholars have suggested that dissatisfaction with national policies and politics may have underpinned the drop in support for integration in the early 1990s. Richard Eichenberg and Russell Dalton, for example, argue that Europeans vented their frustration about prolonged economic recession by souring on the integration project of their national leaders (Eichenberg and Dalton, 1993: 529). To the extent that national concerns determine responses to survey questions about the European Union, the EU cannot be viewed as a locus of identification for Europeans.

Work on public opinion points to an overall drop in support for deeper integration. To what extent, though, does this trend suggest the existence of an EU legitimacy crisis? There are three related grounds for doubt. First, such a conclusion obscures important changes in the meaning of European integration over time. By the 1990s, the integration process had penetrated far deeper into economy and society than at any previous juncture. Since EU policies genuinely have begun to gain relevance in the lives of citizens, what is measured by public approval today is somewhat different from what opinion surveys reflected five years ago.

Second, negative responses to general questions about the EU may represent dissatisfaction with particular EU policies, not the integration process as a whole. For example, low support for deeper integration might reflect dissatisfaction with high rates of unemployment, but those dissatisfied might – if asked – want the EU to do more, not less, to alleviate the problem. Furthermore, expressions of dissatisfaction with the EU may now correspond to the way citizens complain about the performance of their national governments – reflecting concerns about particular policy outputs rather than evaluations of the legitimacy of governing institutions themselves. Previous "cycles" of opinion toward the EU, characterized by downturns in the immediate aftermath of significant steps forward and subsequent consolidation of citizen approval, lend credence to this view (Reif, 1991). Additionally, because of the contested nature of the EU polity, expressed opposition to integration might reflect skepticism about particular interpretations of EU policies, not the policies themselves. Both neoliberals and social democrats appear generally supportive of EMU, for example. But neoliberals, who support a single currency as a means to lock member-state governments into fiscal and monetary discipline, reject it as a necessary step toward deeper political union and a more robust EU social policy – precisely the reason many social democrats support the project. As the integration process penetrates further and further into the lives of Europeans, and particular EU policies become an object of greater political controversy, surveys designed to gauge general levels of support for integration may tell us less and less about EU legitimacy.

Third, the examination of political attitudes cannot capture recognition expressed through patterns of activity. Public opinion surveys provide snapshots of attitudes across a population. As noted above, they often say little about variations in the meanings of key terms like "Europe" or "EU" over time or across different respondents. Even more decisive, from the point of view of this book, a focus on recognition as identification obscures ways in which political activity can contribute to legitimacy. Recognition is revealed not only through subjective orientations; it is also reflected in political practice. Scholarship on political activity within the EU has tended to focus on European Parliament elections, for which turnout indeed remains problematically low. But a concentration on Parliament deflects attention from other patterns of activity, including increasing mobilization of interest groups and parties around EU policies and at various institutional sites, including the Commission and the Parliament. Conceptualizing the EU as a multi-level polity can better capture patterns of contestation and their implications for legitimacy.

The democratic deficit

Work on the "democratic deficit" constitutes a second strand of literature addressing the legitimacy issue, and the problem of representation in particular. Work in this vein tends to trace the EU's crisis of representation back to the elitist design of the European Coal and Steel Community in the early 1950s (Featherstone, 1994). For Jean Monnet and others, efficiency was more important than democracy.

9

Monnet's functionalist approach to building Europe revolved around the ability to attract elites to the European project. Indeed, the centrality of inter-elite bargaining in driving the integration process can be traced through the Single European Act of 1986 and the Maastricht Treaty of 1992 (Sandholtz and Zysman, 1989). From the point of view of institutional critics, the Maastricht ratification controversy demonstrated that the efficient design of European institutions has outlived its usefulness, and that structural shortcomings must be redressed if the EU is to continue to develop.

The discussion of gaps in democracy touches on all of the main EU institutions and generates prescriptions for bridging the deficit that point in all directions. For some, the European Commission is a starting point. Appointed rather than elected and lacking a popular base, it nevertheless initiates and oversees the implementation of policy, activities that require a popular mandate in the national context. Unlike the Commission, the Council of Ministers, the main legislative arm of the EU, is made up of national-government representatives. But these officials, too, are not directly accountable to European citizens. Many view the directly elected European Parliament as a potential source of democratic legitimation at the European level. According to critics of the EU institutional structure, however, the Parliament's powers relative to the Commission and the Council remain too limited, even in the wake of the Maastricht and Amsterdam treaties. And finally, a growing number of observers scrutinize the judgments of the European Court of Justice (ECJ), acknowledge its formative role in the integration process, and raise questions about its accountability.

The diagnosis of a "democratic deficit" has given rise to a variety of prescriptions. Some argue that the key to democratic legitimacy is accountability and that the European Parliament must therefore be entrusted with greater powers to ensure democratic control (Williams, 1991). This would both balance the dominance of national interests represented in the Council and contribute to a process of informed public opinion formation. As another mechanism of enhanced legitimacy, parliamentary debate could help foster informed democratic opinion among citizens. Since European debates tend to take place on narrow technical terms, they typically are exclusionary. In fact, there is no well-developed forum for political debate at a European level; the media contribute to this "political deficit" by paying little attention to European issues relative to national issues (Dehousse, 1995). Other advocates of institutional reform have pressed for a shift away from unanimity toward weighted-majority voting in the Council on a greater number of issues. In this view, the EU might evolve in the direction of a bicameral system in which the executive (Commission) and legislature (Council and Parliament) ensure a high level of representation and legitimacy (Wallace, 1993).

Other scholars have argued that measures should be taken to make national control over EU outcomes more democratic. They have pressed, for example, for greater involvement of national parliaments in EU decision-making (Neunreither, 1994). From this perspective, a shift toward supranationalism, whether through a stronger Commission and European Parliament or through a shift to qualified-majority voting, threatens to undermine representative links between rulers and ruled. Weiler points out that the development of majority voting in the Council raises the prospect of EU legislation that runs counter to the interests of member-state governments and their electorates, raising legitimacy problems in the absence of an overarching European identity or sense of solidarity (Weiler, 1992). In this connection, Dehousse contends that parliamentary majoritarianism can potentially damage the relationship between the Parliament and Commission, on the one hand, and member-state governments, on the other. Since the Commission has derived much of its authority from its multinational, party-neutral composition, enhancing its accountability to a partisan Parliament might render it more of an "alien body in national capitals" and upset the supranational/intergovernmental balance on which the EU system rests (Dehousse, 1995).

Work on the "democratic deficit" tends to distort the nature of the legitimacy problem in the EU in two ways. First, it measures the EU with an inappropriate yardstick of central democratic institutions directly accountable to citizens. The tenacity of nation states and national identities all but rules out the creation of a European super-state with robust democratic institutions, while supranational elements of EU governance make a reassertion of national, democratic control unlikely. The democratic deficit literature not only tends to be inattentive to these constraints; it also puts forward alternative institutional designs ill-suited to the emergent and indeterminate nature of the integration process. Because the EU is a contested polity, with institutions in flux and linked up with national institutions in complex and changing ways, calls for a final institutional solution to the problem of representation, whether through stronger EU institutions or greater oversight by national parliaments, are of limited practical relevance. The literature on the "democratic deficit" points to the problem of representation for EU legitimacy, but not to its resolution.

Second, critics of the "democratic deficit" also tend to obscure the emergence of more pluralist forms of representation in the EU not captured by a focus on formal institutions. Work on multi-level governance has highlighted the importance of informal policy-making channels, mainly involving the European Commission and Parliament in transnational networks of political actors. These are not merely "back-channels," patterns of elite interaction outside of public view. Increasingly, these networks involve established national representative institutions – interest groups and parties, for example – which are coming to participate in European governance. With its focus on formalized channels of representation, the literature on the "democratic deficit" obscures these complex and evolving representative links between EU and national institutions and their actual and potential importance for the political legitimacy of the integration process.

Rethinking legitimacy in a contested polity

Recent work on "multi-level governance" within the EU provides a point of departure for a reconceptualization of the legitimacy problem (Marks, Hooghe and

Blank, 1996; Risse-Kappen, 1996). Growing numbers of EU scholars reject the binary oppositions between national and European institutions, identities, and interests, which inform existing theories and research agendas (Wessels, 1997; Marks *et al.*, 1996; Caporaso, 1996; Rhodes and Mazey, 1995; Kohler-Koch and Jachtenfuchs, 1996). These scholars conceive of the EU neither as the mere creation of nation states nor as a European super-state in the making, but as a complex web of policy and political relationships linking European, national, and subnational institutions. The multi-level perspective does not ignore the importance of formal institutions, such as the European Commission, Parliament, or Court. Nor does this perspective dismiss the importance of national interests in the integration process. But scholars pursuing this approach conceptualize the EU as a fluid polity outside the statist mold, a constellation of institutions embedded in a dense and evolving network of informal interactions that brings together supra-national, national, and subnational actors.

What is the link between the multi-level governance approach and the problem of EU legitimacy? On the one hand, the multi-level approach highlights the existence of new patterns of contestation at the European level. An increasing range of actors has come to acknowledge the EU as an appropriate framework for politics, alongside and not in place of national and subnational levels of government. The activities in which these actors engage – and their capacity to combine existing identities with participation in Europe – have contributed to EU legitimacy conceived as recognition. On the other hand, the institutional structure of the multi-level polity is itself contested, the object of ongoing political conflict. Interactive, decentralized institutions have given rise to complex links between state and society in Europe. Interest groups and parties, while still anchored in national politics, have become more active at the European level. These new forms of representation constitute an important, often overlooked source of political legitimacy within the European Union.

Contestation and legitimacy

The multi-level perspective redirects attention away from popular attitudes and levels of identification to new patterns of political activity that contribute to legitimacy. While the growing policy importance of decisions made at the European level has mobilized political activity, the dispersal of power in the EU system has generated a wide variety of decentralized and evolving political processes (Peterson, 1995; Nugent, 1995; Cram, 1994; Grande, 1996). Since the mid-1980s, policy networks have proliferated. These consist of policy-making "sites" involving the mediation of the interests of interdependent actors, including European and national officials, technocrats, agency officials, representatives of non-governmental organizations and other interest groups, journalists, and academics (Schneider, 1992: 109; Peterson, 1995: 76). In the process of seeking to translate their interests into policies in the context of European institutions, these actors exchange information and ideas (Schneider, 1992: 112). Through their activity, they constitute informal bargaining hubs between institutions and groups at the European level (Grande, 1996; Peterson, 1995: 86–87). Participation in these networks, often encouraged by the Commission in particular, involves recognition of the EU as an arena for politics.

Growing recognition of the EU is not simply the product of its greater salience for economic and social policy in Europe. Since the mid-1980s, the Commission has established its "own sense of purpose" by interacting more intensively with a growing number and range of societal actors in addition to officials of member-state governments (Edwards and Spence, 1994: 11). The increasing involvement of the Commission in policy implementation has also drawn new national and sub-national actors into EU politics and policy-making. The administration of cohesion funds, for example, has served to "break open the mould of the state" (Marks, Hooghe and Blank, 1996: 369) by institutionalizing interactions between the Commission and regional and local actors. National and subnational actors also have come to recognize the EU as a legitimate framework for politics for other reasons. Lower courts have sometimes viewed referrals to the ECJ as a means of circumventing some of the restraints placed on them by higher national courts (Alter, 1996). Policy-makers unhappy with the handling of an issue decided between their own national executive and the Commission have relied on the monitoring activities of the Parliament to shape the agenda of policy reform. And the Commission has served as an alternative vehicle for members of national executives, civil servants, or subnational actors struggling to put their proposals on the policy agenda.

One of the most striking aspects of this political activity is that it has not involved a reorientation of identity from the national and subnational to the European level (Laffan, 1996; Nelson *et al.*, 1992; Wintle, 1996; Garcia, 1993). Government officials, parties and interest groups, and other actors involved in European governance remain anchored in – and primarily identify with – national and subnational political contexts. Recognition of the EU as a legitimate political framework does not, as some have argued, necessitate the creation of an overarching European identity or a shift of loyalties to supranational institutions (Obradovic, 1996; Smith, 1992). There is some evidence of a shift from a national to a European orientation. But there is more evidence that Europeans have come to see integration as compatible with existing identities. The more they participate within European governance, the more that civil servants, parties, and interest groups begin to see themselves inextricably bound within the EU, while still primarily oriented toward the national or subnational levels of governance. In contrast to the history of nation- and state-building, the multi-level perspective points to the "nesting" of compatible regional, national and supranational identities as a viable basis for a stable and legitimate polity.

New patterns of representation

The multi-level governance perspective also points to patterns of representation that constitute sources of legitimacy (Schmitter, 1992; Hooghe, 1995). The evolving architecture of the EU, marked by the coexistence of both nation states and supranational institutions, rules out central forms of democratic representation on the model of the nation state. However, increasing recognition of the EU as a legitimate framework for politics – alongside, not in place of, existing frameworks – has spawned the creation of more informal and fluid forms of representation. The relative autonomy of European institutions, and the creation of policy networks linking those institutions with a variety of actors, has begun to alter the role of parties and interest groups in interest mediation.

In contrast to intergovernmentalist accounts of European integration, which suggest that domestic interests enter EU policy-making only through their impact on the preferences of member-state governments, the multi-level perspective points to a more direct, interactive relationship between national and transnational interest groups and parties, European institutions, and European citizens (Marks, Hooghe and Blank, 1996). The EU level of governance, partly because it is more flexible and evolving, has even proved more responsive to certain societal interests than its national counterpart. For example, organized producer interests relatively entrenched in domestic politics may lose their advantage over broader "civic" interests, such as consumers and environmentalists, in the European arena (Majone, 1996: 67, 77). Moreover, the early process of policy formulation in the Commission tends to be relatively open, making regulatory policy-making at the European level "receptive to the arguments of civic interests" (McGowan and Wallace, 1996: 567). Since the 1980s, the political activities of regional actors and "new social movements" reveal an increasing readiness to bring the concerns of constituents to bear at the European level.

There is also evidence that the European Parliament is emerging as an effective representative institution, even if not in the way many of its proponents traditionally have envisaged (Smith and Kelemen, 1997). The Parliament's increasing competences under Maastricht – and the co-decision procedure in particular – have increased its role in the policy process. The EP has not become a central democratic legislature for Europe. There are other ways, though, in which the European Parliament, as an emerging locus of intensified political activity, is gradually enhancing the democratic vitality of the EU. The activities of the EP in monitoring policy-making, including the Parliament's use of temporary committees of inquiry – a right formalized in the Maastricht Treaty – have enhanced democratic accountability. Moreover, the EP has increased its interaction with national parliaments and has become the focus of more intensive lobbying efforts. The party groups represented in the Parliament have developed clearer policy identities, and strengthened their contacts with existing national parties (Hix, 1995). Formal and informal contacts between EP and national parliamentarians have increased, and the creation of the Committee of the Regions has multiplied contacts with subnational politicians. Growing numbers of interest groups have reacted to changes in the EU legislative process by alerting constituents to the importance of the Parliament in European governance. To a degree that has been underestimated by many observers, the European Parliament has emerged as an important – though not the only important – locus of democratic representation in Europe.

These more informal, fluid forms of representation do not meet the standards of popular sovereignty set by traditional democratic theory. Nonetheless, they reflect the reality of the EU as a polity composed of multiple identities embedded at multiple levels of governance. Representation within the EU does not require the existence of a single European "people" bound by shared cultural and historical roots. Given the multi-level, heterogeneous nature of the European polity, the combination of central institutions and core identity often approximated at the national level is all but impossible. But multi-level politics does not rule out the possibility of European civic identity. As Joseph Weiler has argued, the institution of European citizenship endorsed at Maastricht creates a possible foundation for such an identity despite the persistence of different European peoples (Weiler, 1997b). The persistence of different national and subnational identities – and the different political institutions that they underpin – suggests the importance of EU representation that grows out of, and does not displace, national forms.

Table 1.1 compares the dominant model of legitimacy at the national level with one more appropriate to the EU as a multi-level polity. The table distinguishes the approach to recognition and representation elaborated throughout the volume.

Table 1.1 Models of legitimacy

	Nation state	*Multi-level polity*
Recognition	Shared, organic identity	Recognition through interest articulation and mobilization; multiple, compatible identities
Representation	Central national and subordinate regional institutions; pluralist or corporatist structures	European institutions alongside national institutions; plural and informal forms of representation

Overview of the book

Individual chapters develop and extend the themes set out in the previous section – the emergence of new forms of recognition and representation that contribute to the legitimacy of the EU as a contested, multi-level polity. The chapters explore these issues through a focus on three distinct but interrelated issue areas: policies, institutions, and identities. The accumulation of policy competences since the 1980s has transformed the EU into an important political arena for the contestation of policies. The emergence of this greater contestation has sparked institutional changes at both the European and national levels, as governmental and societal actors have responded to new political opportunities and constraints.

At the same time, multiple identities – European, national, and subnational – have served not to undermine, but to strengthen the cohesion of an unprecedented, multi-level polity. Together, the chapters do not offer an exhaustive approach to the question of EU legitimacy. None, for example, directly addresses the role of the European Court of Justice, the object of a growing scholarly literature in its own right. Instead, each chapter assesses EU legitimacy from a different angle, through a focus on a particular policy area, institutional constellation, or issue of identity.

Policies

The analysis of European policies provides a useful perspective on the problem of EU legitimacy. As EU policies have broadened in scope, extending from economic and social policy to areas such as foreign and cultural policy, the overall impact of the integration process has become more visible. This has led to increasing political contestation: actors at different levels of government and societal organization have clashed more openly over the substance of European policy and the pattern of EU policy-making. For some observers, the contestation of policy threatens legitimacy; incompatible policy priorities threaten to divide and undermine the EU as a whole. In their respective analyses of economic, cultural, and foreign and security policies, Mitchell Smith, Melissa Pantel, and Lily Gardner Feldman examine the implications of this contestation for the problem of legitimacy. They demonstrate how European policies, and the controversy surrounding them, have affected patterns of recognition and representation in the European polity.

Mitchell Smith shows how, in the wake of the Single European Act, political coalitions among diverse EU-level and societal actors have coalesced around contending visions of European economic and social policy. Important segments of Europe's multinational industry, together with the most influential Directorates General within the European Commission, have pursued the single market project as a means to greater economic competitiveness. Others, including the Commission's Social Affairs Directorate General, some Christian democratic political elites, and organized labor, have invoked a "European model of society" that demands a balance between the objective of competitiveness and the demands of greater social cohesion. Mobilization around these perspectives has increasingly generated new patterns of political contestation at the European level. As a byproduct, a broad range of actors on both sides of the political spectrum has created important new representative links between EU governance and European society.

In her discussion of EU cultural policy, Melissa Pantel argues that the Commission's theme of "unity-in-diversity" represents a promising legitimacy-building strategy. Most work on this topic has focused on the EU's attempt to highlight cultural unity and has denied the existence of, and the possibility of creating, a European cultural identity. Without a common culture to bind together diverse Europeans, it is argued, the European polity cannot garner the deep-rooted, long-term support it requires from its citizens. By contrast, Pantel argues that the Commission's theme of "unity-in-diversity" is appropriate for a multi-level, contested polity that does not approximate the nation-state model. EU cultural policy has highlighted not only shared elements of European identity, but also the resilience and importance of national and subnational identities, each with its own rich history and symbols. The Commission has aimed to build legitimacy, not through the imposition of a European identity, but through an emphasis on the compatibility of contrasting identities. Pantel's analysis points to the tensions inherent in the notion of "unity-in-diversity," but suggests that it is well suited to politics in a complex multi-level polity.

In her chapter on the Common Foreign and Security Policy (CFSP) and EU enlargement, Lily Gardner Feldman examines the concept of reconciliation as a source of EU legitimacy. The values of peace and reconciliation, she argues, represent an often overlooked source of internal legitimacy for the EU. Perhaps due to its tranquil nature, peace has not been adequately recognized as a potent source of such sentimental attachment for European publics. Moreover, observers have overlooked the extent to which the experience of postwar reconciliation provides a foundation for difficult but important efforts to coordinate EU foreign policy under the CFSP. Because it reflects the evolving, hybrid nature of a multi-level polity, the CFSP is sharply contested. But it should not be dismissed as a failure. While it cannot match the coherence of *national* foreign policies, it represents a joint effort rooted in the shared experience of postwar reconciliation. EU expansion, Gardner Feldman demonstrates, can be viewed as an effort to extend the postwar legacy of reconciliation to parts of the former Soviet bloc. Whether EU expansion secures the necessary political support will depend in part on whether European leaders can effectively connect it with the theme of reconciliation and peace.

Institutions

Shifts in policy competences since the 1980s have gone hand in hand with institutional changes. This has involved not so much the strengthening of EU institutions as shifts in interinstitutional relations and links back to European society. Most observers have pointed to the ongoing intergovernmental and technocratic character of the EU – the fact that the Council continues to overshadow the Commission, and that the Parliament remains relatively weak. These observers have pointed to a lack of identification with those institutions, on the one hand, and to their weak links with EU citizens, on the other. To some extent, though, this analysis has rested on an oversimplified conception of the European Parliament (EP) as a national legislature writ large. Moreover, the debate between intergovernmental and supranational conceptualizations of European integration has tended to obscure the reaction of important national institutions to deeper integration. National parties, for example, are coming to play a more important role both in placing European issues on national agendas, and organizing politics and shaping policy agendas on the European level. Attention to the changing role of the EP, and to patterns of party politics, national and European, points to modes of recognition and representation not captured in established approaches to the legitimacy problem.

Robert Ladrech argues that the integration process has induced a nascent reorientation of political party activity toward the European level. In recognition of the growing importance of EU policy-making, national political parties concerned about their capacity to shape policy outcomes within national contexts have begun to increase their activities at the European level. While pursuing political goals at home, they have come to recognize the EU as a potentially beneficial arena in which to pursue policy objectives. This is most evident in the emergence of trans-European party activity, as different "party families" seek to shape EU policy outcomes. Increasing involvement of national parties in EU governance is rendering "Europe" less "foreign" for national politicians, and may counteract their tendency to blame the EU for unpopular or failing policies. In an effort to shore up their own legitimacy at home, Ladrech convincingly shows, national parties have ironically buttressed that of the EU as a whole.

Gary Marks and Carole Wilson build on the insight that the emergence of a multi-level polity transforms national politics. In particular, multi-level governance has fostered a tendency for major party families to pursue national political projects through European means. Accordingly, debates about Europe at the national level are less often about the value of the integration process; instead, they increasingly focus on the direction that the integration process should take. Evidence from the orientations of national parties suggests that despite the acceleration of European integration since the mid-1980s, the national/European cleavage has grown less, not more, salient. The major party families have come to recognize the EU as a route to achieving national political objectives through supranational means. In the process, a new left–right cleavage has emerged, in which contestation within the EU pits a diverse center-left coalition which wishes to create a capacity for regulating capitalism at the European level against a right-wing coalition in favor of uncoordinated markets and regime competition. The increasing importance of the traditional left–right spectrum in the EU context refracts European issues through a familiar national lens, making them less distant and abstract to European voters. Moreover, the increasing salience of the European issue in national politics is making national parties more important representative institutions within the Euro-polity.

Wolfgang Wessels and Udo Diedrichs argue that the debate about the "democratic deficit" misconstrues the role of the EP in the legitimation of the EU. Most analysts, informed by either realist or federalist perspectives, focus on the failings of the EP as a central locus of democratic representation within the EU. The authors assert that the EP is in fact essential to a new kind of political system characterized by "fusion," in which the Parliament performs functions involving policy-making, system development, and interaction with citizens. The Parliament has in the post-Maastricht period come to play a much more significant role in the formulation and implementation of policy, and as a consequence it has become a more attractive target for intermediary associations articulating interests at the European level. While the institutional interests of the EP dictate that it often present a united front both publicly and in interaction with the other EU institutions, the emergence in some instances of more partisan debate within the EP, reflecting lines of cleavage familiar to European citizens, can merge the legitimacy of national political institutions with that of the Parliament. Ultimately the result of the fusion process is a polity in which the basis of citizenship is political rather than cultural, religious, or historical, and in which the participation of citizens assumes a diversity of forms, both direct and indirect.

Identities

Issues of identity provide a third perspective on the legitimacy issue. The relationship among European, national and regional identities is central to the question of legitimacy. Both advocates and opponents of deeper integration often have claimed that it requires the creation of an overarching European identity. Advocates have upheld European identity as a goal, while opponents have dismissed it as an impossibility. Both have depicted the absence of such an identity – what Weiler calls the "no demos thesis" – as the source of a legitimacy problem (Weiler, 1997a: 257). While identification with central institutions rooted in an organic or civic attachment eludes the EU, the existence of multiple identities along European, national, and subnational lines does not necessarily threaten the legitimacy of the European project. Actors at all three levels can espouse different identities and still recognize the EU as a productive framework for interest mobilization and political representation. The implications of multiple identities for EU legitimacy are evident in the development of EU citizenship, national ratification controversies, and European political discourse.

Rey Koslowski explores the implications of EU citizenship for European identity and EU legitimacy. With the Maastricht Treaty, the EU created a European citizenship setting out particular bundles of rights – such as the right to live and work throughout the Union and to vote in local and European elections. This extension of rights creates a divergence between nationality and citizenship – categories that traditionally coincide in the context of nation states. In the process, European citizenship sanctions the possibility of multiple, compatible political identities, national and European. Moreover, by extending democratic participation, European citizenship represents a potential source of legitimacy for the integration process as a whole. European citizenship, Koslowski contends, is far more than empty symbolism. It represents a new form of political membership with important implications for the future evolution of the European polity.

Thomas Banchoff examines the efforts of French and German political elites to adapt existing conceptions of national identity in ways compatible with deeper European integration. In order to legitimate the integration process at home, political leaders have sometimes sought to construct a common European identity based on shared historical experience, culture, and political values. More important, and less understood, political leaders also have endeavored to redefine established national identities in ways compatible with the integration process. Through the depiction of integration as an extension of *national* history, culture, and political values, EU supporters in France and Germany have redescribed the nation state as inextricably embedded within European institutions, and have won considerable political support for their perspectives. Banchoff's analysis of ratification controversies surrounding the European Coal and Steel Community in the 1950s and the Maastricht Treaty in the 1990s shows how national political processes – the contestation of contrasting visions of the nation's relationship with "Europe" – can constitute a source of political legitimacy for the EU.

The legitimacy of the EU, John Gaffney argues, also depends on the emergence of a European-level political discourse. National discourses in Europe are deeply rooted and effectively exploited by national leaders. At the European level, the interaction of different languages, histories, and cultures makes discourse more fractured, while the absence of strong central institutions limits the effective use of discourse by EU leaders. While anti-European discourse continues to threaten EU legitimacy, emerging trans-European party families with shared identities may signal the emergence of a European discourse that can buttress legitimacy. European discourse, to be effective in reinforcing EU legitimacy, must grow out of – and not in opposition to – national discourse. It must be attentive to the continued salience of nation states, and national identities, within an emergent multi-level polity.

In assessing the findings of the chapters, the conclusion acknowledges that unfolding developments in European integration – the single currency project and eastward enlargement in particular – harbor the potential to threaten EU legitimacy. However, the evidence reviewed in this volume suggests that the process of integration will continue to involve both national and European institutions in ways that enhance recognition and representation in the European polity.

Bibliography

Almond, G. A. and Verba, S. (1963) *The Civic Culture*, Princeton, NJ: Princeton University Press.

Alter, K. (1996) "The European Court's Political Power," *West European Politics* 19, 3: 458–87.

Andersen, S. S. and Eliassen, K. A. (eds) (1996) *The European Union: How Democratic Is It?*, London: Sage.

Anderson, C. J. (1995) "Economic Benefits and Support for Membership in the E.U.: A Cross-national Analysis," *Journal of Public Policy* 15: 231–49.

Beetham, D. (1991) *The Legitimation of Power*, Atlantic Highlands, NJ: Humanities Press.

Caporaso, J. A. (1996) "The European Union and Forms of State: Westphalian, Regulatory or Post-Modern?" *Journal of Common Market Studies* 34, 1: 29–52.

Caporaso, J. A. and Keeler, J. T. S. (1995) "The European Union and Regional Integration Theory," in C. Rhodes and S. Mazey (eds) *The State of the European Union: Building a European Polity?*, Boulder, CO: Lynne Rienner.

Connolly, W. (1984) *Legitimacy and the State*, New York: New York University Press.

Cram, L. (1994) "The European Commission as a Multi-organization: Social Policy and IT Policy in the EU," *Journal of European Public Policy* 1, 2: 195–217.

—— (1997) *Policy-making in the EU*, London: Routledge.

Dahl, R. A. (1989) *Democracy and its Critics*, New Haven, CT: Yale University Press.

Dehousse, R. (1995) "Institutional Reform in the European Community: Are There Alternatives to the Majoritarian Avenue?" Florence: European University Institute, EUI Working Paper, Robert Schuman Centre, RSC 95/4.

Edwards, G. and Spence, D. (eds) (1994) *The European Commission*, London: Stockton.

Eichenberg, R. C. and Dalton, R. (1993) "Europeans and the European Community: The Dynamics of Public Support for European Integration," *International Organization* 47: 507–31.

Featherstone, K. (1994) "Jean Monnet and the 'Democratic Deficit' in the European Union," *Journal of Common Market Studies* 32, 2: 149–70.

Franklin, M., Marsh, M. and McLaren, L. (1994) "Uncorking the Bottle: Popular Opposition to European Integration in the Wake of Maastricht," *Journal of Common Market Studies* 32, 4: 455–72.

Garcia, S. (ed.) (1993) *European Identity and the Search for Legitimacy*, London: Pinter.

Grande, E. (1996) "The State and Interest Groups in a Framework of Multi-level Decision-making: The Case of the European Union," *Journal of European Public Policy* 3, 3: 318–38.

Haas, E. (1958) *The Uniting of Europe: Political, Social and Economic Forces, 1950–1957*, Stanford, CA: Stanford University Press.

Habermas, J. (1984) *The Theory of Communicative Action*, 2 vols, Boston, MA: Beacon.

Held, D. (1984) *Political Theory and the Modern State: Essays on State, Power and Democracy*, Cambridge, UK: Polity Press.

—— (1995) *Democracy and the Global Order: From the Modern State to Cosmopolitan Governance*, Stanford, CA: Stanford University Press.

Hix, S. (1995) "Parties at the European Level and the Legitimacy of EU Socio-economic Policy," *Journal of Common Market Studies* 33, 4: 527–54.

Hoffmann, S. (1982) "Reflections on the Nation-State in Western Europe Today," *Journal of Common Market Studies* 21, 1: 21–37.

Hooghe, L. (1995) "Subnational Mobilisation in the European Union," *West European Politics* 18: 175–98.

Kohler-Koch, B. and Jachtenfuchs, M. (1996) "Regieren in der Europäischen Union – Fragestellungen für eine interdiziplinäre Europaforschung," *Politische Vierteljahresschrift* 37: 537–56.

Laffan, B. (1996) "The Politics of Identity and Political Order in Europe," *Journal of Common Market Studies* 34, 1: 81–102.

Lindberg, L. N. and Scheingold, S. A. (1970) *Europe's Would-be Polity*, Englewood Cliffs, NJ: Prentice-Hall.

Lodge, J. (1994) "Transparency and Democratic Legitimacy," *Journal of Common Market Studies* 32, 3: 343–68.

McGowan, F. and Wallace, H. (1996) "Towards a European Regulatory State," *Journal of European Public Policy* 3, 4: 560–76.

Majone, G. (1996) *Regulating Europe*, London: Routledge.

Marks, G., Hooghe, L. and Blank, K. (1996) "European Integration from the 1980s: State-centric v. Multi-level Governance," *Journal of Common Market Studies* 34, 3: 341–78.

Marks, G., Scharpf, F. W., Schmitter, P. C. and Streeck, W. (eds) (1996) *Governance in the European Union*, London: Sage.

Martinotti, G. and Stefanizzi, S. (1995) "Europeans and the Nation State," in O. Niedermayer and R. Sinnott (eds) *Public Opinion and Internationalized Governance*, Oxford, UK: Oxford University Press.

Milward, A. S., Lynch, F. M. B., Ranieri, R., Romero, F. and Sorensen, V. (1993) *The Frontier of National Sovereignty: History and Theory 1945–1992*, London: Routledge.

Nelson, B., Roberts, D. and Veit, W. (1992) *The Idea of Europe: Problems of National and Transnational Identity*, Providence, RI: Berg.

Neunreither, K. (1994) "The Democratic Deficit of the European Union: Towards Closer Cooperation between the European Parliament and the National Parliaments," *Government and Opposition* 29: 299–314.

Niedermayer, O. (1995) "Trends and Contrasts," in O. Niedermayer and R. Sinnott (eds) *Public Opinion and Internationalized Governance*, Oxford, UK: Oxford University Press.

Niedermayer, O. and Sinnott, R. (eds) (1995) *Public Opinion and Internationalized Governance*, Oxford, UK: Oxford University Press.

Nugent, N. (1995) "The Leadership Capacity of the European Commission," *Journal of European Public Policy* 2, 4: 603–23.

Obradovic, D. (1996) "Policy Legitimacy and the European Union," *Journal of Common Market Studies* 34, 2: 191–221.

Peterson, J. (1995) "Decision-making in the European Union: Towards a Framework for Analysis," *Journal of European Public Policy* 2, 1: 69–93.

Reif, K. (1991) *Eurobarometer: The Dynamics of European Public Opinion*, New York: St. Martin's Press.

Rhodes, C. and Mazey, S. (eds) (1995) *The State of the European Union: Building a European Polity?*, Boulder, CO: Lynne Rienner.

Risse-Kappen, T. (1996) "Exploring the Nature of the Beast: International Relations Theory and Comparative Policy Analysis Meet the European Union," *Journal of Common Market Studies* 34, 1: 53–80.

Sandholtz, W. (1996) "Membership Matters: Limits to the Functional Approach to European Institutions," *Journal of Common Market Studies* 34, 3: 403–29.

Sandholtz, W. and Zysman, J. (1989) "1992: Recasting the European Bargain," *World Politics* 42, 1: 95–128.

Schmitter, P. C. (1992) "Representation and the Future Euro-polity," *Staatswissenschaft und Staatspraxis* 3: 379–405.

—— (1996) "Examining the Future Euro-polity with the Help of New Concepts," in G. Marks, F. W. Scharpf, P. C. Schmitter and W. Streeck (eds) *Governance in the European Union*, London: Sage.

Schneider, V. (1992) "The Structure of Policy Networks," *European Journal of Political Research* 21: 109–29.

Smith, A. D. (1992) "National Identity and the Idea of European Unity," *International Affairs* 68: 55–76.

Smith, M. P. (1996) "Democratic Legitimacy in the European Union: Fulfilling the Institutional Logic," *The Journal of Legislative Studies* 2, 4: 283–301.

Smith, M. P. and Kelemen, R. D. (1997) "The Institutional Balance: Formal and Informal Change," Centre for European Policy Studies, Brussels, Working Document No. 111.

Taylor, C. (1992) *Multiculturalism and the "Politics of Recognition,"* Princeton, NJ: Princeton University Press.

Taylor, P. (1996) *The European Union in the 1990s*, Oxford, UK: Oxford University Press.

Wallace, H. (1993) "Deepening and Widening: Problems of Legitimacy for the EC," in S. Garcia (ed.) *European Identity and the Search for Legitimacy*, London: Pinter.

Wallace, H., Wallace, W. and Webb, C. (1983) *Policy-making in the European Community*, New York: John Wiley & Sons.

Weber, M. (1978) *Economy and Society: An Outline of Interpretive Sociology*, vol. 1, Berkeley, CA: University of California Press.

Weiler, J. H. H. (1992) "After Maastricht: Community Legitimacy in Post-1992 Europe," in W. J. Adams (ed.) *Singular Europe: Economy and Polity of the European Community after 1992*, Ann Arbor: The University of Michigan Press.

—— (1997a) "Legitimacy and Democracy of Union Governance," in G. Edwards and A. Pijpers (eds) *The Politics of European Treaty Reform*, London: Pinter.

—— (1997b) "The Reformation of European Constitutionalism," *Journal of Common Market Studies* 35, 1: 97–131.

Wessels, W. (1997) "An Ever Closer Fusion? A Dynamic Macropolitical View on Integration Processes," *Journal of Common Market Studies* 35, 2: 267–99.

Williams, S. (1991) "Sovereignty and Accountability in the European Community," in S. Hoffmann and R. A. Keohane (eds) *The New European Community: Decisionmaking and Institutional Change*, Boulder, CO: Westview Press.

Wintle, M. (ed.) (1996) *Culture and Identity in Europe: Perceptions of Divergence and Unity in Past and Present*, Aldershot, UK: Avebury.

Part 1

LEGITIMACY AND
EU POLICIES

2

EU LEGITIMACY AND THE "DEFENSIVE" REACTION TO THE SINGLE EUROPEAN MARKET

Mitchell P. Smith

The closing of French car-maker Renault's assembly plant in Vilvoorde, Belgium, in early 1997 generated a sense of insecurity among Europe's industrial workers that spread far beyond the plant's 3,100 employees. For many observers fearing the demise of Europe's social model, the Vilvoorde closing added to mounting evidence that Europe's internal market is predominantly about securing capital's ease of migration toward regions offering the best investment incentives and least costly labor. Conversely, those who believe the single market has not delivered sufficient market liberalization pointed to the reactions of the European Parliament and Commission which, symptomatic of Union institutions that have an increasing tendency to interfere with market decisions in the name of social and economic cohesion, quickly rose to the defense of the Vilvoorde workers. Dissatisfaction on one side was expressed through trans-European industrial action, legal measures against the company in both Belgian and French courts, and calls for tougher social regulation. In response, business interests called for a true single market with minimal government intervention. Does this unresolved tension over a fundamental dimension of the single European market, and the European Union's seeming inability to satisfy either advocates of freer markets or proponents of greater social protection, reflect a crisis of legitimacy?

As these contrasting perspectives suggest, an increasing number and range of actors are articulating and pursuing their interests concerning social regulation at a European level. On the one hand, there are those actors who believe that the social dimension of Europe's single market has been sacrificed on the altar of market efficiency, lingering only in the rhetoric of European integration. Those who lament the neglect of the social dimension, including a segment of officials within the European Commission, some Members of the European Parliament and its staff, organized labor, and advocates of public services, have coalesced around this critique, which posits that the regulatory activity of the EC has constricted the abilities of member-state public authorities to meet the social welfare needs of their citizens, without adequate replacement policies at the European level. Advocates of a more neoliberal position reside within the business sector.

27

Neoliberals insist that too much weight has been given to the social dimension, with resulting distortions of competition negating many of the efficiency gains promoted by the single market. Situated between proponents of a much stronger social dimension and an exclusive focus on market efficiency, a coalition of Christian democratic and centrist social democratic European political elites, dominant Directorates General (DGs) within the European Commission, and transnational European business elites has promoted a program of liberalization of industry as a solution both to the challenge of industrial competitiveness and the need for social cohesion.

As this chapter examines these contrasting responses to the single market program, it proposes that the "economic constitution" of the emerging European polity has become an object of contestation within European Union institutions and between numerous actors in the EU member states that have been mobilized by the integration process to articulate their interests at a European level. This process of political contestation over the contours of the single European market demonstrates that actors with contrasting economic and social interests increasingly are recognizing the EU as a productive venue for the articulation of their interests.

Mobilization of a diverse European polity around the integration project may be thought of in terms analogous to the widespread reaction against market society that materialized in the nineteenth century. In analyzing the "great transformation" marked by the emergence of market society, Karl Polanyi argued that while liberals condemned the activities of labor unions, socialists, and social reformers for damaging the efficiency of the market machine, the defensive reaction against market society was in fact "universal" and necessary to save market society from itself (Polanyi, 1957). Similarly, while portions of the European Commission press on with efforts to eliminate remaining distortions in the single market, other parts of the Commission, the European Parliament, European political groups, the European Trade Union Federation, portions of the business community, and various citizens' groups have mobilized to contain or control the impact of the single market. Advocates of more thoroughgoing liberalization also have mobilized to bend the single market program to their needs. Ultimately, the public space created by the contention of conflicting views of European integration is integral to the emergence of an increasingly legitimate European polity.

The "great" transformation

During its first quarter-century, European integration was about making war between member states, particularly France and the Federal Republic of Germany, "materially impossible." By the start of the 1970s, the EC largely had achieved this objective, and the Community floundered, aimless amidst severe economic difficulties that challenged member states and pushed them apart rather than together. The entire project was revived in the 1980s, boosted first and foremost by the Single European Act (SEA). For the past decade, European integration has been largely about making a united Europe competitive in the global economy. The focus on competitiveness has translated into a determination on the part of European policy-makers to expose industry and workers more directly to the energizing thrust of market forces.

Substantially a response to global competition, the essential feature of the transformation wrought by the single market program is a shift of market regulation to the European level. The policy problems facing European states have generated a growing demand for Union regulation. This is a result both of the complexity and trans-border scope of policy problems – in areas such as the environment, consumer product safety, financial services, and competition policy – and the demand by trans-European actors – such as firms selling throughout the single market – for European-level regulation rather than a patchwork of national regulations (Majone, 1996: 66; 1994: 86–87). The prospect for increased regulation at the European level is expanded by the "regulatory gap" generated by the development of the single market. The SEA was designed to eliminate non-tariff, essentially legislative, barriers to trade. The prohibition of non-tariff barriers constrains the use of regulatory instruments by member-state governments, creating a situation in which regulatory objectives can best be met at the European level (Dehousse, 1992: 386–87).

The overriding objective of regulation is to establish rules that improve the functioning of markets, an objective that requires credible enforcement (Majone, 1996; McGowan and Wallace, 1996). The European Commission derives much of its authority as the EU's executive from its political neutrality and its credibility as a regulator. This is why the governments of EU member states determined to improve their economic performance chose to vest regulatory authority in the European Commission. In addition, the European Commission's ability to act as a policy entrepreneur has taken market regulation further than the expectations of member-state governments (Majone, 1993; Cram, 1994; Nugent, 1995). Determined to establish their credibility as regulators and to instill trust in the single market, those Directorates General of the Commission charged with overseeing the single market have an institutional interest in pursuing gaps in implementation, even where this involves conflict with member-state authorities. Moreover, officials of these DGs, such as DG III (Industry), IV (Competition), and XV (Internal Market), generally have a deep philosophical commitment to the objectives of an efficiently functioning internal market. The result is a zeal to remove barriers to free competition and the reallocation of public resources to encourage investments that support rather than counteract the market.

Legitimating the single market

The single market's proponents both within and outside the European Commission have, out of fear of politicizing the single market program, denied the tension between efficient regulation and social equity. In response to the conflicting demands of those interests wanting freer markets and those calling for a stronger social dimension, the European Commission and its supporters in the European Parliament and the Council have sought to legitimate the single market idea by arguing that European-level regulation not only can improve the efficient functioning of European markets and thereby create wealth, but also can diminish inequality across regions and broaden economic opportunity. Ultimately, "social cohesion" is best served by permitting more Europeans to share in the prosperity of the Union.

This philosophy of compatibility between economic efficiency and social equality is set out systematically in the European Commission's 1994 White Paper on *Growth, Competitiveness and Employment.* The thrust of the White Paper is that EU member states must undertake reforms to augment the employment-intensity of growth, since even robust economic growth in the context of existing economic structures and policies is unlikely to have a substantial impact on persistently high unemployment. Industrial and labor-market policies across Europe have produced rigidities and lags in structural adjustment that account for the inability of European industry to respond efficiently to intensified international economic competition. Required are: a shift in the locus of taxation from employment and investment to consumption; labor-market deregulation that reduces the risks of hiring faced by employers; austere fiscal policies; and wage restraint (Commission, 1994: 65–67).

The European Council of heads of state and government repeatedly has endorsed the analysis of the 1994 White Paper. The December 1994 Essen Council communiqué posited that competitiveness demands more flexible work organization, wage increases below productivity gains, reductions in non-wage labor costs, and the removal of disincentives to work embodied in income-support policies. These commitments to restrain wage growth and dismantle labor-market rigidities have been reiterated at each subsequent European Council. Moreover, the Council's Resolution on Growth and Employment at the June 1997 Amsterdam European Council echoed the conviction that efficiency and social equity are compatible, stating that "Economic efficiency and social inclusion are complementary aspects of the more cohesive European society that we all seek."[1]

However, results from the Commission's 1996 report on cohesion of EU member states contradict the thesis that economic efficiency complements social cohesion. The report suggests that for the period of analysis, 1983–93, the EU has had admirable success in reducing income disparities between member states, with Ireland and Spain the big success stories. Yet growth in those poorer countries that are the targets of cohesion policy – the so-called "cohesion countries" – has been uneven, widening regional disparities (Commission, 1996d: 24–25).[2] During the decade under study regional income differentials increased in all member states but the Netherlands. While the dispersion of per capita GDP has declined across member states, there has been a slight increase across regions (Commission, 1996d: 134). Disparities in regional unemployment rates have grown not only between member states, but also within EU countries. Overall, while the twenty-five regions with the worst joblessness had an average unemployment level of 17.2

percent in 1983, and the twenty-five best averaged 4.8 percent, by 1995 the twenty-five most heavily afflicted regions had an unemployment rate of 22.4 percent, compared with just 4.6 percent for those with the lowest unemployment.[3] Moreover, with the exception of three of the cohesion countries – Spain, Ireland, and Portugal – the incidence of poverty increased during the course of the 1980s in all member states (Commission, 1996d: 132). And long-term unemployment is particularly acute, accounting for approximately half of unemployment in the EU.[4]

This evidence would seem to be damning for the efforts of the European Commission to legitimize the single market and to regenerate the momentum of the "1992" project in order to complete the single market in concert with the introduction of the euro in January 1999. Were legitimacy defined entirely in terms of support for EU policies, the negative effects of liberalization on social cohesion would potentially pose a threat to EU legitimacy. If, on the other hand, legitimacy is conceived in terms of the articulation and pursuit of interests within the framework of the EU, developments since the 1980s point to the strengthening of legitimacy. Simply put, the shift of economic regulation to the European level has been accompanied by an intensification of political contestation at the EU level. Rather than delegitimating the EU, the debate over the inefficiencies or inadequacies of cohesion policy has drawn a wider range of actors into the debate over the EU's economic constitution. This, in turn, has contributed to the institutionalization of a more pluralistic and inclusive, if contested, European polity.

The single market: regulating for efficiency

The process of contestation that has given substance to the European polity arguably privileges market liberalization over social cohesion, potentially posing a threat to the legitimacy of the integration project. While the European Commission traditionally has presented the objective of deeper integration as ideologically neutral on the left–right spectrum, the Commission's proposals for social regulation "must be compatible with the 'economic constitution' of the Community," in essence "the principles of a liberal economic order" (Majone, 1993: 156; Weiler, 1993: 33). Furthermore, the coalition mobilized around market liberalization, both within and outside the European Commission, is more powerful and cohesive than the forces mobilized on behalf of EU social policy. In the name of industrial competitiveness European multinationals have been prominent in developing elements of the single market aimed at opening markets, fostering an attractive investment climate, and diminishing labor market rigidities. In drafting the single market program itself, executives of European multinationals saw the Commission as an appropriate focal point for organizing a response to the problems of competitiveness, growth and structural adjustment faced by European industry. Representing this perspective, the European Round Table (ERT) of industrialists sought "a restructuring of the regulatory framework of the European Community," in the form of a unified market that would promote "the reindustrialization of Europe" (Cowles, 1995: 503). In particular, these leading industrialists hoped to achieve a reduction in subsidies to uncompetitive industry, and labor-market deregulation that would permit industry the flexibility to undertake necessary structural adjustments (Cowles, 1995: 505).

The ERT's vision resonated with dominant preferences within the Commission, and thereby found support there. Inside the Commission, a shared *Weltanschauung* about the role of the market and a common approach to improving competitiveness foster a cohesiveness between DGs III (Industry), IV (Competition), and XV (Internal Market), while DG V (Social Affairs) remains somewhat marginalized and isolated. While the Commission under the Santer presidency has become a more collegial body, those DGs that are seeking to complete the internal market largely define the agenda.

The coalition between powerful DGs and leaders of Europe's multinational industries benefits from the regulatory basis of Union policy-making. Regulatory governance represents the comparative advantage of the Union; regulatory policy-making is inherently technocratic, based on the articulation and application of clear rules. Most crucially, it is possible to produce and implement regulatory policies with very limited expenditures of financial resources, precisely the sort of constraint faced by the European Commission (Majone, 1993). These factors explain why EU policies in the social sphere have been confined to social regulation and improvement of the allocation function of the economy rather than redistribution or stabilization (Majone, 1993: 157). Thus the policy instruments available to the European Commission and the constraints on Commission competence and resources imposed by member-state sovereignty imply that the Commission can be effective in promoting market liberalization but not in legislating or organizing social or employment policy at a European level.

The Commission has played a central role in securing mutual recognition of minimum product standards (Alter and Meunier-Aitsahalia, 1994), removing other distortions of competition, and fostering liberalization of markets in telecommunications and other sectors. In contrast, the Commission has made little progress in its efforts to promote massive infrastructure investment in trans-European transport as a means of job creation, largely because it lacks the authority to mobilize the vast financial resources required. Where it has substantial resources to promote cohesion – the Union's structural funds – these resources operate largely as side payments to "buy" the poorer member states into the single market rather than more broadly distributing economic opportunity among individuals, groups, or regions within member states. Moreover, these resources are small compared with the vast funds that could be deployed for regional or social objectives by public authorities in member states in the absence of restrictive Union regulation.

The following sections suggest how the Union's policies to promote competition and competitiveness in three policy areas – aid to national industry in the member states; the promotion of market liberalization and privatization of public enterprises; and the procurement of goods and services by public authorities – reflect the opportunities and constraints of regulatory governance as well as the influence of those interests both in society and the European Commission favoring a more liberal economic environment. The strength of these interests has served as an impetus for the mobilization of a defensive reaction to the single market project, as illustrated in the portions of the chapter that follow.

Member state aid to industry

The Treaty of Rome gives the European Commission exclusive competence in the area of competition policy, including the authority to examine member-state industrial aid for its compatibility with the common market. However, the wording of the relevant articles of the Treaty of Rome leaves open the precise powers of the Commission, and until at least the mid-1980s, the Commission's authority remained fairly circumscribed. In concert with the implementation of the single market program, the Commission stepped up the rigor of the state aid regime, bolstered by European Court of Justice decisions sanctioning broader use of the Commission's investigatory authority, and powers to compel member states to provide information and to order recovery of aid granted in violation of the Treaty. The European Commission has emphasized that reduction of state aid that distorts the allocation of resources is a necessary step to promoting the competitiveness of European industry.

In its *First Report on Competition Policy*, in 1971, the Competition Policy Directorate asserted that "the Commission, when examining national initiatives, must never lose sight of the social and human factors involved, which may justify aid beyond what is required by strictly economic reasoning" (Commission, 1971: 18). Consistent with the development of the internal market, in its 1995 Report, the Commission warns that illegal state aid is involved where public funds are "provided to a (public) undertaking on terms more favorable than those on which a private investor operating under normal market conditions would provide them to a private firm in a comparable financial and competitive position" (Commission, 1995: 74, para. 159). Even with a Competition Commissioner originating from a social democratic tradition, the weight of social criteria in state aid regulation has been substantially discounted.

The Commission has developed rules governing aid to promote employment, acknowledging the seriousness of the unemployment problem while simultaneously recognizing the prospect that "boosting employment" can become a catch-all justification for highly distorting state aid. Thus the Commission opposes aid to maintain jobs in a particular firm on the grounds that such aid simply supports unviable enterprises and thereby delays structural change. The Commission judges that "the negative effects of such aid outweigh the possible short-term benefits in terms of maintaining a certain level of employment."[5] Although reining in state aid arguably will improve employment prospects in the long term, both the short-run impact on jobs and the restriction placed on the use of member-state government resources contribute to the disjuncture between European-level regulation and national means of redistribution. This constraint on national social welfare policies has provided an impetus for increasing political activity around Europe's social dimension.

Liberalization and privatization of public enterprises

In 1962, Jean Monnet wrote that "The large market does not prejudge the future economic systems of Europe." Noting that the original EEC Six have substantial nationalized sectors and that some rely on government planning, Monnet asserted that these "are just as compatible with private enterprise on the large market as they are within a single nation" (Monnet, 1962: 20). This can no longer be said about the single market.

While the start of the privatization wave preceded the relaunch of Europe and is substantially independent of the integration process, the commitment to economic convergence and concomitant fiscal austerity has promoted privatization. The Union must remain neutral with respect to ownership status[6] and cannot, for example, make decisions on the compatibility of member-state aid to industry conditional upon privatization. However, approval of aid depends on the Commission's assessment of the long-term viability of an enterprise, and privatization can loom large in such an assessment and therefore determine eligibility for aid (Verhoeven, 1996: 877). In instances of public enterprises seeking restructuring aid for a second or third time, privatization can become a binding condition, since viability may be deemed contingent on the participation of the private sector (Ehlermann, 1995: 1224).

The European Commission also has pursued sectoral liberalization in the utilities sector. While the Commission called for liberalization of the energy market to begin in 1998, the most successful example of Commission-driven liberalization concerns the European telecommunications market. The Commission played a direct role in forcing the pace of market opening in telephone equipment and services. In the process, the Commission overcame the resistance of some member states as well as general opposition to the use of its powers in the field of competition to require liberalization by issuing directives, bypassing the Council of Ministers (Sandholtz, 1993). Though the process proceeded in piecemeal fashion, ultimately the breakup of national monopolies put privatization of telecommunications on the agenda in EU member states. While liberalization may well generate additional jobs in the long term, the short- and medium-term result of privatization is substantial job losses for those employed by the state-owned telecommunications companies.[7] Moreover, telecommunications liberalization has potentially transformative implications for economies with limited private share ownership, especially the German social market economy. In the German case, the sell-off of Deutsche Telekom raised the number of private shareholders in Germany by one-third. The sale was hailed by many German business people as the harbinger of a nation of shareholders, a path that could completely alter the culture of German business and potentially shift its focus from long-term investment to shorter-term profit maximizing.[8]

As for the case of industrial aid to enterprises by member-state governments, the Commission's role in regulatory governance fosters a shift in ownership patterns that may alter the structure of the political economies of member states. In response, societal interests wedded to the protection of public service provision have mobilized at the European level. These interests have articulated their positions through a number of fora, such as within the European Parliament's political groups and in interest associations, both national and trans-European, which interact with EU institutions.[9]

Public procurement

The European Commission's efforts to liberalize national markets for the pro-curement of goods and services by public authorities threatens to supplant the pursuit of social objectives valued by substantial segments of European publics. The Commission's program for public procurement liberalization, a central part of the single market program, has been driven both by the vast size of public pro-curement markets[10] and the conviction that the use of public contracts to meet a range of regional and social policy objectives wastes public resources and renders European suppliers less competitive in the global marketplace.

Public procurement, like state aid, is an instrument of industrial policy. In addi-tion to satisfying the needs of public entities for equipment or services, the process by which public authorities award contracts may be guided by regional develop-ment objectives, any number of social objectives, such as providing jobs for the long-term unemployed, or a desire to sustain or develop particular technical skills as a means of promoting national industrial competitiveness (Crauser, 1991; Winter, 1991). Public contracts may also be used to sustain locally or strategically important companies, for which the public authority may be the chief or sole customer.

Union public procurement directives enacted from the late 1980s onward in concert with the single market program promote more open public contracting processes in which contracts are awarded on strictly economic criteria. In its efforts to institutionalize this policy regime, the European Commission has challenged contract-award processes that appear to diverge from these criteria, in some cases taking public authorities before the European Court of Justice. Court decisions have endorsed the Commission's enforcement of the directives to promote free and fair competition over social or regional objectives. The point is well illustrated by the European Court's 1990 Du Pont de Nemours decision. In this case the Court ruled that an Italian public authority could not reserve 30 percent of its purchases of goods and services for undertakings permanently established in the Mezzogiorno (ECJ, 1990). According to the Court, the 30 percent quota violated Union public procurement rules because it discriminated not only between regions within the country, but also against foreign suppliers (Fernandez Martin and Stehmann, 1991: 218).

The very process of market integration favors industrial centers and thereby harbors an inherent tendency to exacerbate regional inequality (Fernandez Martin and Stehmann, 1991: 236). In the case of Italy, aggregate wealth may be increased by the implementation of the single market while the divergence between Lombardia and the Mezzogiorno widens (Fernandez Martin and Stehmann, 1991: 237). Moreover, the instrument available to the Union to redress regional imbalances – the European Regional Development Fund – is hardly sufficient to offset this effect, amounting in the case of the Mezzogiorno to a small fraction of the transfer implied by reserving 30 percent of public purchases for firms in the south.[11]

While part of the business sector – particularly UNICE, the European employers' federation – has lobbied for more thorough implementation and tougher enforcement of Union public procurement rules, local authorities have been somewhat slow to comply. While mobilization of tens of thousands of local authorities throughout EU countries in opposition to full liberalization of public procurement markets is unlikely due to a serious collective action problem, noncompliance represents a form of passive, unorganized resistance. The Commission, especially as a consequence of pressures brought to bear by the European Parliament for greater attention to the social and regional implications of the Union's public procurement regime (Commission, 1989), has recognized the need to augment consultation of local government authorities and other interests affected by its policies, as illustrated by its use of a Green Paper in November 1996 to stimulate public debate on the objectives of public procurement in the EU (Commission, 1996e).

The "defensive" reaction

The responses of political actors to the liberalizing policies of the single market program and the traditions of the member-state governments comprising the EU indicate that a single European market without a social dimension is unviable. Implicit in the neoliberal claim that any deviation from efficiency criteria is a misstep for Europe is the idea that unfettered market activity is "natural," and intervention a subversion of this state of nature. As Karl Polanyi explained, it was the late nineteenth-century *reaction* to the emergence of market society that was natural (Polanyi, 1957). The same is true for the single market; mobilization at the European level is a natural response to the organization of a European market.

This mobilization is facilitated by the nature of policy-making in the EU, which tends to be very open during the policy-formulation phase, even if closed at the point of decision-making (Peterson, 1995). Organized producer interests relatively entrenched at the national level, especially institutionalized in corporatist systems, may lose their advantage over broader "civic" interests – consumers and environmentalists – at the European level (Majone, 1996: 67, 77; McGowan and Wallace, 1996). The openness of channels of participation in Union policy-making fosters the articulation of interests and contestation of ideas that have emerged in reaction to the single market project.

The following three sections explore the nature of this reaction, first in the realm of rhetoric, then in the more concrete realm of policy, and finally in the mobilization of political activity. These realms are connected, for the notion of a "European model of society," prominent in EU rhetoric, fosters and validates demands for more extensive Union social policies. But most significant for the study of legitimacy, both the demand for a more robust social dimension and the conflicting call for a neoliberal single market have contributed to new patterns of political mobilization and contestation at the EU level.

The "European model" of society

Implementation of the single market program challenged the preference for social cohesion integral to the Christian democratic and Catholic social traditions that have been at the heart of the integration project. The single market project therefore made it urgent for Europe's architects to give additional attention to the social dimension. However, the means by which to do so without disrupting the progress of the single market were not obvious, and much of the early attention to the social dimension was rhetorical. The rhetoric of Europe's architects suggests their wish to find a way of joining economic efficiency with a modicum of equity, typically referred to as "social cohesion." The notion of a "European model" of society is the embodiment of this aspiration.

Speaking before Britain's Trades Union Congress in September, 1995, European Commission President Jacques Santer extolled the virtues of the market, openness, and incentives for entrepreneurship. However, he balanced this tribute to the market with the Christian democratic conviction that the success of the market is sustainable only if "welded and cemented by social solidarity." Underscoring the need to maintain social welfare systems for the benefit of those who do not succeed in the marketplace, Santer added that "It is this humanity, this basic social decency that helps us define what we share in the European Union" (Santer, 1995).

Santer's vision of a Europe characterized by market dynamism and social solidarity echoed the more philosophical vision of his predecessor, Jacques Delors, whose world view is most influenced by progressive Catholicism. For Delors, society consists of a series of interdependent social groups that "owe one another active solidarity" (Ross, 1995: 1). The essence of the European model for Delors is "balance between state and society, between the collective and the individual" (Delors, 1992: 18). Delors invoked a Europe in which individuals not only enjoy rights, but share an awareness of their obligations to their fellow citizens; a society steering a course between "frenzied individualism" and statist collectivism (Delors, 1994: 52). From Delors's perspective, government is responsible for creating conditions that nurture both social solidarity and individual achievement (Delors, 1994: 55). Sustaining the sense of community integral to such a model requires a highly organized and inclusive system of interest intermediation. In this regard, Delors gave particular attention to the role of labor unions as an interlocutor of business, central to promoting industrial modernization. Accordingly, the

Commission's 1994 White Paper, *Growth, Competitiveness and Employment*, engineered by Delors, proposes that the shift in the macroeconomic policy mix and wage restraint should be achieved through broad consensus, "using social dialogue procedures wherever possible" (Commission, 1994: 67). The document invokes the central importance of societal solidarity – between the employed and unemployed; between the sexes; between generations; between prosperous and poorer regions; and between wealthy and poorer individuals (Commission, 1994: 15–16).

While Santer and Delors expressed their dual commitments to market-borne economic dynamism and social cohesion, other prominent architects of European unity also have suggested that the two objectives are complementary. Delivering the 1988 Jean Monnet Lecture, Patrick J. Hillery, President of Ireland and, earlier, Ireland's first member of the European Commission, seconded the concerns of both Monnet and Jacques Delors that in its effort to revive prosperity and promote employment, Europe must not become "a source of social regression." Hillery suggested that rather than there being a tradeoff between economic dynamism and social progress, the two are "inseparably linked." Integration should contribute to greater economic and social cohesion. To accomplish this, the single market "must go hand in hand with the creation of a coherent European social area" (Hillery, 1988: 15). Giovanni Spadolini, President of the Italian Senate, connected the origins of the European model to the values of Christianity and the Enlightenment. These values generate a link "between humanism and Europeanism." Here the confluence of market-based prosperity and social cohesion is reflected in "the dream of building the 'radiant city' . . . the fraternal community of men in the world of Europe" (Spadolini, 1990: 17).

Certainly there are as many European "models" as there are EU member states. Yet as the comments of Santer, Delors, Hillery, Spadolini, and others demonstrate, there are fundamental features common in European – especially continental – conceptions of society, of which the social market economy is the most prominent. As suggested in the European Commission's November 1996 Cohesion Report, solidarity "is given practical effect through universal systems of social protection, regulation to correct market failure and systems of social dialogue" (Commission, 1996d: 14). While the market remains the primary vehicle of resource allocation, government is responsible, through tax and social policies, for the structure of economic incentives; undertakes limited redistribution; and establishes the regulatory framework that encourages social partnership between business and labor. This vision of the European model represents one ideal around which political mobilization and interest articulation have taken place in the European polity.

Promoting social cohesion

Unemployment has been the focal point for efforts to inject a stronger social dimension into the single market. Determined to respond effectively to Europe's largest social problem, and the one given most attention by European publics,

Jacques Santer in 1996 introduced his European Confidence Pact for Employment (Commission, 1996b). Submitting the Confidence Pact to the European Parliament in January 1996, Santer argued that persistent high unemployment "is jeopardizing the cohesion of our society" and "undermining the foundations of our European model."[12]

Despite persistent high-level discussion of employment policy, substantive action has been slow to emerge. In June 1996 the Italian Presidency of the European Council convened a Tripartite Conference on growth and employment, which focused on the broadening of social dialogue as a means of improving job growth. But the conference was limited to endorsing the conclusions of the 1993 White Paper. Representatives of the European Parliament, the Economic and Social Committee, the Committee of the Regions, and the ILO encouraged the heads of state and government to give employment the highest priority and to signal a firm commitment to infrastructure investment at the upcoming Florence Summit. Similarly, in the final text of his Confidence Pact, Commission President Santer called for the Florence Council to "launch a vast mobilization for employment" (Commission, 1996b: 28). The November 1997 Luxembourg Jobs Summit brought about more concrete achievement, with member states agreeing to adopt guidelines on the coordination of annual employment action programs to be monitored by the European Commission, an approach borrowed from the pursuit of economic policy convergence applied in the process of economic and monetary union.

However, other than coordinating activities between member states, the Union does not possess the means to deploy a European-level employment policy; any response to unemployment must come at a lower level of government. Beginning with the June 1996 Florence European Council, member states responded to Santer's proposed local and territorial employment pacts, designed to define specific needs, particularly for services, in local markets, and to channel resources toward those ends. In Florence the Council invited member states to select regions or cities to serve as candidates for pilot projects, and at Amsterdam the Council announced that approximately ninety such projects would be launched toward the end of 1997.

Although the Union's ability to act on unemployment is highly constrained, public attention to the unemployment problem has strengthened the defensive reaction to the single market program in several ways. First, it has sustained the strength of the social dimension lobby within the Commission. Since the seriousness of the unemployment problem is widely acknowledged, DG V (Social Affairs) can keep itself from being shut out of debates about competitiveness by claiming to speak for "public opinion."[13] Additionally, the unemployment issue seems to have given at least a small fillip to the process of social dialogue between UNICE, the European employers' federation, and ETUC, representative of the European trade unions. Although the process of voluntary social dialogue has been tentative and impeded by the lack of commitment by the employers' federation to bargain at the European level and the organizational limits of the union federation to do so, in May 1996 the social partners reached a framework agreement extending enhanced rights to part-time workers. This represented the second accord between UNICE and ETUC, the first a December 1995 agreement establishing a minimum standard for parental and family leave that quickly became a proposed Council Directive (Commission, 1996a).

Perceptions of an imbalance between competitiveness and social cohesion in the implementation of the single market program have spread from the focus on unemployment to other policy areas. For example, the Commission's experience with massive state aid to the French bank Crédit Lyonnais has raised its awareness that the banking sector remains a largely unexplored minefield of state aid. However, at the June 1997 Amsterdam summit, Germany gained support from other member states for a declaration protecting public banks from the Commission's scrutiny, provided member states ensure that these banks are favored only to the extent necessary for them to perform their public service functions.[14]

A measure sponsored by Belgium and the Netherlands similarly shields public broadcasting from the competition rules.[15] This development is closely related to the efforts of the Party of the European Socialists, spearheaded since the May 1997 election by the French government, along with other associations of public services,[16] to defend the role of "services of general economic interest" in European society and prevent their dismantling in the name of competition.[17] The Amsterdam Treaty includes a protocol on public services intended to impede zealous liberalization efforts by the Commission in public services markets.

Finally, influenced by the Vilvoorde episode, the social dimension appears with remarkable prominence in the Commission's June 1997 Action Plan for the Single Market (APSM). Enhancing the social dimension and "safeguarding and developing the European social model" is one of four strategic targets set out in the APSM (Commission, 1997: 2). The Commission recognizes that perceptions are critical for the successful completion of the internal market, and, in an oblique reference to Vilvoorde, the APSM acknowledges that "failure to ensure adequate enforcement of social rules in individual cases can lead to negative reactions and damage to public confidence in the Single Market" (Commission, 1997: 9). The Commission accordingly has resolved to monitor more closely Union rules on worker consultation and to ask member states to enforce the rules more carefully at the national level.

Mobilization of European citizens

The combination of tightened regulatory control over the discretionary use of public resources and circumscribed social policy at the European level has contributed to labor unrest in France, Belgium, Spain, and Greece, and widespread discontent in Austria and in Sweden, where EU membership is seen as a challenge to the valued inclusiveness of "the Swedish way." Large numbers of workers and civil servants disapprove of the austerity that has been wrought in the name of an ever closer Europe.

Along with proximity to Brussels, this welling discontent may explain why the case of Renault's Vilvoorde plant took on such symbolic value in the spring of 1997. In response to the announced plant closure, workers at Renault's production sites in Belgium, France, and Spain coordinated industrial action – the first ever "Euro-strike" – as Renault trade union representatives from across Europe met in Paris.[18] Legal action in French courts by Renault's European works council led to a ruling that the company would have to suspend the plant closure until it met with its works council in accordance with the the EU's 1994 Works Council Directive (*Financial Times*, April 5, 1997: 2). EU Social Affairs Commissioner Padraig Flynn labeled the affair a "sabotage of the construction of Europe,"[19] which demonstrated the critical need for properly enforced social legislation. The European Parliament overwhelmingly adopted a resolution condemning Renault's failure to abide by a Union directive on collective redundancies and the advance-consultation requirements of the European Works Council Directive.

These activities only succeeded in delaying the Vilvoorde closure. But this is not an appropriate measure of their significance. Most critically, the response to Vilvoorde has not been a call to abandon the single market program. Consistent with the trend toward European-level regulation, workers have looked to the European Union to expand social protection across Europe by supplementing existing legislation on works councils and mass redundancies. While UNICE does not share ETUC's demand for tougher legislation, the Vilvoorde episode has intensified the social dialogue between EU Social Affairs ministers, the Social Affairs Commissioner, UNICE and ETUC, who have sought to reach a "common position" on the precise requirements of existing directives. These developments suggest that, despite their very different visions of an integrated Europe, employers' associations and organized labor, along with numerous other actors having a stake in Europe's social dimension, increasingly articulate their preferences and pursue their interests in an arena bounded by European Union policies and institutions.

Concluding implications

This chapter establishes that the reaction to the single market has consisted of conflicting pressures to limit its extent, reform its structure, and extend its reach, rather than demands for its rollback or abolition. One of the principal responses has been a defensive reaction to the single market program which has involved a broadening range of actors in the politics of Europe's social dimension. As in the aftermath of the emergence of market society in the nineteenth century, the defensive reaction to the single market has been widespread, coming not only from labor unions and other "losers" of liberalization, but also from the business sector. Paralleling Polanyi's argument concerning the universal nature of the defensive reaction to the emergence of market society, even neoliberals have come to articulate and promote particularistic interests in the European arena and to promote Union-level regulation. Akin to the nineteenth-century critics of market regulation examined by Polanyi, today's neoliberals assert that the notion of "social and economic cohesion" is so nebulous that it invites "the EC authorities to start pro-grammes and deploy funds in the name of almost every conceivable 'social' purpose" (Streit and Mussler, 1995: 20). For example, neoliberals see an interven-tionist bias in Union activity in the areas of health and safety, and in environmental and consumer protection. At the same time, however, neoliberals both support the single market project and mobilize on behalf of particularistic interests that require protection as the single market develops, in addition to favoring the promotion of economies of scale in European research and technological development.

While these actors are defending diverse and conflicting interests, they all con-tribute to the formation of a public space for political contestation at the Union level. Moreover, this public space has been forged of multiple forms of represen-tation that link European society and EU institutions. The mobilization of diverse actors in response to the single market demonstrates the wide range of formal and informal channels of representation – employers' and labor federations and the voluntarist "social dialogue"; trans-European labor councils; legal instruments available to individual workers and to works councils; public services interest groups; trans-European party congresses – that comprise the European polity and strengthen the democratic legitimacy of the EU despite the relative shortcomings of the European Parliament and other EU bodies as representative institutions.

In the years immediately ahead, the tension between market efficiency and the social dimension of the single market will be exacerbated as the Commission pur-sues full implementation of the single market program and the European Central Bank seeks to establish its credibility in the early years of monetary union. Unemployment may prove stubborn as the many small and medium enterprises that can potentially provide desperately needed jobs bear a disproportionate share of the costs of the introduction of the single currency.[20] If the responses of officials of the EU institutions, as well as European governments, businesses, and workers, follow the pattern of the first post-SEA decade, the result will be an enlarged European public space in which these problems and potential solutions are debated. This tendency for an expanding range of actors to articulate and pursue their preferences at the European level will further signify the growing legitimation of an evolving polity.

Notes

1 Presidency Conclusions, European Council, December 9 and 10, Essen, pp. 4–5; Presidency Conclusions, Amsterdam European Council, European Report no. 2233, June 19, 1997, p. 21.

2 The Cohesion Report offers as an example the disparity between Lisboa, which increased its per capita GDP from 81 percent of the EU average in 1983 to 96 percent in 1993, while the neighboring Alentejo region declined during the same period from 48 percent to 42 percent. See p. 25.

3 Only one of the twenty-five regions with the highest unemployment in 1995 was in east-ern Germany, so German unification does not provide a simple explanation for this widening of regional unemployment disparities. Commission (1996d), Table 2.7, p. 135.

4 The figure is 49 percent, compared with 12 percent in the US. See Commission (1996d: 43).

5 Commission of the European Communities, "European Community Competition Policy (1995)," p. 78.

6 Article 222 of the Treaty of Rome states: "This Treaty shall in no way prejudice the rules in Member States governing the system of property ownership."

7 A private report produced for the European Commission's social affairs and telecommunications Directorates General predicted 275,000 job losses in the dominant national companies. However, the international union confederation, Post, Telegraph and Telephone International, challenged this figure as too optimistic. See *European Voice*, January 16–22, 1997, p. 2. According to the article, British Telecom has eliminated 110,000 jobs since 1990.

8 *Financial Times*, November 19, 1996, p. 1. The German government plans to privatize Deutsche Post by 2000. In response to European Commission investigation of claims that Deutsche Post is using its dominant position in the letters market to subsidize parcels, privatization will sharply restrict Deutsche Post's monopoly powers from the outset. The chairman of Deutsche Post argues that the proposed level of restrictions is inconsistent with Deutsche Post's public service obligations. See *Financial Times*, May 28, 1997, p. 3.

9 Examples include the European Liaison Committee on Services of General Interest and the Initiative for Public Utility Services in Europe.

10 According to the Commission, in 1994 public procurement accounted for 11.5 percent of GDP in EU member states, or Ecu721 billion, the equivalent of the Belgian, Dutch, and Spanish economies combined. See Commission (1996c: 21).

11 According to Fernandez Martin and Stehmann (1991: 237), the ERDF brings Italy about Ecu1 billion annually, while 30 percent of public procurement would amount to between Ecu16 and Ecu24 billion.

12 Official Journal Annex 4–474/2, Debates of the European Parliament, January 31, 1996.

13 Interview with author, May 1997.

14 The Commission earlier had begun to probe possible state aid entailed in government guarantees for some of Germany's Landesbanken, whose public service function is to promote economic development at the Land level. In practice, the Landesbanken compete with the large private banks, and the Amsterdam agreement is likely to anger these banks as well as other member-state governments whose own banks will have a more difficult time competing in the German market.

15 *European Voice*, June 19–25, 1997, p. 5. The debate over public broadcasting has been driven partly by the complaint lodged with the European Commission by private broadcasters in Germany who objected to the use of license-fee funds by public broadcasters to launch new channels that compete directly with the private broadcasters. See the *Financial Times*, May 28, 1997, p. 2.

16 See note 9.

17 In 1994 the European Parliament's Group of the Party of European Socialists launched a Charter for Public Services, based on their observation that the internal market is tending to turn more and more activity over to the private sector, thereby calling into question the future of public services. The 1997 Malmö Declaration of the Third Congress of the Party of European Socialists refers to the need to "put a stop to the erosion of public services."

18 European Report no. 2205, March 8, 1997.

19 European Report no. 2206, March 12, 1997.

20 Firms that produce for the domestic market or provide services in a local market will experience the costs of reprinting price lists and reconfiguring accounting systems, for example, without benefiting from gains of cross-border trade with a single currency.

Bibliography

Alter, K. and Meunier-Aitsahalia, S. (1994) "Judicial Politics in the European Community: European Integration and the Pathbreaking Cassis de Dijon Decision," *Comparative Political Studies* 26, 4: 536–61.

Commission of the European Communities (1971) *First Report on Competition Policy.*

Commission of the European Communities (1989) "Public Procurement: Regional and Social Aspects," COM (89) 400 final, July 24.

Commission of the European Communities (1994) *Growth, Competitiveness and Employment: The Challenges and Ways Forward into the 21st Century.*

Commission of the European Communities (1995) *XXVth Report on Competition Policy.*

Commission of the European Communities (1996a) "Proposal for a Council Directive on the framework agreement on parental leave concluded by UNICE, CEEP and the ETUC," COM (96) 26 final, January 31.

Commission of the European Communities (1996b) "Action for Employment in Europe: A Confidence Pact," CSE (96) 1 final, June 5.

Commission of the European Communities (1996c) "The Impact and Effectiveness of the Single Market," Communication from the Commission to the European Parliament and Council, COM (96) 520 final.

Commission of the European Communities (1996d) "First Cohesion Report," Brussels, COM (96) 542 final, November 6.

Commission of the European Communities (1996e) Green Paper: "Public Procurement in the European Union: Exploring the Way Forward," communication adopted by the Commission on November 27.

Commission of the European Communities (1997) "Action Plan for the Single Market," communication of the Commission to the European Council, CSE (97) 1 final, June 4.

Cowles, M. Green (1995) "Setting the Agenda for a New Europe: The ERT and EC 1992," *Journal of Common Market Studies* 33, 4: 501–26.

Cram, L. (1994) "The European Community as a Multi-organization: Social Policy and IT Policy in the EU," *Journal of European Public Policy* 1, 2: 195–217.

Crauser, G. (1991) "Public Tenders in 1993," *EC Public Contract Law: Public Procurement in Theory and Practice*, 1, 2 (December).

Dehousse, R. (1992) "Integration v. Regulation: On the Dynamics of Regulation in the European Community," *Journal of Common Market Studies* 30, 3: 383–402.

Delors, J. (1992) *Our Europe*, London: Verso.

Delors, J. (1994) "A Necessary Union," address to College of Europe in Bruges, October 17, 1989, reprinted in B. F. Nelsen and A. C.-G. Stubb (eds) *The European Union*, Boulder, CO: Lynne Rienner.

Ehlermann, C.-D. (1995) "State Aid Control in the European Union: Success or Failure?" *Fordham International Law Journal* 18: 1212–29.

European Court of Justice (1990) Case C–21/88 *Dupont de Nemours Italiana SpA v. Unità Sanitaria Locale No. 2 di Carrara*, E.C.R. I–889.

Fernandez Martin, J. Maria and Stehmann, O. (1991) "Product Market Integration versus Regional Cohesion in the Community," *European Law Review* 16: 216–43.

Hillery, P. J. (1988) "Ar Scath a Cheile," or "We are all so interdependent that every action by each one of us affects in some way or other the welfare and destiny of the rest of us," Eleventh Jean Monnet Lecture, European University Institute, Florence, December 1.

Laudati, L. (1996) "The European Commission as a Regulator: The Uncertain Pursuit of the Competitive Market," in G. Majone, *Regulating Europe*, London: Routledge.

McGowan, F. and Wallace, H. (1996) "Towards a European Regulatory State," *Journal of European Public Policy* 3, 4: 560–76.

Majone, G. (1993) "The European Community between Social Policy and Social Regulation," *Journal of Common Market Studies* 31, 2: 153–69.

Majone, G. (1994) "The Rise of the Regulatory State in Western Europe," *West European Politics* 17, 3: 77–101.

Majone, G. (1996) *Regulating Europe*, London: Routledge.

Monnet, J. (1962) "A Ferment of Change," *Journal of Common Market Studies* 1, 1, reprinted in B. F. Nelsen and A. C.-G. Stubb (eds) (1994) *The European Union*, Boulder, CO: Lynne Rienner.

Nugent, N. (1995) "The Leadership Capacity of the European Commission," *Journal of European Public Policy* 2, 4: 603–23.

Peterson, J. (1995) "Decision-making in the European Union: Towards a Framework for Analysis," *Journal of European Public Policy* 2, 1: 69–93.

Polanyi, K. (1957) *The Great Transformation*, Boston, MA: Beacon Press.

Ross, G. (1995) *Jacques Delors and European Integration*, New York: Oxford University Press.

Sandholtz, W. (1993) "Institutions and Collective Action: The New Telecommunications in Western Europe," *World Politics* 45: 242–70.

Santer, J. (1995) Speech to the Trades Union Congress, Brighton, September 11.

Spadolini, G. (1990) "The Crisis of the Societies in the East and the Return to a Common Europe," Thirteenth Jean Monnet Lecture, European University Institute, Florence, November 23.

Streit, M. E. and Mussler, W. (1995) "The Economic Constitution of the European Community: From 'Rome' to 'Maastricht'," *European Law Journal* 1, 1: 5–30.

Verhoeven, A. (1996) "Privatisation and EC Law: Is the European Commission 'Neutral' with Respect to Public versus Private Ownership of Companies?" *International and Comparative Law Quarterly* 45, Part 4: 861–87.

Weiler, J. H. H. (1993) "After Maastricht: Community Legitimacy in Post-1992 Europe," in W. J. Adams (ed.) *Singular Europe*, Ann Arbor: University of Michigan Press.

Winter, J. A. (1991) "Public Procurement in the EEC," *Common Market Law Review* 28: 741–82.

3

UNITY-IN-DIVERSITY: CULTURAL POLICY AND EU LEGITIMACY

Melissa Pantel

Many observers of the European Union (EU) contend that the existence of an overarching European identity is essential for its legitimation. Without a common culture to bind together diverse Europeans, they argue, the European polity cannot garner the deep-rooted, long-term support it requires from its citizens. At the same time, many analysts maintain that efforts to forge such a shared cultural identity are doomed to failure. They see European culture and identity overshadowed by more powerful and resilient national counterparts. It follows that efforts to create a European identity in order to enhance the legitimacy of the integration project are bound to fail. Anthony Smith, for example, terms Europe "deficient" in comparison with "vivid, accessible, well-established" national identities. Joseph Weiler contends that Europe's residents do not feel a sense of "belonging" to their polity. And Daniela Obradovic asserts that there is no common European "myth" that could serve to legitimate the EU in the eyes of its culturally varied citizens (Smith, 1992: 62; Weiler, 1992: 22–23; Obradovic, 1996: 196).

Such views about the links between European identity and EU legitimacy, this chapter argues, obscure the direction and impact of EU cultural policy since the 1980s. The Commission and the Parliament, the two European institutions most active in this field, have indeed sought to foster a sense of European cultural unity rooted in a common history and set of symbols. But those efforts have not aimed to create a European identity over and above existing national ones. The primary theme of European cultural policy – unity-in-diversity – points to another conception of identity politics and its implications for legitimacy. EU policy has underscored not only the existence of a European identity, but also the resilience and importance of national, regional, and local identities, each with its own rich history and symbols. This policy has conceived of European identity not as monolithic, but as internally diverse. EU cultural policy has sought to build legitimacy through an emphasis on the compatibility of contrasting identities.

At first glance, this unity-in-diversity strategy appears problematic. Brigid Laffan, for example, has noted "doubts about the compatibility of national identities with a European identity" (Laffan 1996: 98). How can European unity be *constituted* by European diversity, as EU rhetoric often asserts? The answer lies in abandoning the statist conception of identities as monolithic and hierarchical and viewing them instead as multiple, compatible, and overlapping. From a state-centric perspective, such a conception makes little sense. Historically, the creation of nation states went hand in hand with the construction of national identities designed to replace, not complement, existing regional and local ones.[1] The statist model comprises central political institutions and a core national identity. But that model does not fit the reality of the EU as a contested, multi-level polity. In the current context, the creation of a layer of European cultural identity does not necessarily entail the replacement or diminution of the other layers. If we approach the EU not as a nascent super-state but as a new kind of "polity-in-the-making," the "unity-in-diversity" approach represents a reasonable way – perhaps the only reasonable way – to foster identification with the EU and the legitimacy of the integration project as a whole.[2]

This chapter is divided into three sections. The first section explores the "unity-in-diversity" approach at the level of rhetoric. It provides an overview of EU efforts to construct a common European identity based on shared culture and history and then illustrates a second dimension of EU cultural policy which is less understood: its focus on diversity. The second section moves from the level of rhetoric to that of practice. It demonstrates ways in which the theme of "unity-in-diversity" has informed policies aimed to strengthen identification with the integration project. The final section examines aspects of EU cultural policy deployed as a legitimacy-building strategy by the European Commission and by the European Parliament.

The themes of unity and diversity

European documents on cultural policy elaborate specific conceptions of unity, diversity, and the connection between them. It is impossible to discern a single, unified approach to this thematic complex. Different European institutions, including the European Council, the Council of Ministers, the Commission, and the Parliament, have articulated the themes of unity and diversity in different ways over time. An analysis of rhetoric also reveals variations in nuance within each institutional context. The following discussion focuses on the overall development of the themes since the relaunching of European integration in the 1980s. Through an analysis of official EU statements, it sketches the contours of "unity" and "diversity" and their connection from the time of the Single European Act to the Maastricht Treaty and through the mid-1990s.

The theme of unity

The two key supranational institutions of the EU, the Commission and the Parliament, have been the most assertive in promoting the idea of European cultural unity. Critics consider the current degree of cultural unity inadequate for the task of legitimation, and they consider the construction of a European identity to be a dubious project given the lack of sufficient raw materials. The Commission and the Parliament, on the other hand, have taken a perspective which affirms the capacity to shape and enhance a European identity. Contrary to Laffan's assertion, this does not imply that European leaders are engaged in "a deliberate process of manufacturing and legitimizing a European identity from the 'top down'" (Laffan, 1996: 96). Their approach to the theme of unity, and to the narratives and symbols invoked to support it, is more modest. Promoting European cultural unity has meant encouraging the recognition of existing commonalities rather than imposing something new. EU rhetoric draws connections between shared experiences in the past and the imperative of deeper integration in the present. But it does not seek to synthesize one monolithic identity from contrasting national ones.

Efforts to link the theme of European cultural unity and support for deeper integration can be traced back to the birth of the Community. The founding document of the European Economic Community, the Treaty of Rome (1957), invoked the existence of a "solidarity which binds Europe" (*Treaties Establishing the European Communities*, 1987: 217) which was to be confirmed by the process of integration. But no comprehensive cultural policy or articulation of European identity accompanied the first concrete steps toward deeper integration in the 1950s and 1960s. This began to change after Charles de Gaulle left office in 1969. EC leaders, as part of their efforts to revive the integration process, adopted a Communiqué on European Identity at their 1973 Copenhagen Summit. They pledged to review "the common heritage" of the member states and also "the degree of unity so far achieved" ("The European Identity," 1973: 119). But as European integration flagged during the oil shocks and recessions of the 1970s, little effort was made with respect to these goals. It is no surprise that the persistence of intergovernmentalism within the EC, and the relative weakness of the Commission and the Parliament, militated against the articulation of a European cultural identity.

The relaunching of integration in the 1980s and the increasing importance of the Commission under Jacques Delors breathed life into cultural policy. Quiet efforts to institutionalize the policy had taken place during the late 1970s.[3] But it was only with the drive to complete the single market and accomplish economic and monetary union that cultural policy and the theme of European cultural unity achieved greater visibility. The Commission's 1987 report, "A Fresh Boost for Culture in the European Community," made the case for cultural policy as a "political necessity." The "sense of being part of a European culture," the report maintained, was "one of the prerequisites for the solidarity which is vital if the advent of the large market . . . is to secure the popular support it needs."[4] The European Council and the Council of Ministers, and the national governments they represent, also endorsed the connection between cultural unity and deeper integration. This is evident in their support for the People's Europe initiatives. In addition, with the ratification of the Maastricht Treaty in February 1992, the member states, along with EU institutions, were bound to bring "the common cultural heritage to the fore."[5]

What does EU rhetoric reveal about the content of this shared heritage and the

European unity it constitutes? The 1973 Copenhagen Communiqué underscored the tradition of social justice and a commitment to economic progress ("The European Identity," 1973: 119). In its "Fresh Boost" report, the Commission was more elaborate. It affirmed the existence of a collective consciousness and "special features" of European culture. "Europe's cultural identity is nothing less than a shared pluralistic humanism based on democracy, justice and freedom" ("Fresh Boost," 1987: 5). Another document, entitled "A Human Face for Europe," emphasizes Europe's dedication to human rights and social justice, and freedoms of speech and belief ("A Human Face for Europe," 1990: 5, 12). Together, these features constitute what the "Fresh Boost" report described as the "idea of Europe" ("Fresh Boost," 1987: 6).

EU documents do not only insist on a shared heritage. They also stress the existence of a shared *history*. Joseph Weiler has noted how legitimacy is related to the sense of belonging to a bounded polity, based on "long-term, very long-term, factors such as political continuity, social, cultural, and linguistic affinity, and shared history" (Weiler, 1992: 22). Much of the Commission's and the Parliament's cultural rhetoric attempts to demonstrate that these long-term factors are indeed present in the European Union. It asserts current commonalities, and underscores their roots in centuries of fruitful economic, political, and cultural interaction. For example, a 1993 Commission publication entitled "A Portrait of Our Europe" noted that before "the advent of nationalism, 'European careers' were quite normal" and that "despite the many languages and regional dialects, the knowledge of philosophers and scientists spread everywhere." The report argued that the "peoples of Europe have always been linked together by a shared culture" ("A Portrait," 1993: 5).

Official EU historical accounts do not gloss over Europe's history of bloody conflict. However, they assert that previous wars stemmed from the selfish defense of "misjudged interests," rather than resulting from true differences among states ("The European Identity," 1973: 119). Moreover, they emphasize the ways in which a common history marked by wars and destruction has been superseded by peaceful cooperation and the integration of Europe.[6] Community publications cast the desire to avoid war as a major impetus to integration. The narrative link between war and unity constitutes a significant aspect of efforts to create a sense of shared European cultural identity.

That identity is not only based on history. The Commission and the Parliament also foster unity by alerting Europeans to the presence of dangerous "others" – cultural and economic entities against whom Europe must unite and define itself. The "Fresh Boost" report, for example, referred to the economic "invasion" by American and Japanese programming, and to the "threat to Europe's cultural independence" ("Fresh Boost," 1987: 13). The publication entitled "A Human Face for Europe" noted the importance of an "audiovisual industry capable of expressing and reinforcing the cultural identity of European peoples" and insisted that "a basis for a cultural identity has to be built." It linked the "1992" project to the defense against "creeping cultural asphyxia."[7] The phrases employed in the audiovisual policy literature reinforce the notion that Europeans have not only a common past, but a common present and future.

Though EU rhetoric invokes a shared heritage and history, along with appeals to common external challenges, EU efforts to promote the development of a European cultural identity do not amount to the imposition from above of a clearly defined monolithic notion of "Europeanness." The approach to heritage and history stresses commonalities rather than uniformity; affinities among Europeans, not their cultural homogeneity. This tactic resembles the one Anthony Smith advocates: the promotion of "partially shared historical traditions and cultural heritages" (Smith 1992: 70). Furthermore, EU documents avoid clear delineation of the cultural borders separating Europe from the rest of the world. While the EU rhetoric is sometimes specific about the boundaries of "Europe," limiting it to the member states, at other points the term is used broadly and refers to all of Europe, East and West.[8] Moreover, as the 1995 Transatlantic Declaration showed, EU leaders are not inattentive to cultural commonalities with the United States. The Declaration refers to the values of democracy, human rights, and economic prosperity that are shared by Europe and the United States. Commission President Jacques Santer, in a speech about the Declaration, recalled the "common heritage that binds Europe and the U.S. together."[9]

From a state-centric perspective, this strategy appears rife with contradictions. How can a focus on commonalities rather than unity foster a shared cultural identity? How can the promotion of a European identity succeed if its boundaries are not clear? If EU leaders had ever intended to impose a single conception of European cultural unity, and if this were indeed required to legitimate the EU as a system of governance, these criticisms would have some validity. In fact, an examination of cultural policy rhetoric reveals sensitivity to the reality of the EU as a multi-level, contested polity. The openness and contestation of boundaries – the latter most evident in the context of EU expansion – are essential characteristics of the EU as a polity. And the resilience of national identities, together with the nature of the EU as a multi-level polity, rules out efforts to construct a European identity that would replace national ones. A recognition of these realities has conditioned not only the EU's careful approach to the theme of unity. It has shaped the second major theme of its cultural policy: European diversity.

The theme of diversity

The theme of diversity, like that of unity, can be traced back to the origins of European integration. The founding documents of the Community made it clear that European unity did not imply uniformity. The preamble to the 1957 Treaty of Rome explains an effort "to lay the foundations of an ever closer Union among the *peoples* of Europe,"[10] implying that these "peoples" will retain their distinct identities. While some early documents did mention cultural diversity, at this point "diversity" referred to the diversity of the member states; attention to diversity was meant to assuage the concerns of national leaders with respect to the maintenance of national identities. De Gaulle's vision of a "Europe of Fatherlands," and the more intergovernmental perspective on integration that it entailed, represented the most influential articulation of such concerns. With the 1973 Copenhagen Communiqué, for example, European leaders underscored the central importance of preserving "the rich variety of their national cultures" ("The European Identity," 1973: 8).

With the relaunching of European integration in the 1980s and 1990s, the theme of diversity grew more prominent. In addition, its scope explicitly was extended to encompass regional and local as well as national cultural identities. The 1987 "Fresh Boost" report noted that the "unity of European culture as revealed in the history of regional and national cultural diversity is the keystone of the ambitious construction which aims at European Union" ("Fresh Boost," 1989: 8). And in its official response to the report, the European Parliament stressed that "the essence of Europe is its diversity" and that "not only national values (and cultures) but also regional values (and cultures) are an integral part of our cultural identity" (ibid.: 8, 20). The importance of diversity, and its extension to encompass subnational cultures, found concrete expression in the Maastricht Treaty. Maastricht bound the EU to promote the "flowering of the cultures of the Member States, while respecting their national and regional diversity."

The increasing attention to diversity makes sense against the backdrop of broader national and European political trends. On the one hand, a focus on regional diversity reflected the European realities of the 1970s and 1980s, which saw a reemergence of regional identities and challenges to national authority (Keating, 1995: 3). On the other hand, concentration on diversity, both national and subnational, was meant to address concerns about threats of cultural homogenization within Europe. The passage of the Single European Act meant that "Europe without borders" would soon become reality. The idea of free-flowing European products and citizens provoked anxiety about threats to existing identities. Cultural policy, through its promotion of diversity, could allay such fears.

Recognition of national *and* regional diversity did not imply an endorsement of fragmentation. EU rhetoric conceived of diversity as contributing to and even constituting Europe as a whole. "[T]he essence of Europe is its diversity," the Commission asserted in the 1987 "Fresh Boost" report. "Any commitment to culture," the report continued, "will have to involve making the most of all aspects of this diversity, thereby turning European culture into a culture of cultures" ("Fresh Boost," 1987: 7). The EP, in commenting on the report, reiterated its support for national, regional, and local levels of culture. "'European culture' must be viewed as an intricate nexus of cultures," it insisted ("Fresh Boost," 1989). The notion of a "culture of cultures" seems paradoxical. But given the reality of European diversity, those responsible for cultural policy in both the Commission and the EP believed that a viable conception of European cultural unity could not be monolithic.

European cultural identity should not be thought of, then, as "higher" in some hierarchy of identities, the way many think of national identities as "higher" than the regional sort. While its territorial referent is *larger* than the nation or the region, the European identity should not be conceived as the outer ring of a series of concentric circles comprising local, regional, national, and European identities. Instead, one might think of the European identity as connective tissue in the "body" of Europe, linking the bones and muscles – the regions and nation states – to each other. This tissue is attached to the various bones and muscles in different ways depending on the part of the body, but is common to all of them. The connective tissue allows for the expression of the body's shape and strength, and is essential to its overall coordination. From this perspective, the existence of multiple identities does not threaten the stability of a contested, multi-level European polity; it actually serves to sustain it in practice.

An examination of the rhetoric of European Union cultural policy demonstrates how European institutions, particularly the Commission and Parliament, have created and promoted specific conceptions of European unity and European diversity. Each conception reinforces the other. On the one hand, the theme of unity stresses commonalities, yet does not represent an effort to replace national with European identities. On the other hand, the theme of diversity points to differences which exist alongside, but do not obliterate, those commonalities. The image of European identity that emerges, one of unity-in-diversity, does not fit received statist categories. But it does reflect the reality of the EU as a multi-level, contested polity. Moreover, as the next section demonstrates, it informs the direction of EU cultural policy in practice.

Policies to promote unity amid diversity

The theme of "unity-in-diversity," one might argue, is merely empty rhetoric, an effort to posit European cohesion where it does not exist. But this theme amounts to more than mere words; it has also found expression at the level of practice. Support for cultural exchanges and the promotion of visible European symbols have aimed to foster a sense of cultural unity, while support for regional and local cultures has aimed to sustain an awareness of cultural diversity. The two components of EU cultural policy are designed to be mutually reinforcing. Symbols and cultural exchanges point to (and can generate) commonalities, but in no way erase existing cultural differences. And support for local and regional cultures is linked with efforts to show how subnational identities constitute and contribute to the larger European whole. Examining some of the nuances of this approach to cultural policy will help us evaluate its effectiveness as a legitimacy-building strategy.

Fostering unity

Concrete efforts to foster cultural unity through EU policy began modestly. In the late 1970s, the Commission established a small division to address cultural issues. Its primary task, however, was to develop applications of the Rome Treaty to the sphere of arts and culture (Gelabert, 1993: 291);[11] most attention went to production, distribution, and professional training in the arts and the cultural industries. The Commission highlighted its caution, and denied any attempt to elaborate a cultural *policy*, although it did support cultural and educational exchanges as a means of demonstrating "cultural similarities, links and affinities."[12] In 1982, the Commission explained that "Community action does not expound a philosophy of culture, for it would imply coming out in favor of specific ideological and aesthetic options, which is something the Community has no right to do" (ibid.: 291–92).

An expansion of the scope of cultural policy went hand in hand with broader efforts to revive European integration. A breakthrough came in 1984 with the creation of the ad hoc Committee on a People's Europe (also called the "Adonnino Committee" after its Italian chair) (Commission, 1986). The Committee, composed of personal representatives of heads of state or government and the personal representative of the President of the European Commission, recommended a wide variety of actions. In June 1985, the European Council accepted the Committee's two reports, and requested that the Community institutions and the member states implement the recommendations; most of the measures have been adopted. The People's Europe initiatives most relevant to cultural policy were greater support for cultural exchange and the creation of core European symbols. The Committee backed the development of European audiovisual co-productions, and the pan-European broadcasting of national programs. The Report advocated the "twinning" of towns and schools in order to facilitate youth exchanges. These projects aimed to place as many Europeans as possible "in contact with a different culture and way of thinking" and thus foster a greater sense of shared identity.[13]

In December 1992, the Commission reinforced the direction taken in the 1980s in its "New Prospects for Community Cultural Action." This statement of cultural policy advanced a self-proclaimed "modern" approach to culture with a greater emphasis on educational exchanges (ERASMUS, Youth for Europe[14]), language training (Lingua[15]), information and research.[16] Since 1994, the Commission has drawn attention to three areas: protection of patrimony; the promotion of artistic activities at the European level through the "Kaleidoscope" project; and the diffusion and translation of European literary and theatrical works through "Ariane." Here, too, the goal was the creation of a greater sense of European cultural identity.

The Adonnino Committee, in addition to sparking a drive for more cultural exchanges, supported the creation of European symbols intended to embody European identity: a flag, an anthem, a holiday,[17] and a passport. While the blue flag with twelve five-pointed gold stars had been used by the Council of Europe since 1955, it was hoisted for the first time as the Community flag in May 1986. Along with the flag – for Delors, "a symbol for Europeans of endless hope nurtured by our ideal and our struggle" (Commission, 1987: 4) – the Community also selected a European anthem, the prelude of "Ode to Joy" from Beethoven's ninth symphony. The Community promoted the use of a European passport, the "symbol *par excellence* of membership of that community" (ibid.). And it selected

May 9 as Europe Day, in commemoration of the Schuman Declaration of 1950. The holiday, Delors intoned, should "instigate every year a renewed awakening of European awareness" (ibid.: 4–5). For the Adonnino Committee, these measures were to strengthen European identity through "signs and symbols which help . . . people to express themselves, to communicate and to identify one another in every-day life" ("People's Europe," 1986: 10).

The growing importance of cultural policy from the mid-1980s onward reached its apogee with the Maastricht Treaty.[18] Article 128 placed the field of culture squarely within the range of EU competence, and called on European leaders to place greater emphasis on cultural and educational exchanges. Efforts to foster a sense of European identity in practice through exchanges and symbols do not represent the imposition of a homogeneous European identity from above. Exchange programs are designed to sensitize Europeans to both their commonalities and points of difference,[19] not to engineer a homogeneous European culture. And while critics might perceive that European symbols are intended to *replace* national symbols, the symbols have been constructed and presented in such a way that they are compatible with – not in competition with – national symbols.

Fostering diversity

EU support for cultural diversity also finds concrete expression at the level of practice. At first glance, the application of the principle of subsidiarity (enshrined in the Maastricht Treaty) to the field of culture might be perceived as a limitation on the EU's capacity to direct cultural policy. In fact, subsidiarity helps to foster the kind of multi-layered identity that the EU supports at the level of rhetoric. One jurist, in critiquing Article 128 of the Maastricht Treaty, notes that the EU can only *encourage* cultural action: "the initiative in cultural policy will continue to lie with the Member States" (Lane, 1993: 11). However, the encouragement the Union gives is broad, and includes financial incentives. More importantly, the initiative will also lie with cultural units other than states, fostering diversity. At the same time, the Commission fashions a broader constituency for its cultural initiatives and is empowered to advance its conception of cultural policy as it develops direct con-tacts with actors at the local and regional levels.

Article 128 elaborates a number of other institutional aspects of cultural policy designed to safeguard and promote diversity. For instance, the Council must con-sult the Committee of Regions on cultural action. It cannot seek to harmonize national laws and regulations in the cultural sphere. And the EU is bound to take into account the impact on culture when devising its various policies.[20] As a whole, Article 128 both obliges the EU to respect cultural diversity and gives it occasion to incorporate cultural issues into its dealings with states, regions, and smaller locales. EU cultural policy "should not be confounded with the cultural policies conducted by states or regions"; it should be expanded in ways compatible with them.[21] The Council of Ministers emphasized this compatibility in its insistence that EU cultural policy "should neither replace nor compete" with national and regional activities, "but should bring added value to them and create bridges among them."[22]

Initiatives of this sort can be traced back to the relaunching of European integration in the 1980s. The Council of Ministers of Culture, which began to meet regularly in 1984, approved programs such as the annual "European City of Culture." Each year since 1985, the Community has designated one city to hold cultural events showcasing art, music, drama, literature, cinema, and conferences, and has provided partial funding. These events are designed both to promote the culture of the particular country or region and to advance the notion of a European culture. A 1990 EP report noted that the program as a whole seeks to promote "European cultural appreciation, understanding and integration within the political context of Europe" ("Cities of Culture," 1990: 6). The European City of Culture program therefore provides an excellent example of efforts to promote unity through diversity by emphasizing particular identities and their contribution to the larger European whole.

A variety of programs designed to address regional development are clearly oriented toward regional cultural diversity. For instance, when the EP advocated the development of a system to collect data on cultural awareness and behavior in Europe, one of its goals was the identification of least favored regions for priority action. The plans devised "must focus on their specificity, preserving, promoting and enriching their heritage, using European education and cultural action as means of promoting specific regional identity and regional development" ("Fresh Boost," 1989: 14). In its 1996 document "Cohesion Policy and Culture," the Commission advocated job creation in the cultural sphere, in order to contribute to the preservation of Europe's diverse cultural heritage "which forms a major part of the continent's identity." Through its attention to culture in the context of regional development, the EU respects its pledge in Article 128 to take culture into account in all of its policy spheres.

Another way in which the EU has promoted the "flowering" of regional cultures referred to in Article 128 is in its support for minority languages. In 1982, the initiative of EP members and cultural organizations throughout the Community led to the creation of the European Bureau for Lesser Used Languages (European Bureau, 1995: 3). One of the Bureau's stated goals is to "define legal frameworks that apply to authorities at all levels – the European institutions, the States, the regions, etc. – in order to develop and use their language in everyday life" (ibid.). Directorate General XXII of the Commission provides partial funding for the Bureau, and subsidizes projects designed by Europe's various linguistic communities. The EU also has incorporated the concern for minority languages into other cultural programs, such as those related to the audiovisual and publishing arenas;[23] members of the EP Minority Languages Intergroup work consistently to amend legislation so that it takes regional and minority languages into account.[24] Language policy provides a concrete example of the ways in which EU cultural policy promotes diversity in practice and creates incentives for identity-based mobilization of regional actors at the European level.

In February 1997 the Council of Ministers described culture as "an integral part of Community action [that] contributes to the realization of Community objectives."[25] The greater salience of cultural policy from the mid-1980s onward was evident in two ways. On the one hand, EU leaders sought to foster unity through the promotion of cultural exchanges and visible symbols. On the other hand, they made the promotion of cultural diversity an important policy consideration. These two strategies were mutually reinforcing. Actions to promote unity were designed so as not to overshadow Europe's broad diversity: exchanges and symbols did not aim to obliterate national identities. At the same time, attention to diversity was not intended to foster cultural fragmentation. The promotion of cities' and regions' identities was designed to increase awareness of their links with and participation in a European polity. How is this "unity-in-diversity" strategy related to the problem of EU legitimacy? The next section turns to this question.

Unity-in-diversity: implications for legitimacy

Since the mid-1980s when they relaunched the integration process, Delors and other EU leaders have made it clear that cultural policy is an explicit part of a legitimacy-building strategy. The Adonnino Report, for example, maintained that it is through cultural action, "essential to European identity and the Community's image in the minds of its people, that support for the advancement of Europe can and must be sought" ("People's Europe," 1985: 21). Similarly, the EP indicated that it envisaged Article 128 of the Maastricht Treaty as a "useful reference point for relaunching cultural projects" which might "help to revive the process of European integration, currently mired in economics and monetarism" ("New Prospects," 1992: 16). Despite limited funding and legal restrictions, the Commission and the Parliament have appraised the effectiveness of cultural policy optimistically. As early as 1992, for example, the EP noted that cultural policy had become "an increasingly crucial means of giving effect to policies seeking to foster a union of the European peoples."[26]

When assessed from a state-centric perspective, the results of cultural policy have been minimal at best. European unity has not superseded national and subnational identities in the eyes of most Europeans. Opinion polls since Maastricht show an increasing skepticism of the integration progress and a distrust of European institutions and politicians. However, if the EU is conceived as a multi-level, contested polity, the impact of cultural policy appears more substantial. By definition, such a polity lacks the strong cultural foundation that most nation states have enjoyed. A polity *composed* of nation states must respect their established political institutions and identities. For such a polity to be legitimate, political actors must recognize it as an arena for political contestation alongside others. Also, it must complement – not threaten – the identities established on the national and subnational levels. EU cultural policy provides evidence of both processes of legitimation.

The EU as a framework for contestation

Work on multi-level governance has focused on the development of formal and informal links between European institutions and diverse networks of state and societal actors. Among the most important links are those with regional actors. Through its structural funds, the EU has generated new political and policy ties between Brussels and regions. In the process, it engendered a political reorientation, a shift of relative attention to the European level.[27] Cultural policy has helped to reinforce the idea that the EU constitutes an appropriate framework for contestation. Through a focus on cultural diversity, at the level of both rhetoric and practice, the Commission and the Parliament have encouraged regional leaders to see themselves not only as minorities in national contexts, but also as participants in a broader European polity.

Through its attention to diversity, the EU has encouraged regional actors to consider the EU in two new ways: as a provider of financial and political support and as a source of an identity compatible with their own. The former dynamic has been well documented, while the latter has not. Europe has provided a new layer of identity for those regions that contain cultural minorities and simultaneously has helped to revive and enhance their regional identities. Throughout history, many regional minority populations have had difficult relationships with the respective nation states into which they were incorporated. Various EU programs have allowed for the multiplication of links between regional populations characterized by the same culture but divided by an international border (e.g. Basques, Catalans). This may help to facilitate the development of a European self-image for these regional populations.

The success of EU cultural policy can also be discerned in the behavior of regional actors. Commission administrators publicly encourage regional politicians to seek funding for culture-related projects from the EU's structural funds.[28] By altering the pattern of demands for cultural funding, and encouraging regions to look to the EU rather than to national governments, the Commission facilitates the development of a European cultural identity.[29] The promotion of a "Europe of the Regions," with its concrete expression in the Committee of the Regions, could generate a new conception of the relationship between European unity and European diversity.

It is plausible that the extension of funding and support for culture has spawned the creation of a layer of European identity above both the national and the regional. Yet this is not self-evident: for example, the EP criticized the "European City of Culture" program for often sacrificing the goal of cultural integration for the sake of the city's promotion ("Cities of Culture," 1990: 6, 9). Overall, though, the EU's involvement at the subnational level appears to have had some impact on established perspectives on identity. The presence of symbols such as car bumper stickers depicting both regional and European flags is significant, as is the incorporation of European symbols into the emblems of some regional parties. In quantitative terms, it is worth noting that the "yes" vote in the September 1992

Maastricht Referendum was highest in Brittany and Alsace, two regions of France that benefit from the EU's attention to cultural diversity, particularly through funding for minority language activities and cross-border cultural exchanges.

Multiple identities

The recent clash over European and national symbols on British identity cards is indicative of the frictions generated by the promotion of European symbols by the EU institutions, the different ways in which layers of identity can be juxtaposed, and their ultimate compatibility in practice. In 1996, the government decided to combine new British identity cards with the new EU driver's license, a document which has been envisaged since 1980 (Washington Post Service: August 23, 1996). This provoked debate as to what symbols should appear on the cards; Europhiles, Europhobes, and various regional actors had strong opinions on the matter. The compromise reached allows for each individual to choose one of four options, each of which contains a different mix of three symbols (the Union Jack, the royal crest, and the twelve-star EU emblem). Some actors accept European symbols alongside those which indicate their other loyalties. But even those who do not have been forced to consider the relationship of their primary identities to a European identity.

The compatibility of European and regional identities also illustrates the emergence and persistence of multiple identities. EU efforts to promote a European identity based on both unity and diversity have generated some opposition. Clearly, forces on the far right conceive of integration as a threat to national sovereignty and to national identity. It is striking, however, that this anti-European sentiment has not garnered extensive support in any of the major parties in the EU's leading states. This fact suggests that the conception of European identity articulated by European institutions – and espoused by national parties that favor the integration process – resonates with the population at large. The official EU view that European, national, and regional identities are compatible appears to find considerable support.

Had the EU portrayed European identity as a force which is naturally *in opposition to* national identity, cultural policy might have had different results. While some observers do perceive a decline in national identity (Dogan, 1994), others note its resurgence. Coulby, for example, contends in his discussion of school curricula throughout Europe that nationality and nationalism are actually "resurgent factors in both the politics of Europe and in the shaping of the various European identities" (Coulby, 1996: 2). Moreover, while Europeans feel most attached to their regions and their countries, a significant percentage of respondents *also* identify with Europe. "For nine out of ten Europeans, there is nothing abstract about the regions. Their attachment to them is stronger than it is to Europe, but there is no conflict between the two."[30]

It is impossible to quantify the extent to which European cultural policy has contributed to the compatibility of identities. What is striking, however, is that EU cultural rhetoric and practice have generated little opposition. European cultural policy has provoked some backlash from those who believe that efforts to promote unity undermine individual freedom and constitute an attempt to produce cultural conformity (International Freedom Foundation, 1992: 5). But that backlash has not led to noticeable dividends for anti-Europe parties, most of which continue to reside in obscurity since the Maastricht ratification crisis. Again, this reinforces the notion that a European identity has emerged alongside national ones. The proliferation of European symbols may be a contributing factor. As Michael Billig points out in *Banal Nationalism*, the omnipresence of symbols such as flags serves to reinforce identities; yet, precisely because such symbols are so commonplace, they often go unnoticed (Billig, 1995: 123). Thus, the EU's promotion of European symbols presents less potential to generate opposition, but still makes a contribution to the emergence of a European identity to accompany the national variety.

The lack of opposition to European cultural policy was evident during the 1996–97 Intergovernmental Conference. The IGC provided a forum for EU institutions, member-state governments, non-governmental organizations (NGOs), and citizens to voice their opinions on a wide variety of issues raised by the Maastricht Treaty; cultural policy among them. Given that the inclusion of culture in the Maastricht Treaty was perceived to be relatively controversial, and given some concern about the threat presented to national identities by "Europeanization", it is significant that meetings and publications emerging from the IGC process produced few proposals for change to cultural policy. Most of the proposals came from the Parliament and favored the enhancement of the policy. For example, the Bourlanges–Martin Report suggested that voting on cultural matters should be altered from unanimity to qualified majority.[31] One NGO, in keeping with others, suggested that the Treaty should be amended to provide "a legal basis for a Europe of cultures," particularly regional cultures (Agence Europe, 1996).

While it would be premature to conclude that the apparent lack of opposition to cultural policy in the IGC indicates the wholehearted embrace of the EU's approach to culture and identity, it does indicate a minimum, passive acceptance. Had the Commission and the Parliament endorsed a cultural policy that promoted European unity to the neglect of national and regional cultures, they would likely have met with strong opposition during the IGC. The theme of unity-in-diversity which lies at the heart of EU strategy, then, reflects the EU's political realities: the emergence of Europe as an object of political attention and identification, and the ongoing resilience of nations and regions. EU cultural policy is fostering a new layer of identity that complements the others without replacing them.

Conclusion

This study of European Union cultural policy has revealed a conscious legitimacy-building strategy on the part of the European Commission and the European Parliament. By promoting a European identity, these two institutions hope to contribute to a broader legitimacy-building effort. The European identity cannot and should not be compared to any national identity: it is inherently different, just as the EU is a polity inherently different from the nation state. Against this back-drop, the "unity-in-diversity" strategy is the only one suitable to the creation of a meaningful European identity. It leaves this identity open to multiple interpreta-tions and juxtapositions. European cultural policy has encouraged regional actors, in particular, to conceive of their identities in new ways which include a European component.

The 1996–97 IGC produced one small but significant change for cultural policy. The Treaty of Amsterdam modified Article 128 to read: "The Community shall take cultural aspects into account in its action under other provisions of this Treaty, *in particular in order to respect and to promote the diversity of its cultures.*"[32] This amendment to Article 128 marks the culmination of a trend since the 1980s: European cultural diversity is to be a concern in *all* EU policy spheres. This most recent development in cultural policy is emblematic of the way in which "unity-in-diversity" has been employed as a legitimacy-building strategy: through gradual change and the advo-cacy of inclusivity, cultural policy aims to increase identification with the EU and legitimate the integration process as a whole.

In the European context, cultural policy modeled on national policies would be doomed to fail. To argue that the EU has sought to forge a European identity on the national model and has failed or that the absence of sources of organic unity leaves the EU with no basis for legitimacy obscures the political context within which its cultural policy unfolds: the continued salience of national and subnational institutions and identities. Laffan argues that "just as nation-states are 'imagined communities'," official policy in the Union is to construct such a community (Laffan, 1996). While Benedict Anderson's "imagined community" holds in the EU context, the comparison with the nation state does not. National identity – actual or ideal-typical – is not an appropriate benchmark for the assessment of the nature and effectiveness of European cultural policy. In the EU's ongoing quest for legit-imation, Europe must be imagined, but in new ways.

APPENDIX

Treaty on European Union, Article 128, "Culture" (Office for Official Publications of the European Communities, 1995: 261–62).

1   The Community shall contribute to the flowering of the cultures of the Member States, while respecting their national and regional diversity and at the same time bringing the common cultural heritage to the fore.

2   Action by the Community shall be aimed at encouraging cooperation between Member States and, if necessary, supporting and supplementing their action in the following areas:
    • improvement of the knowledge and dissemination of the culture and his-tory of the European peoples;

- conservation and safeguarding of cultural heritage of European significance;
- non-commercial cultural exchanges;
- artistic and literary creation, including in the audiovisual sector.

3 The Community and the Member States shall foster cooperation with third countries and the competent international organizations in the sphere of culture, in particular with the Council of Europe.

4 The Community shall take cultural aspects into account in its action under other provisions of this Treaty.

5 In order to contribute to the achievements of the objectives referred to in this Article, the Council:

- acting in accordance with the procedure referred to in Article 189b and after consulting with the Committee of the Regions, shall adopt incentive measures, excluding any harmonization of the laws and regulations of the Member States. The Council shall act unanimously throughout the procedures referred to in Article 189b;
- acting unanimously on a proposal from the Commission, shall adopt recommendations.

Notes

1 There are, of course, no "pure" nation states in existence; inhabitants of modern states already deal with multiple layers of identity. But since the nineteenth century, the national layer has proved ascendant. See, for example, Hobsbawm (1992), and Smith (1991).

2 For a discussion of cultural policy that conceives of the EU in the "process of state formation in Europe," see Shore (1993).

3 See discussion below in the section entitled "Fostering unity."

4 "A Fresh Boost for Culture in the European Community: Commission Communication to the Council and Parliament transmitted in December 1987 (COM(87) 603 final)," *Bulletin of the European Communities Supplement* 4/87, p. 5 (hereafter, "Fresh Boost," 1987).

5 "Treaty on European Union," Article 128 in *European Union: Selected Instruments*, 1995, pp. 261–62.

6 See, for example, the treaty establishing the European Coal and Steel Community: "resolved to substitute for age-old rivalries the merging of their essential interests; to create, by establishing an economic community, the basis for a broader and deeper community among peoples long divided by bloody conflicts" (*Treaties Establishing the European Communities*, vol. 1, Luxembourg: Office for Official Publications of the European Communities, 1987, p. 25.)

7 "A Human Face for Europe," European Documentation, Periodical 4/1990, pp. 44–45. During the late 1980s, the EC was in the midst of battles with the USA over audiovisual policy and "culture quotas" in the context of the GATT. See Filipek (1991), p. 323.

8 See "Documents concerning the proceedings of the ad hoc Committee on a People's Europe," S. 7/85, (1985), p. 21; European Parliament, "Report of the Committee on Youth, Culture, Education, the Media and Sport on European Cities of Culture," Doc A3–0296/90, (1990), p. 10; European Parliament, "Report drawn up on behalf of the Committee on Youth, Culture, Education, Information and Sport on a Fresh Boost for Community action in the cultural sector," PE Doc A2–287/88, 1989, p. 16.

9 The text of the Transatlantic Declaration and the speech of November 30, 1995 by Santer can be found on the website of Directorate General I (http://europa.eu.int/en/comm/dg01/eu-us.htm).

10 Preamble, Treaty of Rome, *European Union: Selected Instruments*, Luxembourg, Office for Official Publications of the European Communities, 1995, p. 103 (emphasis added.)

11 For specifics, see the discussion in "Community action in the cultural sector: Commission Communication to the Council," *Bulletin of the European Communities Supplement* 6/77, 1997.

12 Ibid., p. 21. In the same document (p. 5), the Commission noted: "Just as the 'cultural sector' is not in itself 'culture,' Community action in the cultural sector does not constitute a cultural policy."

13 "Human Face," 1990, p. 34. Unfortunately, the Commission does not have information on the number of students who have participated in such exchanges since the inception of these programs. However, they do note that the number is relatively small, but that there is a "knock-on" effect, i.e. youth who have participated in exchanges share their experiences with their peers when they return home.

14 ERASMUS is the European Community Action Scheme for the Mobility of University Students; Youth for Europe is a program which facilitates exchanges for disadvantaged youth.

15 "Lingua" is a European Action Programme in support of the teaching and learning of foreign languages in the member states of the European Union.

16 European Parliament, "Report of the Committee on Culture, Youth, Education and the Media on the Commission communication to the Council, the European Parliament, and the Economic and Social Committee entitled 'New Prospects for Community Cultural Action,'" Doc A3–0396/92, December 3, 1992, p. 16. These particular programs are discussed in "Education and training in the approach to 1992," *European File* 5/90, Commission of the European Communities, April 1990.

17 These three symbols are discussed in the "Documents concerning the proceedings of the ad hoc Committee on a People's Europe," S. 7/85, p. 29.

18 See Appendix to this chapter for text.

19 RAPID, "Actions en Faveur de la Culture," 1994, Ref: IP/94/751. DO5372–NT, 94/07/27.

20 See "Premier rapport sur la prise en compte des aspects culturels dans l'action de la Communauté Européenne," Brussels, 1996, COM(96)160.

21 RAPID, "La Commission Adopte le Premier Rapport sur la Dimension Culturelle des Politiques de la Communauté," 1996, Ref: IP/96/316, April 17.

22 Conseil des Ministres, "Conclusions des Ministres de la Culture Réunis au Sein du Conseil du 12 novembre 1992 sur les lignes directrices d'une action culturelle de la Communauté," 92/C 336/01, p. 1.

23 For example, in a program funding translation of literature, the top three priorities are: translating works written in a Union minority language into more widely spoken languages; translating works in minority languages into other minority languages; and translating works in widely spoken languages into minority languages (Commission, "Support for the Translation of Contemporary Literary Works," October 5, 1993, IP(83) 831.)

24 European Bureau for Lesser Used Languages, *Annual Report*, 1995, p. 37.

25 "Resolution du Conseil du 20 janvier 1997 sur l'integration des aspects culturels dans les actions de la Communauté," *Journal officiel des Communautés européennes* No. C 36/4, February 5, 1997.

26 Ibid., p. 5. On this theme, see also "Fresh Boost," 1989, p. 11; and European Parliament, "Report of the Committee on Culture, Youth, Education and the Media on Community policy in the field of culture," Doc A3–0386/93, December 1, 1993, pp. 6–7.

27 See, for example, G. Marks (1992), "Structural Policy in the European Community," *Euro-Politics: Institutions and Policy-making in the "New" European Community*, A. Sbragia (ed.), Washington: Brookings Institution.

28 P. Nicolas, Directorate General XVI, Speech given at "Culture, collectivités territoriales et construction européenne," March 24–25, 1995, France.

29 The collection of comparative European data on culture began only recently. For information on country expenditures, see ERIES–DAFSA, 1996, *Cultural Statistics in Europe: First Data*, Paris: Documentation française. Funding from national governments ranges from approximately 0.7 percent (Portugal) to 1.2 percent (Denmark) of total national expenditures. It is extremely difficult to ascertain the total amount of EU funding for culture, particularly since different kinds of program have cultural components. What is certain is that those in the cultural sector benefit from this new funding source.

30 A Commission document based on a 1991 Eurobarometer survey reports that 87 percent of those interviewed felt very or fairly attached to their region; 88 percent felt very or fairly attached to their country; and 48 percent felt very or fairly attached to Europe or the European Community (Directorate General for Regional Policies (DG XVI), document B–526-92.)

31 EP Commission Institutionelle, "Rapport sur le fonctionnement du Traité sur l'Union européenne dans la perspective de la CIG de 1996," J. L. Bourlanges et D. Martin, rapporteurs (hereafter, "Bourlanges–Martin Report"), 1995, p. 123.

32 Italics indicate the new portion of Article 128 (4).

Bibliography

Primary sources

1973 "The European Identity," *Bulletin of the European Communities* 12–1973.

1977 "Community action in the cultural sector: Commission Communication to the Council," *Bulletin of the European Communities Supplement* 6/77.

1985 "Resolution of the Ministers responsible for Cultural Affairs, meeting within the Council, of 13 June 1985 concerning the annual event 'European City of Culture,'" *Official Journal of the European Communities* No. C 153/2, June 22.

1985 Documents concerning the proceedings of the ad hoc Committee on a People's Europe, S. 7/85.

1986 Commission of the European Communities, "Towards a People's Europe," *European File* 3/86.

1987 "A Fresh Boost for Culture in the European Community: Commission Communication to the Council and Parliament transmitted in December 1987 (COM (87) 603 final)," *Bulletin of the European Communities Supplement* 4/87.

1987 Commission of the European Communities, "European Identity: Symbols to Sport," *European File* 6/87, March.

1987 *Treaties Establishing the European Communities*, vol. 1, Luxembourg: Office for Official Publications of the European Communities.

1988 Commission of the European Communities, "The European Community and Culture," *European File* 10/88, May.

1988 Office for Official Publications of the European Communities, "Report drawn up on behalf of the Committee on Youth, Culture, Education, Information and Sport on Community education policy: medium-term perspectives (1989–92)," PE Doc A 2–285/88, December 1.

1989 European Parliament/Office for Official Publications of the European Communities, "Report drawn up on behalf of the Committee on Youth, Culture, Education, Information and Sport on a Fresh Boost for Community action in the cultural sector," PE Doc A 2–287/88.

1990 "A Human Face for Europe," European Documentation, Periodical 4/1990.

1990 European Parliament, "Report of the Committee on Youth, Culture, Education, the Media and Sport on European Cities of Culture," Doc A3– 0296/90.

1992 Council of Ministers of Culture, "Communication sur les lignes directrices d'une action culturelle de la Communauté," *Journal officiel des Communautés européennes* No. C 336/1, December 19.

1992 European Parliament, "Report of the Committee on Culture, Youth, Education and the Media on the Commission communication to the Council, the European Parliament, and the Economic and Social Committee entitled 'New Prospects for Community Cultural Action,'" Doc A3–0396/92, December 3.

1993 European Parliament, "Report of the Committee on Culture, Youth, Education and the Media on Community policy in the field of culture," Doc A3–0386/93, December 1.

1993 European Commission, "A Portrait of Our Europe," Office for Official Publications of the European Community.

1995 European Parliament Commission Institutionelle, "Rapport sur le fonctionnement du Traité sur l'Union européenne dans la perspective de la CIG de 1996," Jean Louis Bourlanges et David Martin, rapporteurs.

1995 *European Union: Selected Instruments Taken from the Treaties*, Luxembourg: Office for Official Publications of the European Communities, book I, vol. I.

1996 Communication from the Commission to the Council, European Parliament, Economic and Social Committee, and Committee of the Regions, "Cohesion Policy and Culture: A Contribution to Employment," COM (96) 512 final, Brussels, November 20.

1997 Council of Ministers, "Resolution du Conseil du 20 janvier 1997 sur l'integration des aspects culturels dans les actions de la Communauté," *Journal officiel des Communautés européennes* No. C 36/4, February 5.

Secondary sources

Agence Europe (1996) (EU)CIG 1996/CULTURE: Propositions de la Fondation, "Europe des Cultures – 2002," Brussels, April 12.

Anderson, B. (1991) *Imagined Communities* 2nd edn, London: Verso.

Billig, M. (1995) *Banal Nationalism*, London: Sage Publications.

Buchwalter, A. (1992) "Introduction," in A. Buchwalter (ed.) *Culture and Democracy: Social and Ethical Issues in Public Support for the Arts and Humanities*, Boulder, CO: Westview Press.

Coulby, D. (1996) "Warfare by Other Means: Unity and Fracture in European Education," unpublished conference paper presented at "Why Europe? Problems of Culture and Identity," Keele University, UK, September 6–9.

De Witte, B. (1993) "Cultural Legitimation: Back to the Language Question," in S. Garcia (ed.) *European Identity and the Search for Legitimacy*, London: Pinter.

Dogan, M. (1994) "The Decline of Nationalisms within Western Europe," *Comparative Politics* 26, 3: 281–305.

Europe (1997) (EU)PE/CULTURE: "Le Parlement indique des mesures concrètes pour renforcer les aspects culturels de l'union," No. 6905, February 1.

European Bureau for Lesser Used Languages (1995) *Annual Report*, Baile Atha Cliath, Ireland: European Bureau.

Filipek, J. (1991) "'Culture Quotas': The Trade Controversy over the European Community's Broadcasting Directive," *Stanford Journal of International Law* 28, 2: 323–70.

Franklin, M., Marsh M. and McLaren L. (1994) "Uncorking the Bottle: Popular Opposition to European Unification in the Wake of Maastricht," *Journal of Common Market Studies* 32, 4: 455–72.

Gelabert, E. (1993) "The Arts and Culture under the European Community," in J. Huggins Balfe (ed.) *Paying the Piper: Causes and Consequences of Art Patronage*, Urbana and Chicago: University of Illinois Press.

Hobsbawm, E. J. (1992) *Nations and Nationalism since 1780*, 2nd edn, New York: Cambridge University Press.

Holm, E. (1994) "Europe, a Political Culture? Fundamental Issues for the 1996 IGC," London: Royal Institute of International Affairs.

Howe, P. (1995) "A Community of Europeans: The Requisite Underpinnings," *Journal of Common Market Studies* 33, 1: 27–46.

International Freedom Foundation (1992) "Culture Vultures: The EC's Imposition of Cultural Conformity," London: International Freedom Foundation.

Keating, M. (1995) "Europeanism and Regionalism," in B. Jones and M. Keating (eds) *The European Union and the Regions*, Oxford, UK: Clarendon Press.

Laffan, B. (1996) "The Politics of Identity and Political Order in Europe," *Journal of Common Market Studies* 34, 1: 81–102.

Lane, R. (1993) "New Community Competences under the Maastricht Treaty," *Common Market Law Review* 30: 939–79.

Obradovic, D. (1996) "Policy Legitimacy and the European Union," *Journal of Common Market Studies* 34, 2: 191–221.

RAPID (1994) "Actions en Faveur de la Culture," Ref: IP/94/751. DO5372–NT, July 27.

RAPID (1996) "La Commission Adopte le Premier Rapport sur la Dimension Culturelle des Politiques de la Communauté," Ref: IP/96/316, April 17.

Shore, C. (1993) "Inventing the 'People's Europe': Critical Approaches to European Community 'Cultural Policy,'" *Man* 28, 4: 779–800.

Smith, A. D. (1991) *National Identity*, Reno: University of Nevada Press.

Smith, A. D. (1992) "National identity and the idea of European unity," *International Affairs* 68, 1: 55–76.

Washington Post Service (1996) "A UK Identity Crisis: Choice of ID Cards Divides Britons," *International Herald Tribune* August 23.

Weiler, J. H. H. (1992) "After Maastricht: Community Legitimacy in Post-1992 Europe," in W. J. Adams (ed.) *Singular Europe: Economy and Polity of the European Community after 1992*, Ann Arbor: University of Michigan Press.

4

RECONCILIATION AND LEGITIMACY

Foreign relations and enlargement of the European Union

Lily Gardner Feldman

The shrillness of public and policy debates over Economic and Monetary Union (EMU) and the viability of the post-Cold War European Union has obscured one of the EU's fundamental achievements and core legitimating values: the development of a "peace community" entailing reconciliation between former enemies. As John Mueller has noted in his magisterial analysis of peace in the twentieth century: "Because it is so quiet, peace often is allowed to carry on unremarked" (Mueller, 1989: 5). This chapter is an effort to recognize the value of a particular kind of peace in the EU, what Kenneth Boulding has called "stable peace" (Boulding, 1989). Stable peace differs from the absence of war; it suggests a qualitatively and structurally new relationship among former combatants. Unlike limited or unstable peace, whose very fragility renders it visible to public opinion, stable peace remains hidden (Zielinski, 1995: 11). Yet, invisibility means neither non-existence nor inauthenticity. An exploration of the dynamics of reconciliation in the EU reveals its actual and potential role in the legitimation of the integration project.

This chapter addresses the relationship between reconciliation and legitimacy at two connected levels: within the EU, and in its external dealings. How does reconciliation contribute to the internal legitimacy of the EU? Recent scholarly discussions have centered on the affective aspects of community in the EU context – the need, beyond material benefits, for "shared" or "symbolic" values that reflect or sustain public support (Wallace, 1993: 100; Laffan, 1996: 83; Obradovic, 1996: 191). Perhaps due to its tranquil nature, peace has not been identified as a potent source of such sentimental attachment for European publics. Obradovic, for example, argues that "mythological discourse, so sorely needed for establishing Union policy legitimacy, cannot . . . be derived from the Community's foundational ideals: peace, prosperity and supranationality" (Obradovic, 1996: 212). This chapter counters Obradovic's thesis about the irrelevance of "peace" for the internal legitimacy of the EU. It argues that the success of peace and reconciliation within the EU has sustained the success and durability of the entire integration project. And it shows how both remain salient values that resonate for European elites and public opinion. Attention to peace and reconciliation points to an important source of internal legitimacy for the EU, not as a static supranational or intergovernmental structure, but as an ongoing and open historical process.

Reconciliation also contributes to the legitimacy of the EU externally – in two ways. The legacy of reconciliation makes possible external relations (supranational Pillar I) and a Common Foreign and Security Policy (CFSP) (intergovernmental Pillar II) in the first place. Employing established statist criteria, some observers deem the CFSP an abject failure and insist that nation states remain the primary legitimate actors in European international relations. Philip Zelikow, for example, refers to the discrepancy between Europe's high aspirations and its actual achievements (Zelikow, 1996: 9). However, critics who equate the fragmented nature of the CFSP with its ineffectiveness and illegitimacy obscure its inherent limits, its concrete achievements, and its growing international recognition. Because it reflects the evolving, hybrid nature of the EU, the CFSP is sharply contested. While it cannot match the coherence of national foreign policies, it nevertheless represents a common effort grounded in the shared experience of postwar reconciliation. The CFSP has endured several highly publicized failures, in the Balkans in particular, but has been effective in many lesser-known contexts. And it has contributed to the growing recognition of the EU as a legitimate international actor in its own right.

The legacy of reconciliation not only makes it possible for European states to work together in a variety of international areas. It also provides EU foreign policy with a distinctive content – a focus on peace and development, on the one hand, and the creation of cooperative institutional structures, on the other. From a traditional realist perspective, the perceived fraying of foreign policy cooperation is an inevitable outcome of the Cold War's disappearance. After all, realists argue, the post-Second World War evolution of peace in Western Europe, including the European Community, was a by-product of the Cold War and nuclear deterrence. Even those, like Philip Gordon, who acknowledge and appreciate the non-traditional strengths of the EU's external activities, privilege the military dimensions of the CFSP, and judge the EU accordingly (Gordon, 1998). The image of the EU advanced here is fundamentally different from the realists' conception. The analysis features the EU as a hybrid or nuanced actor (Hill, 1997: 86; Ginsberg, 1996a: 1). It assumes that peace-building has possessed a genuine and not instrumental purpose, that it crosses the 1989 divide, that it encompasses a differentiated set of actors and institutional activities. This focus on peace and reconciliation is a source of the EU's legitimacy in the eyes of other international actors, and in the eyes of its own citizens.

After setting out the links between reconciliation and legitimacy – both internal and external – this chapter illustrates them through an analysis of the EU expansion debate. Expansion represents an effort to extend the postwar legacy of reconciliation eastward to encompass parts of the former Soviet bloc; it promotes the legitimacy of the EU in the eyes of Central and East Europeans and the international community as a whole; and it has the potential to garner widespread public support within existing member states. Whether EU expansion secures the necessary support will depend in part on whether European leaders can effectively connect it with the theme of reconciliation and peace. The legacy of reconciliation represents a real but still largely untapped political resource for EU leaders seeking to increase the legitimacy of the integration process.

Reconciliation and internal legitimacy

The concept of "reconciliation" has been used most frequently in the context of international relationships, and increasingly is applied in national settings.[1] With less frequency and less elaboration, "reconciliation" also has been applied by founders, current officials, and analysts to the European Union (both to Franco-German relations and the larger framework in which they rest) (Duchêne, 1995: 203, 309, 395, 396; Monnet, 1978: 306; Schuman, 1961: 346; Dinan, 1994: chapter 1; Campbell, 1989: 14–15, 74, 78, 95). The centrality of reconciliation between France and Germany for American postwar policy toward European integration has also been clearly noted (Schwabe, 1995: 130–31). However, its implications for the legitimacy of the integration project have not been the focus of scholarly attention. Here, the focus is on reconciliation as a constitutive dimension of the EU itself, and as an object of broader societal identification.

The central relevance of reconciliation for the European Union

The concept of reconciliation captures a central dynamic of the postwar integration process. In his examination of the causes of peace, Zielinski notes the utility of the term "peace community" in certain multilateral settings such as the European Union (Zielinski, 1995: 15). Rittberger has referred to the EU as an example of Kant's "pacific union" (Rittberger, 1997: 14). Both wrestle with the Deutschian choice of labelling the EU as either a "pluralistic" security community (sovereignty retained) or an "amalgamated" security community (sovereignty surrendered). EU officials have characterized the EU in similar terms. In a November 1994 speech, for example, Commissioner van den Broek called it a "genuine security community in which the very idea of war between any members can be dismissed out of hand. Indeed I would describe the Community as the greatest confidence building measure in the history of Europe" (van den Broek, 1994). The concept of reconciliation, then, provides insight not only into the history of the EU but into its very substance.

How relevant is the incipient conceptual literature on "reconciliation" in the European context? Two schools have emerged. One focuses on forgiveness as the catalyst that allows former combatants to forget the past source of conflict and to return to a prior peaceful state; the end point of the process of forgiveness is reconciliation. The other equates reconciliation with rapprochement and is oriented to temporally limited, post-conflict negotiation of differences. The "forgiveness" school does not ignore pragmatic considerations but emphasizes moral imperatives rooted in religious thought. The "rapprochement" school is much more interest-based. While it breaks with a power-centered realism, it nevertheless focuses on material "inducements" and "incentives" for transforming enmity into amity. The first school stresses reconciliation between societies while the second features reconciliation between political elites. Both schools refer to reconciliation as a process. And both identify the need for a major "reconciliation event" that signals publicly the willingness and commitment to change.[2]

While useful departures, the extant approaches are insufficient because neither addresses fully the notion of transformation – the creation of new political structures and systems that make war impossible. The "forgiveness school" focuses on overcoming the immediate past while the "rapprochement school" has a limited sense of the future. Judging by the reality of other cases of reconciliation (both well-established examples and more recent efforts) as a transformative process, reconciliation involves ongoing, dynamic, long-term confrontation: with the painful past, and with serious conflict. Diversity is accepted and expected; harmony is not the goal. Creative, new institutions are geared to the reconfigured relationship.[3] As a process of political and societal change, reconciliation must also find broad, but by no means unanimous, support among publics, and include extensive, regularized, and structured networks of transnational ties.[4]

In applying the concept of reconciliation to European integration, it is important to keep both dimensions of reconciliation in mind – the philosophical/emotional and the practical/material. (These dimensions mirror the two German terms for reconciliation, *Versöhnung* and *Aussöhnung*; see Hajnicz, 1995: 142–61). Thus, in giving prominence to reconciliation and peace as new lenses for viewing the Union, one need not overlook the economic origins of the Union, its utilitarian methods, or its economic, financial, and commercial priorities. While they also have a prominent life of their own, these elements are intimately connected to reconciliation in three ways: as instruments of exchange between societies; as the stimulus to organized networks; and as the focus of elite policy interaction. In his elaboration of "pacific union," Rittberger has reminded us of the "inseparably linked" triumvirate of democracy, economic exchange, and peace (Rittberger, 1997: 3). As a process and set of activities, then, reconciliation points to the dual nature of the EU – as a set of states pursuing material interests while simultaneously committed to the construction of new institutions that mark a break with a destructive past.

The features of this more elaborate, long-term notion of reconciliation can be found in the historical development of the EU. The motivations for the Schuman Plan, the "reconciliation event," were both pragmatic and moral: it was designed both to make war between France and Germany impossible and to spur postwar economic recovery (Duchêne, 1994). The decades after 1950 saw further efforts to institutionalize cooperation and a series of major crises rooted in contrasting interests – the EDC crisis of the 1950s, the empty chair crisis of the 1960s, the Eurosclerosis crisis of the 1970s, the budget crisis of the 1980s, the financial market crisis of the 1990s. New decision-making institutions continue to be devised, and societal relations and networks are expanding and highly institutionalized (Kohler-Koch, 1994: 10, 20; Laffan, 1996: 91; Risse-Kappen, 1996). The historical development of the EU has generated an appreciation of both the pragmatic and moral dimensions of reconciliation – as a proven source of security and prosperity and a break with age-old national animosities. Reconciliation is both a historic achievement and an ongoing source of internal stability and legitimacy for the EU.

Reconciliation, public attitudes, and legitimacy

Reconciliation not only provides a conceptual lens for rethinking the EU outside of traditional statist categories; it also helps to explain societal support for that project over the postwar period. European political elites have placed peace and reconciliation at the center of their articulation of the integration project, and their views have resonated within the public as a whole. Peace stands out still today as a key objective of EU elites. A spring 1996 Eurobarometer survey of top decision-makers revealed that "the establishment and maintenance of peace" was the top priority for the next ten years, together with fighting unemployment, crime, and terrorism (European Commission, 1996c: 5). Responses in Eurobarometer surveys in 1995 and 1996 also reveal a high attachment to peace on the part of the public. More respondents in 1995 (46 percent) chose peace as a priority for the next ten years than chose ten other items (promoting economic growth in the EU was viewed as a priority by only 29 percent) (European Commission, 1996a: Table 3.15, B.52). In 1996, the figure had risen to 88 percent (now peace shared a second ranking with fighting terrorism, drug trafficking and organized crime; fighting unemployment was first with 89 percent of respondents considering it a priority) (European Commission, 1996b: Table 3.10, B.36).[5] A year later, the response remained at the same high level (European Commission, 1998: Table 3.7, B.39).

Other public opinion evidence reveals the extent to which support for peace dovetails with an appreciation of the EU as a source of postwar reconciliation. Whereas the priority question related to a geographically broad application of peace ("to help establish and maintain peace throughout Europe"), a 1995 question on attitudes toward peace concerned the EU specifically. When asked to choose between "One of the main reasons for the EU is to avoid war between member states" and "Even if the EU were dissolved tomorrow, a future war between any of its member states is unthinkable," 49 percent of respondents selected the first statement and 26 percent the second. Only 14 percent disagreed with both statements; a large proportion of respondents viewed the EU as a framework for peace, and a large plurality viewed its continued existence as essential to that objective (European Commission, 1996a: Table 3.16, B.52).

This evidence suggests that the concept of reconciliation not only provides a lens through which to view the integration process, but represents a reservoir of actual and potential political support for it. Europeans appreciate the material dimensions of reconciliation – the fact that it has brought their states economic prosperity and military security. But they also value reconciliation in moral terms as a break with a terrible past and a starting point for further cooperation in the present and the future. Bringing in the concept of reconciliation casts the legitimacy problem in a new light. It suggests that the untidy, multilevel structure of the EU is not an obstacle to its internal legitimacy. Postwar reconciliation, which preserved existing nation states while transforming their relations with one another, ruled out the creation of a supranational EU that could become the object of direct affective identification. At the same time, however, the reconciliation process itself constituted – and still constitutes – an important source of support for and identification with the European Union.

Reconciliation and external legitimacy

So far I have considered links between the themes of peace and reconciliation and the internal legitimacy of the EU. An analysis of the practice of foreign relations and CFSP reveals other, external links between reconciliation and legitimacy. The success of postwar reconciliation has fostered the recognition of the EU as a legitimate international actor in two ways. On the one hand, reconciliation has made foreign policy cooperation possible, allowing the contestation of foreign policy within the EU to coexist with its emergence as a major economic, political, and security actor in international politics. In this connection, EU legitimacy has been defined either explicitly or implicitly in terms of the "perceptions of other actors in the international system" (Rhodes, 1998: 6; Hill, 1996: 13), a variant of Philippe Schmitter's "externalization" thesis (Ginsberg, 1996b: 11–16). On the other hand, the experience of reconciliation has shaped the specific content of EU foreign policy in ways that have enhanced its legitimacy. In particular, the EU's efforts to foster peace internationally and to strengthen international institutions have increased its recognition abroad. Both dimensions of external legitimacy have implications for internal legitimacy: an awareness of the EU's international role, and the central place of reconciliation within it, represents a further source of public support for and identification with the integration process.

Dimensions of an international role

The postwar integration process drove the gradual emergence of the EC as a crucial and increasingly recognized actor and "presence," in both economic and political terms (Ginsberg, 1989; Rummel, 1990; Hill, 1993, 1996; Holland, 1995, 1997; Piening, 1997; Herrberg, 1997; Landau and Whitman, 1997). With 20 percent of global exports, the EU is the world's biggest trading bloc, outstripping the United States with 16 percent and Japan with 12 percent. The EU's GDP is double

71

that of Japan, and one-third larger than the US figure; it possesses 37 percent of international financial reserves; and manufactures 27 percent of all automobiles (Cameron, 1998: 21; Van Oudenaren, 1997: 124–25). The EU is a regular, and influential participant in the most important international economic and financial fora: G-7, G-10, World Trade Organization, International Monetary Fund, and World Bank. In recognition of the EU's role, the World Bank set up a liaison office in Brussels in September 1996. While the United States remains an economic and financial leader, the EU has increasingly established its own international profile.[6] It brings a particular style and purpose to the international arena deriving from its social market economy base. Overall, the EU's established economic persona and specific economic instruments facilitate the crafting of an EU international political profile, particularly with respect to Central and Eastern Europe.

The EU is not only an economic "giant" (Cameron, 1998: 42); it is also an increasingly recognized international actor in other areas. Quantitative indications of EU political and security activity do not adequately convey its character, but do give some indication of its scope. By the end of 1996, 164 foreign missions were accredited to the European Communities, and the Commission was represented in 126 countries and international organizations. The EU is active in the UN and its specialized agencies and fora such as UNCTAD, UNIDO, FAO, UNESCO, Law of the Sea Convention – as well as the OSCE and the Council of Europe. From November 1993, the date of the Maastricht Treaty's implementation, until November 1996, within the framework of the CFSP there were 40 joint actions, 25 common positions, and 98 declarations (European Union, 1996a; 1996d; 1996e).

What are the contours of European foreign policy in particular cases? While Europe does not possess the policy coherence and military instruments of a superpower like the United States, it has been able to apply three tools of the CFSP – declarations, joint actions, and common positions – to a variety of long-established and new international problems. In the Middle East, for example, joint statements have been a staple of European policy since the beginnings of European Political Cooperation (EPC) in the 1970s. The EU has regularly sent Troika missions to the Middle East, and in October 1996 appointed a special envoy to the peace process. Moreover, the EU has been an important player in both the bilateral and multilateral aspects of peace-making, including the Regional Economic Development Working Group. It is the main supplier of assistance to the Palestinian Authority, and in February 1997 concluded with the Palestinian Authority an Interim Association Agreement that is comparable to the agreement the EU already has with Israel.

The Balkans provide another important recent example of EU foreign policy. In the years after the outbreak of civil war in Yugoslavia in 1990–91, European leaders combined joint declarations with a diverse set of responses: an arms and military equipment embargo; suspension of financial protocols; suspension of trade and cooperation agreements; convening of a peace conference; facilitation of cease-fires; dispatch of cease-fire monitors; diplomatic missions; and the creation of both guidelines for recognition of new states and an arbitration commission for their implementation. While it is the United States and NATO that have been the principal military actors, since the 1995 conclusion of the Dayton Accords the EU has led the non-military reconstruction efforts. Its civilian initiatives have been coordinated through the activities of the EU's High Representative in Bosnia-Herzogovina, while its economic efforts have unfolded through its own PHARE program, its joint convening with the World Bank of the ministerial conferences of donor countries, and the preparation of new trade and cooperation agreements with the successor states. The EU also has aided reconstruction in the region through physical and financial support of the OSCE's preparation and monitoring of elections, and through support for international aid convoys.

In two other cases that caught international attention in 1997, the EU also demonstrated its "civilian power" capacity. In the Albanian case, joint statements were accompanied by EU evaluation missions to the region, the approval of humanitarian and development aid, and supportive and cooperative activities with the OSCE. Statements, Troika missions, and the activities of a special envoy (Aldo Ajello) defined the EU approach to the Great Lakes region and eastern Zaïre. The EU has sought "a constructive relationship" with the new Democratic Republic of Congo.

Contestation and legitimacy

These activities give some indication of the emergence of the EU as an important and recognized international actor. Yet, many scholars, drawing on state-centric assumptions, point to continuing divisions within the EU as an example of its international weakness. Even scholars fully cognizant of the international role of the EU tend to obscure the particular nature of European foreign policy. For example, Carolyn Rhodes's depiction of the EU as a dynamic, multi-faceted international actor represents an important break with realist thinking that either ignores the EU internationally or finds it deadly deficient. But she, too, tends to apply traditional nation-state images that focus on the need for institutional and policy coherence and characterize different national histories as an obstacle.

There is no doubt that European foreign policy does not present a picture of coherence. Realists' image of EU foreign relations as highly disputed is largely correct. As Christopher Hill has noted, interests are "inevitably contested" within the context of the CFSP (Hill, 1997: 86). Contestation can be explicit, as in the failure to come up with a comprehensive, unified EU policy. Or it can be implicit, as when countries take initiatives without recourse to discussion with other member states. In a variety of regional settings, from Albania and the former Yugoslavia in Europe, to the Middle East and Africa there has been marked disunity within the EU. The most severe differences have emerged over the use of military force – for example, in Bosnia repeatedly since 1991, in eastern Zaïre in November 1996, and in Albania in February and March 1997.[7]

However, it is misleading to equate the contested nature of EU foreign policy with its insignificance. The existence of sharp divisions on military issues is hardly surprising given that military security still does not lie within the EU's supranational competence. Even in fully functioning federated systems, such as the United States and Germany, military issues can be particularly rending, as demonstrated by the Gulf War. In the looser, European context, the existence of differences does not amount to an absence of policy. The tendency of national and European officials toward self-criticism heightens the appearance of disunity. Both Delors and Santer, for example, have criticized the disarray of European policies toward the Middle East and former Yugoslavia at certain junctures. What is most striking, though, is the determination to seek agreement, not the existence of discord. Against a backdrop of reconciliation, European elites have increasingly come to recognize the EU as a framework for foreign policy contestation. To focus on that contestation as evidence of illegitimacy is to miss the broader context of cooperation within which it is embedded.

Critics of European foreign policy have focused not only on the existence of discord, but also on the historically grounded differences underlying it. There is little doubt that divergent historical experiences and relationships place limits on the possibilities of a single European foreign policy in practice. Prime Minister Chirac, for example, noted France's "historic ties to the region" in explaining the French attempt to negotiate between Israel and the Hezbollah in Lebanon. A similar pattern is evident in France's relations with its former colonies in Africa, and in Germany's close ties with Central and Eastern Europe. The most publicized example of different historical perspectives undermining joint efforts was EU policy toward the civil war in Yugoslavia. A number of commentators construed the German desire to recognize Croatia and Slovenia as a function of historical affinities and French and British reticence as a reflection of their traditional links with Serbia (Newhouse, 1992: 61–64).

Clearly, an EU foreign policy undertaken by different states will encompass different views of history and its lessons. And those views of history will sometimes create divisions and undermine joint efforts. At the same time, however, the diversity of historical perspectives also has the potential to increase the legitimacy of the EU as an international actor. French links with its former colonies, for example, have provided a source of strength and legitimacy for the EU in its relations with Africa. And German links with Central and Eastern Europe have a similar potential. Moreover, the existence of different historical perspectives does not rule out some convergence over time. Within the CFSP, Hill points out, "member states have no choice but to become closely acquainted with each others' positions and outlooks" (Hill, 1997: 91). In this connection, too, the historical process of reconciliation has fostered legitimacy. Over time, postwar reconciliation gradually drove some convergence of foreign policy perspectives, though not without contestation. As a result, the EU is increasingly recognized as a legitimate foreign policy actor – by Europeans and the rest of the world.

Foreign policy contestation, then, is not an indication of the illegitimacy of the

EU as an international actor. The EU is not a foreign policy actor on the model of a great power, as its policies in the Balkans vividly demonstrated. There, differences of strategic outlook and historical perspective precluded any effective resolution of the conflict. From a statist perspective, these difficulties disqualified the EU as an effective foreign policy actor. When one acknowledges the particular, multi-level structure of the EU, however, it is the presence of a foreign policy rather than its absence that is most striking. Despite their differences, European states have managed to work together effectively in an increasing number of foreign policy areas – including reconstruction in the Balkans. The historical process of reconciliation – not to be confused with the absence of conflict and contestation – has made an extension of foreign policy cooperation possible. In the process, it has contributed to the growing legitimacy of the EU as an international actor.

Distinctiveness and legitimacy

Links between reconciliation and external legitimacy are evident not only in the form but also in the content of EU foreign policy. An examination of the Union's foreign relations reveals how some of the character of the EU as a system of reconciliation and a peace community is translated into specific policies in the external arena. In an address to the European Parliament in 1995, German President Roman Herzog noted that the "message of reconciliation still remains the best message Europe can offer the world" (Herzog, 1995: 2). Ginsberg points to the existence of "principles underlying EU foreign policy activities." The EU, he argues, "is a symbol of structural peace and reconciliation among ancient enemies" (Ginsberg, 1996a: 5).[8] Two distinctive dimensions of EU foreign policy reflect the experience of reconciliation: a multifaceted approach to the promotion of peace; and the institutionalization of cooperative international ties at both the governmental and societal levels. In practice, the principles of peace and cooperation reinforce the legitimacy of the EU as an international actor.

Consistent with the notion of it as a principled player, or what others call a "civilian power," the EU has sought to promote peace abroad in a variety of ways: through conflict management; human rights; and development assistance and humanitarian aid.[9] At least since the mid-1980s, the EC/EU has viewed itself explicitly as a model for regional integration and conflict resolution. This vision has been especially obvious in German leaders' references from the late 1980s through to today to "peace initiatives," "peace community," and "role model" of the EC (Press and Information Office, 1988: 343–44, 349; Ungerer, 1988). President Delors referred to the Community as "a focus of attraction in Europe and throughout the world, a model of regional integration serving the interests of peace" (Commission, 1992a: 15; 1992b: 44). In 1995, Foreign Minister Kinkel amplified the point at the UN: "The European Union is intensifying its political, economic and cultural cooperation with other regions of the world. In Asia, Africa and Latin America, it is already a model for peace, prosperity and regional integration" (Kinkel, 1995: 3). Such a vision has stimulated the EU's extensive declarations on regional conflict in every region of the globe and its formal participation in the peace process, for example, in the Middle East and in Bosnia, as noted above.

In terms of human rights, EU activity has included election monitoring – in 1996, for example, in Guatemala, the Dominican Republic, Ghana, and for the first elections to the Palestinian Council. This activity also has included statements condemning human rights violations, for example, in Myanmar/Burma, Burundi, and China. The human rights area suffers from inconsistency: whereas the EU was able to issue a declaration in November 1996 strongly criticizing the sentence passed on Wang Dan, it was severely divided in April 1997 on supporting a UN Resolution condemning China's human rights record (*European Report*, 1997b). Yet, the EU does exhibit the capacity to link economic relations and development assistance to human rights observance, and to elaborate graduated responses to violations. The suspension of cooperation with Niger in January 1996 provides an example.

Development assistance and humanitarian aid also figure prominently in the EU's activities. As the US role in development assistance continues to decline (USAID, 1996: 5), the EU will continue as a primary player in development assistance. It already accounts for 53 percent of all official development assistance and the Lomé Convention has been called "the largest single aid program in the world" (Cameron, 1998: 22). In 1996 the EU became the leading international donor to the Palestinian Territories. Humanitarian aid is funneled through the European Community Humanitarian Office (ECHO). In 1995, the EU was the single biggest donor in ex-Yugoslavia, Afghanistan, Sierra Leone, southern Sudan, and Liberia (Commission, 1996). In 1996, the Great Lakes region of Africa, Bosnia, and the Caucasus were singled out for attention.[10] In 1996 a combination of EU support and member-state bilateral assistance made the EU "the world's top humanitarian aid donor" (European Commission, 1997b: 301–03). According to the Commission, humanitarian aid had "contributed to fostering the first fragile moves towards peace, reconciliation and reconstruction" around the world (Commission, 1996: ii).

Alongside a multifaceted approach to the promotion of peace, the EU's focus on institutional cooperation reflects its historic experience with reconciliation. The EU has sought in particular to institutionalize its links with regions of conflict, so as to facilitate transparency and consistency and allow the EU to link economic incentives to political behavior. Most extensive of all is the EU's multifaceted relationship with sixty-nine African, Caribbean, and Pacific states. The EU also has institutionalized ties of varying degrees, formats, and regularity, with at least a dozen other regional groupings: EFTA, the Council of Baltic Sea States, the MEDA (twelve Mediterranean partners), the Gulf Cooperation Council, the Euro-Arab Dialogue, ASEAN, the San José Group (Central America), the Rio Group, Mercosur, the Andean Pact, the West African Economic and Monetary Union, and the OAU (European Union, 1996b, 1996c). At the individual country level, there is a long list of trade agreements, financial cooperation arrangements, and political dialogue. The EU also encourages institutional contacts at the societal level. For example, approximately 400 representatives of non-governmental organizations from Europe and the ACP countries convened in Brussels in April 1997 to chart a course for EU–ACP relations after the expiration of Lomé IV in 2000 (*European Report*, 1997b: 2–3). Similarly, some 170 non-governmental organizations act in partnership with ECHO to confront the challenges of humanitarian assistance (Commission, 1996).

The EU also has fashioned a series of regularized bilateral dialogues with Japan, Canada, and the United States. Here, too, governmental and societal links develop side by side. The New Transatlantic Agenda covers a broad range of institution-alized ties at various levels of government, in the business community, between political elites, and among non-governmental actors. The "people-to-people" aspect of the New Transatlantic Agenda was showcased in a May 1997 Washington conference, designed to illuminate and expand societal exchange. Business elites are an integral part of the New Transatlantic Agenda via the Transatlantic Business Dialogue, and industrial elites are also active in traditional security relations (Chilton, 1996: 223, 230–33).

Both dimensions of EU foreign policy, the focus on the promotion of peace and the institutionalization of cooperative ties, reflect the Union's own experience with reconciliation. They represent a conscious effort to increase the geographical scope of the "peace community" achieved within the European context. These efforts have contributed to the external legitimacy of the EU in important ways. The EU is increasingly recognized as an active force for peace and development in the world. And its increasing web of institutional links, both with the developing world and with other industrial democracies, has buttressed its role as an important international economic and political actor.

Links between external and internal legitimacy

External legitimacy – the increasing recognition of the EU abroad – has helped to reinforce internal legitimacy – the degree of support for and identification with the EU at home. Positive public attitudes regarding the EU's external relations stand in sharp contrast to public views of EMU.[11] In a 1996 Eurobarometer survey, for example, 79 percent of respondents considered it a "key priority" that the EU should be "keeping peace by intervening more firmly in possible conflicts." Of the thirty-three possible priorities, only four received marginally greater responses: fighting organized crime (87 percent), fighting against drug trafficking (86 percent), fighting against cancer and AIDS (86 percent), and fighting against unemployment (85 percent). In a set of for-or-against questions in specific policy areas, the response remained high, both for "one common foreign policy towards countries outside the Union" (66 percent) and even for a "common defence and military policy" (60 percent) (European Commission, 1996b: Tables 3.11 and 3.13, B.38–B.46). A US government poll of European attitudes showed equally high responses (USIA, 1997: 6).

With respect to more specific areas of principled activity set out above, acceptance of EU competence was also high. For example, 71 percent of respondents preferred joint EU decision-making on Third World cooperation; only 20 percent thought it should be a national competence (European Commission, 1996b: 59). In the fall of 1996, 83 percent of respondents were in favor of an increase in the EU budget for development assistance. Africa should be a focal point according to 69 percent of respondents whereas Central and Eastern Europe should not (only 1 percent emphasized it) (European Commission, 1997a). The weak public support for aid to Central and Eastern Europe may be related to the nature of the public debate on enlargement, a topic covered below in more detail. Discussion has centered almost exclusively on the economic costs, and has neglected the political necessity and benefits of anchoring Central and Eastern Europe into regional institutions. An itemization of the costs of non-enlargement also has been lacking, although German leaders in particular increasingly identify the dangers of excluding Central and Eastern Europe, and stress the region's centrality for European stability (Herzog, 1995: 3; Kinkel, 1996a; Kohl, 1996: 117).

An examination of public opinion, then, suggests the interdependence of both the internal and external dimensions of legitimacy. European citizens identify with the values of peace and reconciliation – values which contributed to the internal development and success of the Union through time. At the same time, they support the extension of those values to the foreign policy of the EU itself. As a component of EU foreign policy, then, reconciliation not only contributes to the legitimacy of the EU as a significant actor in the eyes of other states and international organizations; it also contributes to the recognition of the EU on the part of the European public.

The case of enlargement

Enlargement to Central and Eastern Europe provides a crucial example of the links between reconciliation and legitimacy in practice.[12] Eastern expansion represents a greater challenge than previous enlargements in light of the number of applicants, the magnitude of economic and social differences between applicants and current members, the combined size of population, and the vastness of territory (Commission, 1995b: 4–7). The process of enlargement contains elements of contestation and of distinctiveness similar to the characteristics of the EU's foreign relations in general. That is, the ends and means of enlargement are disputed, yet the process reflects an effort to foster peace and reconciliation on the continent. Here, too, both contestation and distinctiveness provide evidence of external legitimacy. Despite their differences, EU leaders have been able to reach agreement on the contours of an expansion strategy. And the distinctive focus on peace and cooperation – as well as the promise of material benefits – has heightened the legitimacy of the EU in the eyes of most Central and Eastern Europeans. External and internal legitimacy are linked through efforts to extend the experience of postwar reconciliation to the rest of Europe.

The contestation of enlargement

Enlargement is a divisive issue, as Commissioner van den Broek acknowledged in December 1995: "I cannot pretend that a consensus has yet been reached among the fifteen member states on all points" (van den Broek, 1995: 2). Differences over enlargement, rooted in divergent interests and historical perspectives, have since complicated, but have not precluded, the emergence of a common approach. Four main cleavages have been evident through the mid-1990s: integrationists vs. intergovernmentalists; bold vs. cautious integrationists; richer vs. poorer countries; Central and Eastern Europe proponents vs. Mediterranean Europe boosters (Dauderstädt and Lippert, 1996). It is striking, though, that contestation across these cleavages has not derailed the expansion project. A determination to overcome the division of Europe, and a recognition of the EU as an appropriate means to do so, has generated a high degree of underlying consensus on the issue.

Moving along the first cleavage, Germany, for reasons of stability related to history and proximity, belongs to the integrationists who view enlargement as an opportunity to deepen unification (Kohl, 1997: 750–51; Kinkel, 1996a: 738). Germany also has promoted actively in the East the EU's internal reconciliation model (Ischinger and Adam, 1995; Kohl, 1997: 751). Britain belongs to the intergovernmentalist core who would like to use the process to dilute integration. Along the second cleavage, it is Germany and France that provide the contrasts. Germany has been bold in its advocacy of enlargement and of deepening. While supporting the overall objective of expansion, France has been more cautious; for example, its early confederation initiative was deemed a tactic to delay (but not derail) the enlargement process (Cameron, 1995: 23). The highly integrationist small states have been concerned that enlargement could stimulate voting reform to reduce the disproportionate and growing weight of small states (Baldwin, 1994: 181). The most obvious split over enlargement falls between the richer member states and the poorer countries who see expansion as a threat to their receipt of structural and regional funds and their status as low-wage locations. A final cleavage exists over historic and geographic priorities for external engagement, with Germany emphasizing Central and Eastern Europe and France highlighting the Maghreb. Both Germany and France have sought to minimize this difference through the creation of the Weimar triangle among Germany, France, and Poland to develop common projects; the attention to Asia and to the "special relationship" with the Mediterranean during the 1994 German Council presidency when the CEEC pre-accession strategy was outlined; and the progress in CEEC preparation for accession during the French Council presidency when the Mediterranean Initiative was announced. The cleavages are deep and the stakes are higher than ever, yet past enlargements suggest that contestation can be surmounted through negotiation, money, and compromise (Ginsberg, 1997).

Despite the very real differences in perspective that have rendered the approach cautious and gradual, the EU member states have crafted a comprehensive enlargement strategy toward Central and Eastern Europe since 1989 comprising six stages:

1   the creation of a new relationship between 1989 and 1991 through trade and cooperation agreements and development assistance;
2   signalling the possibility of membership through the negotiation and conclusion of much more comprehensive Europe Agreements, largely in the period 1992–93;
3   a commitment to the prospect of membership under specific conditions presented at the June 1993 Copenhagen European Council;
4   a detailed map of the paths necessary for adaptation to Union norms and *acquis*, beginning with the endorsement of a pre-accession strategy at the December 1994 Essen European Council, continuing with the presentation of specific papers at the June 1995 Cannes European Council and the December 1995 Madrid European Council, and finally involving detailed country, economic sector, and budget analyses that culminated in the Commission's July 1997 "Agenda 2000" opinions;
5   the final European Council December 1997 deliberations and decisions in Luxembourg; and
6   the actual negotiations with the first five candidates – Hungary, Poland, the Czech Republic, Estonia, and Slovenia – at the end of March 1998, and the creation of Accession Partnerships, a unified framework for all resources and forms of assistance in the preparation of CEEC membership.

(European Commission, 1997d)

The course of the enlargement debate underscores the compatibility of contestation with EU legitimacy. Whatever their particular differences, EU leaders have managed to cooperate in a sensitive foreign policy area. Divergent economic, political, and security interests made some conflict inevitable. But decades of cooperation, and the experience of postwar reconciliation, ultimately facilitated a joint approach. Moreover, the contestation of policy has not detracted from the legitimacy of the EU internationally. Central and East European states continue to seek membership, and the prospect of enlargement increased the political weight of the EU in its dealings with the United States and Russia in particular. The slowness of the EU's long-term orientation has frustrated Central and Eastern Europe applicants and some US officials in Washington, but reflects the multifaceted, complex, and dense nature of the EU's identity. Despite some frustration, the United States recognizes the unique contribution EU enlargement can make to the stability of Central and Eastern Europe, and Europe as a whole, and broadly supports the EU's elaborate program to prepare the countries for accession (Eizenstat, 1996: 1).

Distinctiveness and enlargement

The distinctive content of the enlargement process also reinforces the legitimacy of the EU as an international actor. Here, too, reconciliation is central. In addition to the goals of embedding democratic polities and market economies in Central and Eastern Europe through the process and achievement of enlargement, the EU wants to create in the East a psychological environment of "mutual trust," a "feeling of belonging" (Commission, 1994: 4; European Commission 1994: 12). Enlargement also provides a political–spiritual opportunity to "undo the wrongs of half a century" (Brittan, 1995: 5). Enlargement is not only about economic and political stability but about extending the postwar legacy of reconciliation – a point reiterated regularly at European Council meetings and in Commission documents since the June 1993 Copenhagen Summit.

The instruments and activities the EU has chosen for the pursuit of its objectives reveal the principles of its external activity – on both the governmental and societal levels. EU projects, economic and political, aim to foster prosperity and stability, but also to institutionalize a variety of new cooperative institutional ties in Europe.

The Europe Agreements have embraced cooperation in the political, scientific, technical, environmental, and cultural arenas, with the core comprising economic partnership to embed the CEECs in the flow of trade and to facilitate gradual economic restructuring. Aid, principally through the PHARE program (subsequently applied to the rest of the region beyond Poland and Hungary), was one of the first instruments the Union employed to support the process of economic and political reform in the CEEC and remains vital to helping them assume the *acquis communautaire* (European Commission, 1995b; 1997c). In trade and aid, the EU is by far the most important partner for the CEEC (Burghardt and Cameron, 1997: 7; Cameron, 1998: 24–25). Together with the "structured dialogue," aid, and the Europe Agreements, the Commission's May 1995 White Paper formed the essence of the EU's pre-accession strategy by setting out both the provisions of the Rome Treaty and the key secondary legislation relating to the internal market (Commission, 1995a).

The structured dialogue, the Stability Pact, and the EU's regional cooperation strategy all reinforce the economic activity outlined above, but their agenda is also political and they promote security in both broad and narrow senses. The structured dialogue has entailed participation of a consultative and advisory nature by CEEC ministers and heads of state or government in a whole range of EU functional areas spanning the Union's three pillars; this dialogue also has fostered coordination between the EU and the CEEC in international organizations like the OSCE and the UN and in third countries. The March 1995 Pact on Stability in Europe has incorporated peace and security through trade, functional and administrative cooperation, and good-neighborly relations while also attending to ongoing disputes over borders and minorities, as in the case of Romania and Hungary (Conférence, 1995: Annex 1 – Part (b): 5–7, 8–12). Launched as a French initiative and embroidered by the EU, the Stability Pact is now housed within the OSCE. Transborder projects stimulate societal relations, but cannot promise ultimate public support for widening (European Commission, 1995c).

In seeking to develop habits of peaceful cooperation and close institutional links between the Union and the CEEC through the structured relationship, the EU is implicitly applying postwar lessons. The legacy of reconciliation sheds light on both the means and ends of EU policy toward East and Central Europe. While the end is overcoming the division of Europe and broadening the space of Europe's "peace community," the means are those neofunctional and networking lessons gleaned from decades of incremental integration. This approach to expansion is well tailored to foster the legitimacy of the EU as an international actor. Through their efforts to join, Central and East European states have recognized the EU as a crucial partner. And US officials, too, have recognized the full significance of EU efforts in the region. On his departure from Brussels, Ambassador Stuart Eizenstat noted that the "overarching achievement of the EU is the maintenance of peace on the European continent by uniting the energies, integrating the economies, and forging a common destiny for formerly centuries-old enemies and bitter antagonists" (Eizenstat, 1996: 3).

Public support and enlargement

To what extent has external legitimacy redounded to the benefit of internal legitimacy in the context of enlargement? The evidence is mixed. Public opinion displays variation across countries, and, to complicate matters, surveys show dramatically different results. According to the EU's polling in 1995, only in a minority (six) of the fifteen member states has opposition to Eastern enlargement reached above 15 percent, with the highest figures registered in France (24 percent), Austria (22 percent), and Belgium (22 percent). However, low opposition figures cannot be taken at face value, for the "Don't know" answers are dramatically high in several countries where there is low opposition (Spain: 4 percent opposition, 44 percent uncertain; Greece: 10 percent opposition, 32 percent uncertain; Ireland: 8 percent opposition, 40 percent uncertain; Portugal: 12 percent opposition, 42 percent uncertain). And when asked about specific countries in fall 1997, only for the Czech Republic, Poland, and Hungary did EU15 favorable responses exceed 40 percent (European Commission, 1998: Table 4.4, B.53).

Majorities nonetheless prevail on the question of whether Central and Eastern European countries "should become member states of the European Union" if we aggregate the three time horizons of "less than 5 years," "next 5 to 10 years," and "over 10 years." Sixty-five percent of respondents in the EU15 support membership (broken down as 14 percent in the first time category, 31 percent in the second, and 20 percent in the third). Aggregate majorities range from 53 percent in Spain and Ireland to 85 percent in Finland and 86 percent in the Netherlands. In all countries except Spain, most respondents cited mutual security reasons for Central and Eastern Europe's membership, with member states evenly divided in assigning second place either to economic interest or moral obligation. For the EU15 as a whole, 49 percent cited mutual security, 23 percent emphasized moral duty, and 20 percent chose economic interest (European Commission, 1996a: Tables 3.11, 3.12, B.46–B.47). In a 1997 survey, 59 percent of respondents agreed that an enlarged EU would guarantee "more peace and security in Europe," and 67 percent felt enlargement would make the EU "more important in the world" (European Commission, 1998: Table 4.1, B.47–48).

American government surveys in 1997 portray a quite different picture which may result from the specificity of the question posed (the preamble ran: "Keeping in mind that we might have to pay higher taxes to admit new members") and the limited range of respondents (Britain, France, Germany, and Italy). When asked "Please tell me how you would vote if there were a referendum tomorrow on including the following countries as members," only in Italy was there significant support for Hungary, Poland, and the Czech Republic. In France and Germany, opposition to Polish and Czech membership ranged from 53 percent to 69 percent (USIA, 1997: 9).[13] American polls suggest, then, that the EU will have an uphill battle in the next stage of enlargement and will have to muster all of its intellectual, leadership, and public education resources to avert a calamity.

Whether the enlargement process tests the legitimacy of the EU or contributes to it may depend on the tenor of the political debate. Evidence suggests that the themes of peace and reconciliation resonate with European publics. At the same time, however, public controversy about enlargement has tended to focus on its costs. By communicating the links between reconciliation and enlargement more effectively, European leaders might be able to secure the necessary public support. Given its pervasive and widely acknowledged role in Europe's post-1945 revival, it is surprising that EU elites have not grounded public debate and policy rationale – on expansion and other issues – more in the bedrock of reconciliation. The prospect of economic costs and sacrifices obviously does not garner support for the EU project from public opinion, as is clear with EMU. Yet, a variety of surveys indicate that publics can be mobilized around issues of peace, security, and reconciliation. It would behoove EU and national leadership to hear what energizes European publics and to develop priorities and policies accordingly.

Conclusion

This chapter has developed the notion of reconciliation as a basic legitimating value for the EU internally and externally. Contrary to the realist filter of a unitary, undifferentiated, traditional nation state, I have described and interpreted the EU through the lens of peace and reconciliation. Conceiving of integration as an ongoing process in which states seek to overcome past antagonisms and build common institutions – while maintaining their separate identities – places the issue of EU legitimacy in a different light. Because the EU incorporates both unity and diversity, its foreign policy has been, and will likely continue to be, sharply contested. But that contestation does not imply a lack of legitimacy. While they differ on a variety of foreign policy issues, EU governments increasingly recognize the CFSP as a framework for contestation. Moreover, the values of peace and reconciliation – both common foundations upon which differences are articulated and a core content of the CFSP in practice – contribute to the recognition of the EU as an important actor internationally and to overall support for integration at home.

The outcome of the June 1997 Amsterdam Summit reinforces these conclusions. Neither "maximalists," who wanted to make the CFSP supranational, nor "minimalists," who preferred the intergovernmental approach, prevailed. Some changes took place, including the appointment of a High Representative for CFSP (the Secretary-General of the Council), the establishment of a Policy Planning Unit, and expanded financial support. However, the ideal of perfect fusion, rationality, and unity remains chimerical. The CFSP chapter of the Treaty reiterated the "unity and diversity" motif. That motif is not, as some critics have charged, simply an effort to paper over the inherent contradictions of European foreign policy. It reflects the reality of foreign policy in a hybrid polity that does not – and cannot – fit the model of the nation state. The legacy of reconciliation provides the context within which unity and diversity can be combined. It represents not only an impressive historical achievement, but also an actual and potential resource for European leaders in their efforts to boost the legitimacy of the EU at home and in world politics.

Notes

1 The term has been employed by both participants and analysts to characterize Germany's relations with France, with Poland, and with the Czech Republic (Brandt, 1971: 110; Campbell, 1989: 12; Ackermann, 1994; Hajnicz, 1995; Kohl, 1997: 751; Kinkel, 1996b: 2–3; Havel, 1995). The term has also been applied to post-apartheid South Africa (Tutu, 1991), including the creation of a Truth and Reconciliation Commission; and most recently to post-civil-war Bosnia (the US Institute of Peace project directed by Harriet Hentges). For broad treatment of cases in a variety of geographic settings at both the international and national level, see Shriver, 1995; and Frost, 1991.

2 Most of the literature on reconciliation centers on forgiveness. See: Kraybill, 1988; Frost, 1991; Assefa, 1993; Shriver, 1995. The chief example of the "reconciliation as rapprochement" school is Rock, 1989 (Introduction). He does offer a two-stage approach (initial "motivating factors" followed by "facilitating factors" that turn commitment into action), but centers his investigation on the first stage (Rock, 1989: 11–12). A recent quantitative assessment of reconciliation between international dyads straddles the two schools by defining reconciliation as "returning to peace, harmony, or amicable relations after a conflict" (Brecke and Long, 1997: 1), and narrowing analysis to a "reconciliation event" between elites and not to subsequent implementation.

3 While this literature refers to transformation at the personal level (especially by those, like Montville, 1990, who take a psychological approach), it deals with neither aggregation of individual and group change nor institutions for enforcement/maintenance of a new condition. One exception is Assefa, 1993, but most of his observations relate to internal transformation within states.

4 This differs from Deutsch's notion of communication and transaction links between societies which are often ad hoc or accidental.

5 There was an increase in all items, in part because of the changed wording of the question. In 1995, the question was: "Which of the following aims should be given priority in the European Union over the next ten years?" In 1996, it was reworded: "Please could you tell me whether you view the respective points as having a high priority, a low priority or neither a high nor a low priority?" (European Commission, 1996a: Table 3.15, B.52; European Commission, 1996b: Table 3.10, B.36).

6 For regular details of the EU as an international economic and financial actor, see the sub-sections on "international organizations and conferences" and "common commercial policy" in the section on "Role of the European Union in the World" in the Commission's *General Report*, and in the monthly *Bulletin*.

7 For information on the nature of disagreement and the various country groupings, see: *European Report*, 1997a (Albania); Gaunt, 1996; Reuter, 1996 (Iraq; Lebanon; Middle East Peace Process); McEvoy, 1996 (eastern Zaïre); Edwards, 1997 (ex-Yugoslavia). On some major issues, the EU has exhibited relatively small degrees of contestation; for example, over South Africa (Holland, 1995).

8 "Structural peace" was coined by Johann Galtung. I prefer the less static term "structured peace" because it reflects a conscious and deliberate process of engagement to structure peace.

9 For a discussion of "civilian power," see Gardner Feldman, 1992: 143–53.

10 For regular details of humanitarian assistance, see the *ECHO Annual Review* and quarterly *ECHO News*.

11 For detailed analysis of the evolution of public support for a common foreign and security policy beginning in the 1980s, see Eichenberg, 1997.

12 For the EU "Central and Eastern Europe" covers the following ten countries: Bulgaria, the Czech Republic, Hungary, Poland, Romania, Slovakia, Slovenia, plus the three Baltic states of Estonia, Latvia, and Lithuania. The common EU acronym is CEEC (Central and Eastern European Countries).

13 In Germany, there was marginally higher support than opposition for Hungary (41 percent support; 40 percent oppose).

Bibliography

Ackermann, A. (1994) "Reconciliation as a Peace-building Process in Post-war Europe: The Franco-German Case," *Peace and Change* 19, 3, July: 229–50.

Assefa, H. (1993) *Peace and Reconciliation as a Paradigm*, Nairobi Peace Initiative Monograph Series, no. 1, Nairobi.

Baldwin, R. (1994) *Towards an Integrated Europe*, London: CEPR.

Boulding, K. E. (1989) *Stable Peace*, Austin: University of Texas Press.

Brandt, W. (1971) *Peace. Writings and Speeches of the Nobel Peace Prizewinner*, Bonn–Bad Godesberg: Verlag Neue Gesellschaft.

Brecke, P. and Long, W. J. (1997) "War and Reconciliation," paper presented at the 38th Annual Convention of the International Studies Association, Toronto, March 18–22.

Brittan, L. (1995) "The Next Enlargement: Challenges and Opportunities," speech to Europolitischer Kongress, CDU/CSU Group in the European Parliament, Ref: 95/163, September 11.

Buchman, F. N. D. (1961) *Remaking the World*, London: Blandford.

Burghardt, G. and Cameron, F. (1997) "The Enlargement of the European Union," European Commission, Brussels, April 11.

Cameron, F. (1995) "The Bureaucratic Politics of CFSP in the European Union: The Roles of Germany, France and Britain," in *The European Union's Common Foreign and Security*

Policy: Central Issues . . . Key Players, Carlisle, PA: The Strategic Studies Institute, US Army War College.

—— (1998) "The European Union as a Global Actor: Far from Pushing its Political Weight Around," in C. Rhodes (ed.) *The European Union in the World Community*, Boulder, CO: Lynne Rienner.

Campbell, E. S. (1989) *Germany's Past and Europe's Future. The Challenges of West German Foreign Policy*, McLean, VA: Pergamon–Brassey's International Defense Publishers.

Chilton, P. (1996) "A European Security Regime: Integration and Cooperation in the Search for Common Foreign and Security Policy," *Revue d'integration européenne* XIX, 2–3, winter–spring: 221–46.

Commission of the European Communities (1992a) *From the Single Act to Maastricht and Beyond. The Means to Match our Ambitions*, COM (92) 2000, Brussels.

—— (1992b) *1992: A Pivotal Year*, address by Jacques Delors, President of the Commission, to the European Parliament, February 12, *Bulletin of the European Communities*, supplement 1/92.

—— (1994) "The Europe Agreements and Beyond: A Strategy to Prepare the Countries of Central and Eastern Europe for Accession," Communication from the Commission to the Council, COM(94) 320 final, Brussels, July 13.

—— (1995a) White Paper on "The Preparation of the Associated Countries of Central and Eastern Europe for Integration into the Internal Market of the Union," COM (95) 163 final, Brussels, May 3.

—— (1995b) "Interim Report from the Commission to the European Council on the Effects on the Policies of the European Union of Enlargement to the Associated Countries of Central and Eastern Europe," CSE (95) 605, Brussels, December 6.

—— (1996) *Annual Report 1995 on Humanitarian Aid*, report from the Commission to the Council and the European Parliament, COM (96) 105 final, Brussels, March 18.

Conférence sur la stabilité en Europe (1995), Paris, March 20–21.

Dauderstädt, M. and Lippert, B. (1996) "No Integration without Differentation. On the Strategy for a Scaled Eastern Enlargement of the European Union," Friedrich–Ebert–Stiftung, London Office, February.

Dinan, D. (1994) *Ever Closer Union? An Introduction to the European Community*, Boulder, CO: Lynne Rienner.

Duchêne, F. (1994) *Jean Monnet. The First Statesman of Interdependence*, New York: W. W. Norton.

Edwards, G. (1997) "The Potential and Limits of the CFSP: The Yugoslav Example," in E. Regelsberger, P. de Schoutheete de Tervarent and W. Wessels (eds) *Foreign Policy of the European Union. From EPC to CFSP and Beyond*, Boulder, CO: Lynne Rienner.

Eichenberg, R. C. (1997) "Do European Citizens Want a Common Security Policy (Anymore Than They Ever Did?)," paper prepared for delivery to the Convention of the International Studies Association, Toronto, March 19–23.

Eizenstat, S. E. (1996) "Farewell Remarks to the EU Committee of the American Chamber of Commerce," Brussels, February 8.

European Commission (1994) *Bulletin of the European Union*, number 12, vol. 27, Brussels.

—— (1995a) *Eurobarometer*, results of Standard Eurobarometer number 43 (April–May 1995), early release, Brussels, July 27.

—— (1995b) *Phare 1994 Annual Report*, Com (95) 366 final, Brussels, July 20.

—— (1995c) *Phare Cross-border Cooperation Programme*, Brussels.

—— (1996a) *Eurobarometer*, report number 44, Brussels.

—— (1996b) *Eurobarometer*, report number 45, Brussels.

—— (1996c) *Eurobarometer, Top Decision Makers Survey, Summary Report,* Brussels, September.

—— (1997a) *Eurobarometer Survey: Europeans in Favour of an Increase in Development Aid Budget,* rapid text file, Brussels, April 15.

—— (1997b) *General Report on the Activities of the European Union 1996,* Brussels.

—— (1997c) *The Phare Programme: An Interim Evaluation,* Evaluation Unit DG1 A/F5, June.

—— (1997d) *Agenda 2000. For a Stronger and Wider Union, Bulletin of the European Union,* supplement 5/97, Brussels.

—— (1998) *Eurobarometer,* report number 48, Brussels.

European Report (1997a) no. 2210, March 26.

European Report (1997b) no. 2214, April 9.

European Union (1996a) Secrétariat General du Conseil, "Liste des positions communes adoptées par le conseil depuis l'entrée en vigueur du traité sur l'union européenne," Brussels, November 6.

—— (1996b) Secrétariat General du Conseil, "Dialogue politique, engagements au niveau d'experts," Brussels, November 8.

—— (1996c) Secrétariat General du Conseil, "Dialogue politique, engagements avec autres pays tiers," Brussels, November 11.

—— (1996d) Secrétariat General du Conseil, "Liste des actions communes adoptées par le conseil depuis l'entrée en vigueur du traité sur l'union européenne," Brussels, November 12.

—— (1996e) Secrétariat General du Conseil, "Déclarations," Brussels, November 12.

Frost, B. (1991) *The Politics of Peace,* London: Darton, Longman and Todd.

Garcia, S. (ed.) (1993) *European Identity and the Search for Legitimacy,* London: Pinter.

Gardner Feldman, L. (1992) "The EC in the International Arena: A New Activism?" in *Europe and the United States: Competition and Cooperation in the 1990s,* study papers submitted to the Subcommittee on International Economic Policy and Trade and the Subcommittee on Europe and the Middle East of the Committee on Foreign Affairs, US House of Representatives, Washington, DC, June.

Gaunt, J. (1996) "EC Struggles to Find a Common Diplomacy," Reuter, September 12.

Ginsberg, R. H. (1989) *Foreign Policy Actions of the European Community. The Politics of Scale,* Boulder, CO: Lynne Rienner.

—— (1996a) "The European Union's Common Foreign and Security Policy Before, During, and After the Turin Debates: the Politics of Reform," paper presented at the European Community Studies Association Workshop on the Role of the European Union in the World Community, Jackson Hole, Wyoming, May 16–19.

—— (1996b) "The European Union in International Politics: A Theoretical Excursion," paper presented at the 92nd Annual Meeting of the American Political Science Association, San Francisco, August 29–September 1.

—— (1997) "The Impact of Enlargement on the Role of the European Union in the World," in J. Redmond and G. Rosenthal (eds) *The Expanding European Union: Past, Present, Future,* Boulder, CO: Lynne Rienner.

Gompert, D. C. and Larrabee, F. S. (eds) (1997) *America and Europe: A Partnership for a New Europe,* New York: Cambridge University Press.

Gordon, P. H. (1998) "The Limits of Europe's Common Foreign and Security Policy," in A. Moravcsik (ed.) *Centralization or Fragmentation? Europe before the Challenges of Deepening, Diversity, and Democracy,* New York: Council on Foreign Relations.

Hajnicz, A. (1995) *Polens Wende und Deutschlands Vereinigung. Die Öffnung zur Normalität 1989–1992,* Paderborn: Ferdinand Schöningh.

Havel, V. (1995) "Czechs and Germans on the Way to a Good Neighbourship," speech given at Charles University, Prague, February 17.

Herrberg, A. (1997) "The European Union in its International Environment: A Systematic Analysis," in A. Landau and R. G. Whitman (eds) *Rethinking the European Union: Institutions, Interests and Identities*, London: Macmillan.

Herzog, R. (1995) Address to the European Parliament, Strasbourg, October 10, *Statements and Speeches*, German Information Center, New York, vol. XVIII, no. 16.

Hill, C. (1993) "The Capability–Expectations Gap, or Conceptualizing Europe's International Role," *Journal of Common Market Studies* 31, 3: 305–28.

—— (1997) "The Actors Involved: National Perspectives," in E. Regelsberger, P. de Schoutheete de Tervarent and W. Wessels (eds) *Foreign Policy of the European Union. From EPC to CFSP and Beyond*, Boulder, CO: Lynne Rienner.

—— (ed.) (1996) *The Actors in Europe's Foreign Policy*, London: Routledge.

Holland, M. (1995) "Bridging the Capability–Expectations Gap: A Case Study of the CFSP Joint Action on South Africa," *Journal of Common Market Studies* 33, 4: 555–72.

—— (1997) *Common Foreign and Security Policy: The Record and Reforms*, New York: Pinter.

Ischinger, W. and Adam, R. (1995) "Alte Bekenntnisse verlangen nach neuer Begründung," *Frankfurter Allgemeine Zeitung*, March 17.

Kinkel, K. (1995) "Speech at the Fiftieth Session of the United Nations General Assembly," New York, September 27, *Statements and Speeches*, German Information Center, New York, vol. XVIII, no. 15.

—— (1996a) "Vorbereitung der Europäischen Union auf die Osterweiterung," speech in Alpbach, Austria, August 28, *Bulletin*, Presse- und Informationsamt der Bundesregierung, Bonn, no. 68, September 3.

—— (1996b) "Address at the Fifty-first Session of the United Nations General Assembly," New York, September 25, *Statements and Speeches*, German Information Center, New York, vol. XIX, no. 13.

Kohl, H. (1996) "Erklärung der Bundesregierung vor dem Deutschen Bundestag," December 12, *Bulletin*, Presse- und Informationsamt der Bundesregierung, Bonn, no. 103, December 16.

—— (1997) "Das transatlantische Netzwerk ausbauen und verstärken," speech to the Chicago Council on Foreign Relations, June 19, *Bulletin*, Presse- und Informationsamt der Bundesregierung, Bonn, no. 63, July 30.

Kohler-Koch, B. (1994) "The Evolution of Organized Interests in the EC: Driving Forces, Co-evolution or New Type of Governance," paper presented at the XVIth World Congress of the International Political Science Association, Berlin, August 21–25.

Kraybill, R. (1988) "From Head to Heart: The Cycle of Reconciliation," *MCS Conciliation Quarterly* 7, 4: 2–3, 8.

Laffan, B. (1996) "The Politics of Identity and Political Order in Europe," *Journal of Common Market Studies* 34, 1: 81–102.

Landau, A. and Whitman, R. G. (eds) (1997) *Rethinking the European Union: Institutions, Interests and Identities*, London: Macmillan.

McEvoy, J. (1996) "EU Fails to Back Eastern Zaïre Initiative," Reuter, November 7.

Monnet, J. (1978) *Memoirs*, New York: Doubleday.

Montville, J. V. (1990) *Conflict and Peacemaking in Multiethnic Societies*, Lexington, MA: D. C. Heath.

Moravcsik, A. (ed.) (1998) *Centralization or Fragmentation? Europe before the Challenges of Deepening, Diversity, and Democracy*, New York: Council on Foreign Relations.

Mueller, J. (1989) *Retreat from Doomsday. The Obsolescence of Major War*, New York: Basic Books.

Newhouse, J. (1992) "The Diplomatic Round. Dodging the Problem," *The New Yorker*, August 24.

Obradovic, D. (1996) "Policy Legitimacy and the European Union," *Journal of Common Market Studies* 34, 2: 191–221.

Piening, C. (1997) *Global Europe: The European Union in World Affairs*, Boulder, CO: Lynne Rienner.

Press and Information Office of the Federal Government of Germany (1988) *European Political Cooperation*, Bonn.

Redmond, J. and Rosenthal, G. (eds) (1997) *The Expanding European Union: Past, Present, Future*, Boulder, CO: Lynne Rienner.

Regelsberger, E., de Schoutheete de Tervarent, P. and Wessels, W. (eds) (1997) *Foreign Policy of the European Union. From EPC to CFSP and Beyond*, Boulder, CO: Lynne Rienner.

Reuter (1996) "Santer Gently Rebukes French on EU Foreign Policy," October 10.

Rhodes, C. (ed.) (1998) *The European Union in the World Community*, Boulder, CO: Lynne Rienner.

Risse-Kappen, T. (1996) "Exploring the Nature of the Beast: International Relations Theory and Comparative Policy Analysis Meet the European Union," *Journal of Common Market Studies* 34, 1: 53–80.

Rittberger, V. (1997) "Europe at Century's End – Anarchy or Pacific Union?" paper presented to the Center for German and European Studies, Georgetown University, March 18.

Rock, S. R. (1989) *Why Peace Breaks Out. Great Power Rapprochement in Historical Perspective*, Chapel Hill: University of North Carolina Press.

Rummel, R. (ed.) (1990) *The Evolution of an International Actor. Western Europe's New Assertiveness*, Boulder, CO: Westview.

Schuman, R. (1961) "Foreword," in F. Buchman, *Remaking the World*, London: Blandford.

Schwabe, K. (1995) "The United States and European Integration: 1947–1957," in C. Wurm (ed.) *Western Europe and Germany, 1945–1960*, Oxford, UK: Oxford University Press.

Shriver, D. W., Jr (1995) *An Ethic for Enemies: Forgiveness in Politics*, New York: Oxford University Press.

Tutu, D. (1991) "Foreword," in B. Frost, *The Politics of Peace*, London: Darton, Longman and Todd.

Ungerer, W. (1988) "EC Progress under the German Presidency," *Aussenpolitik* 39, 4: 311–22.

United States Agency for International Development (1996) *Agency Performance Report 1995*, Washington, DC.

United States Information Agency (1997) *West European Attitudes Toward the European Union*, Washington, DC, April.

van den Broek, H. (1994) "The Future of the European Union," speech to the Nederlands Genootschap voor Internationale Zaken, The Hague, European Commission, Brussels, Ref: IP/94/1095, November 24.

—— (1995) "The Challenge of Enlargement," speech to the East–West Institute, Brussels, Ref: 95/264, December 1.

Van Oudenaren, J. (1997) "Europe as Partner," in D. C. Gompert and F. S. Larrabee (eds) *America and Europe: A Partnership for a New Europe*, New York: Cambridge University Press.

Wallace, H. (1993) "Deepening and Widening: Problems of Legitimacy for the EC," in S. Garcia (ed.) *European Identity and the Search for Legitimacy*, London: Pinter.

Whitman, R. G. (1997) "The International Identity of the European Union: Instruments as Identity," in A. Landau and R. G. Whitman *Rethinking the European Union: Institutions, Interests and Identities*, London: Macmillan.

Wurm, C. (ed.) (1995) *Western Europe and Germany, 1945–1960*, Oxford, UK: Oxford University Press.

Zelikow, P. (1996) "The Masque of Institutions," *Survival* 38, 1: 6–18.

Zielinski, M. (1995) *Friedensursachen*, Baden-Baden: Nomos Verlagsgesellschaft.

Part 2

LEGITIMACY AND INSTITUTIONS

5

POLITICAL PARTIES AND THE PROBLEM OF LEGITIMACY IN THE EUROPEAN UNION

Robert Ladrech

European integration has brought into question the relevance of national political parties as organizations promising purposive action in national government. This questioning of political parties has become intertwined with the legitimacy of the EU as the provider of certain collective goods. A resolution of this two-level legitimation predicament is thus a prime motivation for party elites to come to terms with the EU, and, in the process, perhaps confer some form of enhanced acceptance of EU policies among their electorates. In a manner reminiscent of Milward (1992), the need to strengthen domestic positions, in this case the national "party" interest, may be brought about by engaging at the European level to obtain resources required to deliver collective goods. This process may generate as a by-product the organizational development of European-level partisan organizations,[1] which are best placed to serve as intermediaries between actors in the EU Commission and Parliament and national party elites. In addition, the demonstration of a supranational "will" to support national actors, that is, a tangible linkage between parties and the EU issue agenda, may help legitimate the EU as a framework for political contestation.

The situation in which mainstream political parties find themselves within their national contexts, one fraught with questions about their own popular legitimacy (Mair, 1995), has origins apart from the issue of European integration. Popular disenchantment with political parties, perhaps even their (alleged) decline, has several causes, but it is the contention of this chapter that increased policy competence by the EU *aggravates* this situation by emphasizing the image of the irrelevance of national parties in various policy sectors, especially economic. By the same token, the problems encountered in building EU legitimacy cannot necessarily all be laid at the doorstep of EU institutions; some are unjustifiably attributed in the sense that the EU does not have a leading role or full competence in the area in question. This chapter argues that on certain high-visibility issues party elites have begun to make a case for their involvement, though indirect, in EU agenda-setting to the extent it serves explicit national interests. This is very different from early neo-functionalist predictions of a "shift of loyalties, expectations and political activities"

(Haas, 1958) toward a new center, and the type of involvement may be said better to reflect a strategy of operating at both national and European levels.

The chapter begins with a presentation of the EU's legitimacy problem as reflected in the attitudes of European citizens toward European integration and the expectation of material gain. This section will further develop the point that public expectations unjustifiably attributed to the EU add to legitimacy problems. The second section will introduce the theme of national party difficulties, especially the potential for growing *irrelevance* as a consequence of increasing EU policy competence. The third section will then explore attempts by national party elites to influence the policy agenda of the EU. Here special focus is given to the manner in which transnational and supranational partisan organizations were mobilized to achieve national goals in the context of the 1996–97 Intergovernmental Conference (IGC). Finally, the conclusion will address the implications of a more partisan EU – in particular, the potential benefit for the legitimation of the EU that could follow from the introduction of national cleavages into EU politics.

The EU and the problem of legitimacy

The notion that the EU, as a "contested polity," can serve as the object of shared identification and legitimacy, and in fact that contestation itself can reinforce, not undermine, legitimacy, rests upon several factors. The one most pertinent to this analysis is that in which the EU level is reinforced by patterns of contestation at the national and regional levels. As the introductory chapter suggests, as national actors engage increasingly in the multiple levels of the EU–national matrix, the "EU becomes less foreign and more a part of the domestic political sphere." Moreover, "the legitimacy of the EU is enhanced, not as it necessarily assumes greater control of more and more policy, but as its politics become linked up and identified with those of the nation state." This definition, especially support for European policies, is most relevant for my discussion because party elites[2] are most likely to be able to refer to specific national or EU policies as part of their political discourse. Although symbols and certain narratives may support such articulation, connecting their partisan or ideological position with material interests will be the most familiar manner in which party elites present their own goals.

This analysis considers that the European Union's apparent growing intrusion into the lives of citizens via its policies, but more importantly the cost entailed by those policies, for example, the single market project's "rationalizing" of industrial sectors and subsequent unemployment, lays the foundations of the current legitimacy problem. If the "permissive consensus" has indeed shattered, since the early 1990s we might say that it is "plausible that European publics approach the integration process with somewhat of a cost-benefit calculus in mind" (Anderson and Kaltenthaler, 1996: 193). If this is so, performance criteria now become a key focus for the issue of EU legitimacy, hence the linkage of support for European integration and the expectation of material gain suggested above. The more visibly intrusive the EU's policies have become, the more ambivalent are the public's

attitudes.[3] Further, as the effects of these policies begin to generate *political* opposition, as was seen in the referendums on the Maastricht Treaty and anti-EU party
formation during the 1994 European Parliament elections, such developments
raise the critical question asked by Beetham and Lord: "what right does the Union
have to make such momentous decisions about individual life-chances and the distribution of key values, imposing sacrifices on some and opening opportunities to
others?" (Beetham and Lord, 1996: 16). It is precisely at this moment, when the
EU has entered a new phase of its development, that rethinking the concept of
legitimacy for the EU becomes necessary.

The term "permissive consensus" has been used to describe public support for
the EC that was widespread but not necessarily deeply rooted – a situation in
which the management of European integration was left to political elites[4]
(Lindberg and Scheingold, 1970). In the post-Maastricht referendum period, one
with an awakened and more contradictory public opinion, the technocratic aspect
of EU decision-making has become accentuated, thus altering the bases of public
support. Together with the higher and more visible costs of present EU policies, a
type of legitimation that was heretofore absent is required, at the very least because
the EU itself has moved far from its early mission of negative economic integration
and more into positive integration (Scharpf, 1996). Addressing the "internal legitimacy crisis" of the EU that has emerged with this shift, Shackleton succinctly
defines the problem as a:

> product of the realization that we do not yet have the means to move
> from a system essentially concerned with the *administration of things* to one
> concerned with the *governance of people*. Administration can have conse-
> quences, often important ones, for individuals . . . Nevertheless, it is a
> process that is essentially justified by reference to criteria of effectiveness,
> efficiency or fairness. Governance, on the other hand, needs broader
> support within society, a support that can only be acquired through some
> form of democratic legitimation.
>
> (Shackleton, 1994: 5)

Beetham and Lord have suggested that the "criteria of normative justifiability
(authorization and performance standards) . . . provide the key site for the analyses of legitimacy, since it is problems in this domain that typically find expression
in breaches of legality or acts of delegitimation." Authorization relates to repre-
sentativeness and accountability, while performance criteria incorporate popular
expectations along with mechanisms for the "removal of those who have 'failed'"
(Beetham and Lord, 1996: 2). A much broader range of groups and individuals
now feel the impact of the EU on their affairs, and whereas before the single
market project the "permissive consensus" allowed the "administration of things,"
performance criteria *and* mechanisms of democratic legitimation, that is, normative justifiability, are now necessary. The performance of EU policies, both in their
desired result and appropriateness of responsibility, now engage more explicitly the

interests, and thus expectations of material gain, of EU citizens. As Shackleton implies, it is now necessary for the EU to acquire the means to legitimate this shift.

Legitimacy and the attribution of issues

The problem of EU legitimacy is exacerbated by citizens' perceptions that *incorrectly* attribute policy area competences to the EU. Sinnott labels as *attributed internationalization* the process by which public opinion attributes policy-making or problem-solving to an international agency. What matters is "how the public thinks problems ought to be tackled rather than how it perceives the actual competences of various levels of governance, perceptions which may be more or less in accord with reality" (Sinnott, 1995: 247). The potential for public perceptions to be inconsistent with reality is genuine. According to Sinnott, this has a "particular bearing on legitimacy because it contains explicit demands for internationalized action which are neither rooted in the nature of the issues involved nor in competences claimed by the agency of internationalized governance" (Sinnott, 1995: 253). In the case of the EU, this state of affairs complicates the analysis of performance and legitimacy because it unfairly punishes the EU for policy failures not of its doing. According to Sinnott, attributed internationalization can have damaging consequences for legitimacy precisely because it pertains to critical issues such as unemployment (Sinnott, 1995: 271).

Because the EU does not possess clear institutional and/or procedural means for sanctioning failure, that is, an effective European Parliament or elections removing from office the perpetrators of policy failure, the legitimacy of EU action itself is called into question. Policy is seen to be developed in a popular vacuum by technocrats enjoying immunity from accountability. Whom and what ends do they serve? Political opposition, manifested by new party creation or tensions within mainstream parties, grows apace as a result. Anti-EU parties and tendencies are therefore in a position reasonably to invoke protection of national identity as well as a policy or programmatic orientation, for example, a left-wing economic agenda.

To summarize, the EU increasingly has developed a high-visibility profile in policy areas affecting ever broader numbers of organized groups and individuals. The intrusion of the EU into the lives of citizens elicits an attitudinal orientation in response to the policies themselves, as well as, rightly or wrongly, expectations of action upon which judgment will be pronounced using criteria of efficiency and fairness and increasingly criteria derived from norms of democratic accountability. The failure of the EU to demonstrate positive change poses the danger of delegitimation, depending especially upon the salience of the issue(s). The EU's weakness in terms of representation and accountability, the so-called "democratic deficit," further exacerbates the situation. This is the conventional understanding of the EU's legitimacy problem. But, as this chapter demonstrates for the case of national political parties, the very fact that this politicized atmosphere has elicited reactions which acknowledge the EU's institutions as arenas in which to articulate interests and contest policies fosters the legitimation of the EU.

Party relevance and European integration

How has the alleged "decline of party" motivated national parties to begin to intensify their involvement in political contestation at the European level? Simply put, decline is associated with the diminished ability of parties to aggregate interests and present distinctive programs that satisfy constituents' demands. The EU provides a forum in which parties may be able partly to reclaim these functions.

As stated at the outset of the chapter, public disenchantment with political parties preceded the post-Maastricht politicization of European integration. The most frequently cited causes of "party decline" include: changes in the social structure of European countries; patterns of individual behavior; and the behavior of political parties together with the issues that concern them (Gallagher, Laver and Mair, 1995). In addition, some analyses point to anti-party sentiment mobilized by political elites "who genuinely and fundamentally challenge party government or even democracy"[5] (Poguntke, 1996: 340). Katz and Mair also have advanced the thesis of an emergence of a new model of party organization and party democracy, the *cartel party*. The chief characteristics of this party model, as compared with the previous mass and catch-all party models, are its position between civil society and the state – "Party becomes part of state" – and its representative style – "Agent of state" (Katz and Mair 1995: 18). The cartel party model is primarily characterized by the "interpenetration of party and state, and also by a pattern of inter-party collusion" (Katz and Mair, 1995: 17).

The significance of this perspective on the relationship between parties and citizens is the emphasis on the diminution of *choice*. Mair has elsewhere elaborated upon the impact of parties' remoteness from civil society on their legitimacy. Although drawing a distinction between party *change* and party *decline*, he nevertheless suggests the possibility of this state of affairs "undermin[ing] the legitimacy of party government itself" (Mair, 1995: 54). The apparent paradox is that in some ways parties have not declined, rather they have strengthened certain functions, for example, the recruitment of political leaders and the organization of government. At the same time, other classic functions such as the articulation of interests and the aggregation of demands, and, to a certain extent, the formulation of public policy, have eroded. It is in this sense that parties become "less relevant."

When speaking of the danger of eroding party relevance, Mair points to the representative aspect of parties. More precisely, one of the chief characteristics of parties as representative agencies is their "relevance in purposive terms" (Mair, 1995: 46). The capacity of parties in government to guide and control domestic policy-making has been affected by forces such as globalization. This in turn, according to Mair, influences the capacities of parties in government in two ways. First, the scale of penetration of domestic economies by transnational actors and financial flows means that "they cannot always respond to domestic demands in a way which fully satisfies the local interests on which they depend for their legitimacy and authority." Second, the sheer "complexity of the global economy leads to severe problems for the monitoring and control of the policy-making process, and hence undermines the capacity for effective and authoritative action" (Mair, 1995: 47). The result of these trends is twofold: parties are seemingly less able to convince voters of their partisan intent while at the same time electorates question the efficacy of party government.

The development of the EU is implicated in this deterioration of national party efficacy. The growing scope of EU policy-making and consequent transfer of national policy competences to EU institutions results in much less maneuverability for governments in selected areas. Because the EU is more readily identifiable to citizens than the impersonal forces of globalization, the lack of partisan influence in EU decision-making is made all the more apparent. Indeed, "precisely because decision-making within Europe itself is not seen to be mediated by party . . . this is likely to undermine even further the relevance of party in representative terms" (ibid.: 47–48).

National political parties are thus subject to multiple pressures on their capacity to "deliver the goods" once in government. The Europeanizing of policy-making (Andersen and Eliassen, 1993), the growing complexity of issues, and the enhancement of executive and bureaucratic power over parliamentary authority all combine to undermine the role of party in democratic society. Jacques Delors commented recently on the "weakening of democracy," implicitly endorsing the idea that party cartels have wrought damaging consequences:

> It is impossible to speak of citizenship in Europe without posing the question of the current weakening of democracy within each of our countries. This weakening is worsened by the widening distance between the governed and their governments. Parliaments are weaker. Meanwhile, because decisions become more and more complex, this favors the emergence of experts, bureaucrats and technocrats. This weakening causes the dangerous emergence of new extremist parties.
>
> (*The European*, October 24, 1996)

Although some scholars advance the thesis that the development of the EU has in fact strengthened national member states by transferring certain problematic policy responsibilities to the EU (Milward, 1992), another version of this phenomenon suggests that enhanced power has accrued more precisely to national executives (Moravcsik, 1994). Regarding the issue of the "democratic deficit" and implications for EU legitimacy, Moravcsik has asserted that the efficiency of EU policy-making over the past three decades is positively attributable to the fact that "insulated executives can resist pressures from particularistic groups, pursuing policies in the interest of a broader spectrum of society." As a consequence, "while democratization may create greater legitimacy in the short term (though this remains to be seen), a possible, but paradoxical consequence in the long term may be a further erosion of precisely the popular support that democratization seeks to restore" (Moravcsik, 1994: 56-57). The validity of Moravcsik's thesis appears to be time-bound by historical stages in the development of the EC/EU. The strengthening of the executive, that is, may have been operable during the period of generally quiescent public opinion on Europe – that is, the period of the permissive consensus. The Maastricht referendums and the very high-profile government actions to achieve EMU membership on schedule mark watersheds in public attitudes toward the EU. The very efficiency of the EU to launch policies of a historic nature in fact draws attention to its weak democratic basis. In the case of national parties, whether in government or opposition, they are "pushed" for practical purposes into coming to terms with this phenomenon, and in the process link their concerns with the legitimacy of the EU.

Thus, as EU visibility has grown, the ability of parties to influence the increasingly pervasive effects of EU legislation in any appreciably partisan direction has diminished. Even worse, once in power, governments disingenuously blame the EU for the resulting hardships (Smith, 1997). This tactic presumably deflects attention from the fact that member state executives desire the policies in the first place. In the short term this may indeed seem a rational policy, but the accumulation of "don't blame me, blame Brussels" defenses serves only to highlight national impotence, a state of affairs contributing to the legitimacy problem of party government.

This development coincides with the evolution of the EU away from the "administration of things" and towards a form of governance. Because of the EU's increasingly intrusive impact on daily lives it has entered a new, more politicized phase where its policy orientation is challenged by expanding numbers of domestic groups. While this development has unfolded, the role of political parties has come under substantial pressure in the areas that most precisely affect their basis of popular legitimacy, that is, performance.

Is there a solution to this double legitimacy bind? The rest of this chapter concentrates on evidence of efforts by national parties to adapt to the wider political environment of the EU in order to try to bring a partisan influence to EU policy-making, and thus reassert their relevance. In this fashion, though it may be strictly speaking a by-product of this involvement, the European level may develop clearer linkages with national actors and thereby foster mutual legitimation.

Party networks and the EU policy agenda

The process of national party involvement at European level is complicated by the non-parliamentary composition of the EU polity, which impedes normal channels of party activity. Nevertheless, party adaptation means adapting precisely to given institutional dynamics. In this regard, the EP may be seen as a nexus or site for a network of partisan organizations which exist within the EP – party groups – and outside of it – national parties and transnational party federations. Their contribution to EU policy-making or governance is less significant for the details of EP legislative work than in shaping the EU's medium-to-long-term issue agenda – what Peterson (1995) characterizes as "policy-setting." The nature of their activities, with regard to issues of political-institutional development as well as public policy, their dissemination and mobilization among potential audiences at the national and European levels, marks out a role somewhat different from our traditional understanding of the functions of parties (Hix, 1995). Indeed, Abélès (1995: 75) remarks that the European level of political activity "implies a profound transformation in traditional conceptions of politics, such as it is practiced at the national level."

Furthermore, party activities at the European level do not constitute a form of "Europeanizing" domestic political actors in the neofunctionalist sense articulated by Haas. Rather, these activities comprise an indirect Europeanization in which various actors are routinely exposed to and increasingly participate in transnational and supranational partisan forums for instrumental reasons. In certain respects, then, the European level is introduced as a legitimate environment in practical problem-solving by national actors. Confronted with challenges to their relevance, the "Euro-option" is approached for precisely national benefits (Ladrech, 1994; 1997). In the process, partisan activity at the European level – political contestation – indirectly legitimates the EU as a practical political framework. Moreover, the partisan dimension of the problem-solving process may have an effect upon the nature and style of EU policy-making, shifting a publicly perceived technocratic domination viewed by some as in competition with the domestic arena on to political axes much more familiar and thus identifiable to voters. Issues considered pertinent to this argument are, then, those of a broad programmatic nature, for example, the role for the EU in employment, the role of public services, the management of monetary union, the desired outcome of the IGC on institutional matters, and so on.

But how might national parties go about this task of political engagement in EU policy-making? As the European Parliament is but one institution in the EU set-up, and at that not the most significant, it would be understandable that the other institutions critical in the process be "penetrated." However, neither the Council of Ministers nor the Commission is amenable to the exertions of party actors. Indeed, Hix points out that with regard to transnational parties, "the institutional system determines that without real decision-making power in the European Parliament, and with a fusion of executive and legislative functions in the European Council, parties at the European level must change their strategy to be able to have an impact on the EU policy agenda" (Hix, 1995: 546). The question of how national parties influence policies at the European level therefore becomes more perplexing. Hix (1995: 547) has suggested that "the increasing organization of the party federation leaders' summits immediately before or after . . . each European Council meeting" is empirical evidence of such a new strategy. I would accept his point but vastly expand the scope of partisan activity within the interstices of the EU. More than simply organizing party leaders' summits, the activities of transnational parties, EP party groups and national parties together constitute networks of partisan activity building points of contact that bring national parties into cooperation with European actors on issues that are important to each side. The EP, one of the key sites for this activity, therefore becomes much more important for its "system-transformative role in the EC" (Lodge, 1993) than as a legislature.

Transnational parties as national instruments

National parties in this analysis stand alongside two other partisan organizations: transnational party federations and EP party groups. Transnational parties are particularly significant in this analysis because although they transcend any one national party, their activities and organizational structure are dependent upon national party agreement. Transnational parties stand at the intersection of national parties and EP party groups, allowing a form of communication not mediated by the institutional dynamics between national parties and the parliamentary agenda of the EP groups. In this section I provide an account of this communication process. I then offer evidence of the broadening scope of party network activities. To accomplish this, I first describe the two most relevant transnational parties, the Party of European Socialists (PES) and the Christian Democrat European People's Party (EPP), both of which have strengthened their internal organizations since 1992, that is, in the wake of the Maastricht Treaty.

The PES

The PES, along with the EPP and Liberal party federations, was created in the late 1970s in anticipation of the 1979 direct elections to the European Parliament. Named (in English) the Confederation of Socialist Parties of the EC (CSPEC), its secretariat was small and its ability to influence the program for the 1979, 1984 and 1989 EP elections negligible (as witnessed by the number of national party opt-outs or exemptions in the manifesto). For the Socialist federation in particular, this reflected at the time the great variance among the member parties on ideological grounds, in particular the hostility of the British Labour and Danish Social Democrat parties to deeper EC integration. Unanimity was required for decision-making in the CSPEC bureau, and so this divergence of party views essentially prevented it from expanding its operation or developing a well-defined role.

By 1989 a process of organizational enhancement was set into play, and with it a new sense of mission for the party federation and also for all the relevant Socialist actors in the EU system. Two developments combined to revive interest in the transnational organization. First, changes within member parties opened up possibilities for organizational transformation. This includes primarily the British and Danish parties' turn from hostility to at least a qualified embrace of the EC (Haahr, 1993). Second, there appears to have been a growing realization among party leaders themselves that the EC was now of greater importance than had been the case when only party "Euro-experts" would pay much attention to issues of integration, especially political. This recognition was made explicit at a party leaders' summit in 1990 in Madrid when their unanimously approved declaration opened with the statement:

The ever increasing internationalization of the economy and inter-dependence of our societies at every level means that it is increasingly difficult to respond on a national level to the new challenges which arise. Democratic control of the future remains possible, provided that those elements of sovereignty which can no longer be exercised in a purely national framework are pooled.

(PES Leaders' Declaration, 1990)

This summit was scheduled before the opening of the 1991 IGC, thus allowing a higher than usual profile for a party leaders' summit of this kind (Ladrech, 1993). In November 1992, CSPEC was transformed into the Party of European Socialists, and majority voting was introduced on those issues upon which the Council of Ministers also employs qualified majority voting. Additionally, national party opt-outs on the EP election manifesto were prohibited, as exemplified in the 1994 manifesto.

The EPP

The EPP incorporated the word "party" into its title at the outset. To a greater degree than the Socialists, Christian Democratic parties had as part of their national programmatic identity a commitment to a unified Europe, and together with a generally more pro-business attitude, were in far greater agreement over the course of European integration (Hanley, 1994). Despite the fact that many of these parties were in government throughout the 1980s, thereby allowing party leaders to interact at a government-to-government level, an emphasis on organizational enhancement did not occur until the post-Maastricht period (EPP officials make references to "catching-up" with the PES on organizational grounds). By the mid-1990s Christian Democratic national governmental presence had been reduced (Netherlands and Italy), and with anti-Maastricht sentiment in many countries growing, party leaders called for a revival of the pro-integration movement. Germany's CDU was particularly crucial in this regard. Consequently, in 1995, the EPP adopted a revised organizational format. The leadership structure was streamlined and meetings arranged more frequently, increasing the EPP's ability to respond more flexibly to emerging issues. In addition, the link between the transnational organization and the national parties was strengthened by more frequent meetings between the presidium and the chairmen of the member parties. These meetings comprised the EPP Council, which was empowered to make polit-ically binding decisions. Justifying these changes, the EPP asserted that "To be a truly effective European party, the EPP needs direct contact with the leadership of member parties. The EPP has no desire to be an umbrella organization, but rather a political force" (EPP News, no. 36, 1995).

Between 1992 and 1995 the European party federations that had remained essentially dormant throughout the 1980s were upgraded both organizationally and in terms of activities deemed necessary to promote member parties' interests.

Organizational enhancement included an emphasis on more effective decision-making, and this resulted in the adoption of majority voting at the bureau level. As the EPP's 1995 reforms make clear, the mandate that has developed for both the PES and EPP is to be more a political force than simply an organizational shell for limited "get-togethers" of national party leaders for publicity purposes twice a year. "Networking" operates along two dimensions: party-to-party and institutional. Party-to-party networking includes the activities of transnational parties, which in addition to the biannual party leaders' summits,[6] organize a number of working groups or parties under their auspices. These occasions for collaboration in small-group working environments bring prominent national party figures into more intimate contact with colleagues from other parties, as well as MEPs. Parties themselves have used the increased organizational collaboration fostered by the transnational party secretariats to hold joint meetings, usually focused on one or two significant issues. PES leaders employ a "conclave" style of meeting on an occasional basis, and party-to-party initiatives may be launched from such discussions. Institutional party networks include: EP party groups and their involvement in the legislative process; the EP committee structure itself, which represents a more focused form of collaboration; and COSAC, the body created in 1989 bringing together individuals from the various committees in the national parliaments specializing in European affairs with their counterparts from the EP. Overall, the amount of organized partisan activity in various contact points within the EU machinery has increased, and one can expect to witness these efforts affecting those issues most amenable to partisan contestation.

National parties have, in an instrumental fashion, used these transnational parties to "network" with other actors in the EP and elsewhere. This process of bringing partisan national concerns more directly into the process of political contestation at the European level was particularly acute in the context of the 1996–97 IGC because of its singular potential to alter the institutional and policy landscape of the EU.

Networking and political mobilization

A central assumption in this analysis is party leaders' motivation to benefit their domestic situation – aggravated by EU dynamics – by influencing the EU's issue agenda in such a way as to link their and their voters' interests with the direction of EU policy. Given the direction of economic liberalization, deregulation and privatization, parties on the left may have a greater incentive to influence such programs, including the application of a future monetary union, than conservative parties. Thus we see more of an effort on the part of the PES to "relate their policy proposals on the socio-economic issues to their historically defined ideological positions [which] may create a legitimizing link between public value orientations and EU policy-making" (Hix, 1995). The policy issues that have been promoted by the PES and EPP are then items which reflect a consensus among party leaders, and their respective networks are employed to promote these issues in the national–transnational–supranational matrix. Apart from the organizational changes to the transnational parties over the past few years, substantive policy propositions were linked to the 1996–97 IGC. In other words, the IGC represented a catalyst in the development in their respective issue agendas by deepening and extending party network activity. This, in turn, presents the EU to party leaders as a pragmatic problem-solving arena, and this demystification further strengthens the legitimacy of the exercise itself.

The PES network and issue agenda

EMU and the convergence criteria

The public perception that the convergence criteria for monetary union contained in the Maastricht Treaty are aggravating already high rates of unemployment (and thus undermining EU legitimacy) affects PES party leaders directly because they are on record supporting monetary union. Their quandary is obvious: they are seen as supporting the very policies injuring their core constituencies. The response has been to develop a common position on how to manipulate monetary union so as to derive benefit from it while at the same time embedding it into a wider economic logic. The first significant effort in this direction reflecting use of the Socialist network was the Larsson Report, adopted at the PES Leaders' Summit of December 1993 as the PES "European Employment Initiative." The initiative behind the Report emanated from a PES party leaders' conclave in September 1993, when the Swedish Social Democratic Party offered the services of former finance minister Allan Larsson to chair a working group charged with drafting a common program for generating employment, integrating a European strategy with national approaches. The subsequent report was a product of consultation at the highest levels of party and government. The ad hoc group was composed of the main economic policy advisers in the PES member parties, representatives of Commission President Delors and the EP Socialist Group, and a guest from the European Trade Union Confederation (ETUC). Due to the involvement of the Delors cabinet, which itself was drafting the future White Paper on *Growth, Competitiveness and Employment*, one can assume a cross-flow of ideas and information.

Another example relates more specifically to the future EMU. During the period leading up to the launch of the 1996 IGC, the Socialist network sought to influence the multiple points at which the IGC agenda was being developed. The participation of French Socialist MEP Elisabeth Guigou in the Reflection Group which composed the formal agenda, together with Socialist party government representatives from ten other member states, ensured that Socialist concerns were introduced, even though the manner in which the Final Report was written excluded detailed positions and numbers backing them. Nevertheless, a majority of the Reflection Group did call for a strengthening of the legal basis for employment policies, with the Swedish Social Democrat-led government proposing the inclusion of a specific chapter on employment in the Treaty.[7]

In a document adopted just before the Reflection Group began its work in June 1995, the EP Socialist Group emphasized its support for balance between the demands of EMU for economic convergence and the need to promote social protection and a high level of employment stipulated in Article 2 of the EMU provisions in the Treaty (PES Group, "An initial approach to the 1996 Treaty Review Conference"). In December 1995 PES party leaders (including prime ministers from Austria, the Netherlands, Denmark, Portugal, Finland, Sweden, Spain, and Greece) endorsed this position in a communiqué adopted unanimously at their Party Leaders' Summit. In addition to calling for EMU to begin "with the highest number of Member States," party leaders pronounced that "The implementation of Monetary Union should be accompanied by increased coordination of economic, budgetary, fiscal, employment and social policies to ensure that the convergence criteria for sound economic performance are sustainable" (PES Leaders' Conference, "Bringing the European Union into Balance").[8]

The EP's Bourlanges–Martin Report preceding the official launch of the IGC also states that EMU and the convergence criteria "should not be modified but the monetary policy provisions should have their counterweight in reinforced economic policy coordination and a clear link to Article 2 of the Treaty." The similarity in language suggests that overlapping membership allowed all points in the network to agree on a generally similar approach and promote these positions to their target audience: for the EP, to give direction to its members on the IGC Reflection Group as well as to position the EP itself vis-à-vis the other European Union institutions; for the Socialist Group in the EP, to influence the overall EP position as well as to strengthen this position with member parties as MEPs explained the Group's position at national party meetings; and for the party leaders themselves, especially those wielding national governmental authority, to begin preparing their governments' positions for the IGC negotiations.

Although these examples involve national party actors interacting with supranational institutional actors on the issue of employment and monetary union, party-to-party, or transnational, networking has also been employed, usually originating as an initiative in a summit of party leaders. For example, at the June 1995 Party Leaders' Summit, Austrian Chancellor Vranitzky agreed to prepare a report under the title, "The social compatibility of EMU," for discussion by party leaders at a conclave scheduled immediately prior to the opening of the 1996 IGC. The meeting was attended by Socialist party leaders of nine EU member states, and in press reports Vranitzky stated that he and his colleagues would, during the IGC negotiations, try to obtain the inclusion of full employment among the objectives of the EU. Justifying this approach, Vranitzky asserted that "This is not a question of transferring to Brussels the tasks of national governments, but of using the 'European dimension' in the matter" (Agence-Europe, January 29/30, 1996).

Other issues upon which European Socialist parties through their EP Group and the PES adopted positions in the context of the IGC include the role of public services, the powers of the European Parliament, enlargement, and justice and home affairs. Nevertheless, of those issues for which a significant effort has been made to mobilize party resources, as well as those which are historically connected to a Socialist political identity, the emphasis on employment has been central. Indeed, these initiatives reflect the fact that "a new cross-national dialogue has emerged between the member states on employment topics," and that "Fresh ideas and proposals are likely to come out of this pan-European exchange of information and experience" (Teague, 1994: 343). These efforts of the parties of the center-left to combat party decline at the national level through closer engagement in Europe via the activities of the PES have broadened the range of actors who view the EU as a productive locus of political contestation.

The EPP network and issue agenda

As mentioned above, introducing new items on to the IGC agenda was less of a priority for the EPP because the general economic orientation of the EU satisfies the domestic agendas of the member parties. Nevertheless, two issues were highlighted by the EPP network in which their position diverged from that of the PES. Both issues concern the decision-making structure – the first for the Common Foreign and Security Policy (CFSP); the second for justice and home affairs, especially for questions related to Europol and asylum. One might notice the domestic priorities of the German government reflected in the choice of issues given emphasis, and indeed, the EPP's basic document spelling out their positions was the product of a working group chaired by MEP H.-G. Pöttering of the CDU.

CFSP

In all policy documents concerning the CFSP produced by the PES and EPP respectively for the IGC, the EPP took a more detailed and ambitious position. Whereas the PES party leaders stated that the EU's "capacity to take action at international levels needs to be strengthened considerably," and that the question of the role to be played by the Western European Union (WEU) "will have to be decided in the context of the 1996 Intergovernmental Conference," the EPP more specifically asserted that "The European Union must be enabled to take joint action in the field of foreign, security and defense policy, as elsewhere." The EPP stipulated that the Council should abandon unanimity in order to accomplish this, and that "It should be possible to decide on 'joint action' in the form of diplomatic, humanitarian or military measures by a qualified or reinforced majority" (EPP, 1995: 10). Further, the EPP called for integrating the WEU into the European Union (EPP, 1995: 11). These two positions are consistent with the views of several EPP member parties, but especially reflect the German government's positions, made all the more explicit by a foreign policy pact with France announced on February 27, 1996 in preparation for the IGC (*Financial Times*, February 28, 1996).

Justice and home affairs

The EPP developed specific proposals in the area of justice and home affairs, whereas the PES position reflected a lack of consensus among party leaders (less so in the EP group). The EPP stated categorically that "Starting with asylum policy, visa and emigration policy, border controls, judicial and internal affairs necessitating the harmonization of policy must be progressively absorbed into Community procedure (Article 100c of the Treaty) and placed under the political control of the European Parliament, and judicial control of the European Court of Justice." This would transform Europol into a European police authority with operational powers (EPP, 1995: 9). These positions are very detailed compared with the PES leaders' declaration, which after acknowledging that the EU has followed through very few initiatives with regard to "crucial issues like police cooperation, combating fraud, terrorism and drugs trafficking," simply cites the need to develop "a European strategy" for immigration and asylum (PES, 1995: 5). EPP party leaders were able to reach a consensus on these issues, and were better able as a bloc to push these positions at the IGC, while the Socialists were unable to agree that this level of transnational policy was suitable for all concerned. However, in the end, Chancellor Kohl's backdown on putting asylum and immigration under Union competence undercut the EPP's position.

The effect of this type of coordination among Socialists and Christian Democrats in the European Parliament and in national governments and oppositions was to enhance the input of those participating in the IGC. The development of common positions beforehand raised the possibility of influencing the overall agenda. National party leaders, the instigators of policy change, increasingly turn to party networks. The post-IGC political situation, coinciding with historic EMU membership decisions, will certainly politicize EU–national relationships as parties take positions that may be the product of European-level consultation, such as a French PS–German SPD manifesto.

To what extent does the introduction of party-political activity at an agenda-setting stage and the success of transnational party networks in attaining some of their objectives in the IGC contribute to the transformation of governance in the EU? Three consequences may follow this development, each of which helps structure the EU as a polity characterized by intensified political contestation and interaction among the multiple levels of governance. First, success may breed continued and deepened "networking." The organizational changes adopted by the EPP in December 1995, the creation of a high-level "Council" of party leaders, is one of the means by which it seeks to insure a permanent political presence. Similarly, the June 1997 PES Congress reviewed the efficacy and impact of its 1992 rules changes in response to the feeling that "European integration has become such a dominant phenomenon and important political feature that there is an urgent need for a [PES] which is active on a much larger scale than we have achieved so far" (PES Bureau, 1996/7).

Second, by introducing a socio-economic dimension at the European level resembling the traditional political cleavages found in national systems, the multi-level structure of EU governance can contribute to the legitimation of the EU as a polity. As Hix argues, "if the EU socio-economic policy agenda can reflect a majority of party family opinion, a connection may be made between enduring political attitudes and EU decisions" (Hix, 1995: 547). This may take place particularly in response to increased powers for the European Parliament that make it a more significant target for lobbying. Such a development would facilitate the introduction of a more coherent and, for citizens, more familiar pattern of agenda-setting in the EU (Peters, 1994: 16).

Lastly, evidence of change derived from the application of party networks as problem-solving activities benefiting national party agendas furthers a type of Europeanization which makes the professional intermingling of national, transnational, and supranational actors all the more routine. This process may alter the popular perception of "Brussels" as a foreign and external competitor to domestic interests. Instead, at least in the minds of national party elites and mid-level activists, the EU could become another playing field for partisan forces to reach consensus and coordinate mobilized action at the pressure points of the EU system. It is from this form of legitimation that the EU, as a contested polity, benefits.

Conclusion

This chapter began by arguing that the legitimacy problem of the EU and that of national parties in EU member states are linked. As the institutions of the EU are at best semi-autonomous, the resolution of legitimacy problems is likely to emanate from national actors. In this regard, the activities documented in this chapter on the part of the two major party families – Socialists and Christian Democrats – to construct a presence at the EU level in order to influence the general direction of EU policies may contribute to the growing legitimation of the EU as a polity. The motivation to enhance the instruments of collective partisan action on a European level is self-interest on the part of party leaders. In particular, the realization that high-profile EU policy-making contributes to the image of partisan irrelevance and reduced maneuverability in government stimulates party leaders to reassert some form of control over the wider environment. The activities of Social Democratic and Christian Democratic parties represent innovative (transnational) organizational responses to new environmental (European Union) inputs. If we assume organizations – including political parties – seek to control their environment (Panebianco, 1988), then the explanation for enhanced party networking becomes clearer.

What, then, are the consequences of transnational party activity for the legitimacy of the EU? On the one hand, some scholars have suggested that politicization would foster delegitimation, particularly by damaging the relationship between the EU's supranational institutions and member-state governments. On the other hand, the argument advanced in this chapter suggests that the intensification of national party activity at the European level can strengthen the link between European electorates and EU policy-making.

Focusing on the potential introduction of a more parliamentary institutional logic resulting from a boost in the powers of the European Parliament,[9] Dehousse (1995) believes this would itself lead to legitimacy problems. To the extent the European Commission is closer to member states given the process by which Commissioners are selected, it has a form of legitimacy that rests upon a national foundation. The development of a more parliamentary institutional logic would shift the legitimate basis of Commission endeavors (e.g. the Work Program) closer to the European Parliament, as it would need the support of a parliamentary majority. While politicization both of EP membership and the Commission's annual Work Program would perhaps reduce the "political deficit" encountered by voters, this could well come "at the expense of good relations with national government" (Dehousse, 1995: 128). The majoritarian logic introduced by a more partisan and parliamentary EU could, according to Dehousse, put in jeopardy relations between the Commission and national governments because it would no longer be seen as an "honest broker," a mediator among national interests. Thus the strengthening in horizontal institutional ties between Commission and Parliament would threaten to cause tensions for the supranational–national relationship.

Dehousse notes that the type of parliamentary system that could evolve at the European level remains indeterminate, depending upon such factors as "the cohesiveness of political parties or the type of coalition that will be formed" (Dehousse, 1995: 129–30). Nevertheless, if party-political activity is directed toward influencing the EU policy agenda along partisan lines, and majoritarian support is a necessary ingredient, the framework most identifiable for voters at a national level paradoxically could undermine the legitimacy of the supranational level of decision-making.

It is also possible that the party-political activity described in this chapter not only brings more clarity to the European voter concerning the political basis of EU policies, but in fact contributes towards the legitimation of the process itself. Beyond introducing familiar cleavage patterns onto EU issues, the ability of parties and their leaders to demonstrate that organized partisan pressure is at least partly responsible for policy "success" (again, defined more in terms of shifts in direction of primarily economic issues) could link the EU level with familiar national political actors. Wessels, for example, has pointed out the importance of this type of representation for the relationship between citizens and the political class (Wessels, 1996: 64).

Moreover, a more politicized rather than technocratic arena does not inevitably lead to confrontational, majoritarian parliamentary dynamics. Indeed, one of the defining characteristics of EU decision-making is its complexity, and "the absence of a separation of powers within the 'triangle of institutions' ensures more room . . . for the search for compromise over the exercise of powers of arbitration" (Mény et al., 1996: 16). Thus collective transnational partisan efforts to influence the EU policy agenda are not governance in the national sense of the word, and compromise among political forces may result in shifting coalitions depending on the policies debated, thereby resembling multi-party coalitions rather than Westminster-type politics. In this fashion, the role and aim of parties in EU politics is less to "occupy the state" than to impart a more open and competitive partisan logic to its socio-economic agenda. As argued in the introduction to this volume, the result may be to strengthen the development of the EU as an object of shared identification.

In the absence of a "European public sphere" for the articulation of organized interests, political parties – the accepted organizational vehicle for the aggregation and articulation of interests – are forced to adapt to the non-national institutional terrain of the EU. In so doing their activities take on a logic different from their national responsibilities – running campaigns and organizing the parliamentary process. Ultimately the ability to convince voters there is, however, a means by which to bring a partisan logic to the EU may very well validate both parties and the EU process.

Notes

1 On October 30, 1996 the European Parliament's Committee on Institutional Affairs adopted a report on the constitutional statutes of European political parties, calling among other things for a framework regulation on the legal status of these parties and a regulation on their financial situation. See EP Report A4-0342/96, D. Tsatsos, rapporteur.
2 The set of parties I include in this analysis excludes those self-declared as anti-EU.
3 It has been suggested elsewhere that support for the EU is correlated with economic prosperity. Good times equal (roughly) support for European integration. See Eichenberg and Dalton (1993). I argue that the more politicized the EU has become, the more complex will be the relationship between support and economic development.
4 Though the EC was essentially "built" by Social Democrat and Christian Democrat politicians, the motivation for European construction, at least in its formative years, had more to do with perceived "national interests" than partisan motivation, especially for Social Democrats.
5 Although this chapter is not concerned directly with anti-EU party formation, there is an overlap between these and protest parties. See, *inter alia*, Betz (1994).
6 The PES and EPP include relevant EC Commissioners and officials such as the president of the EP and president of the respective EP party group.
7 The idea of an employment chapter or charter subsequently became a fixed item in the negotiations.
8 The French Socialist prime minister, Lionel Jospin, has made a concerted effort to ensure that the new Council of the Euro, dubbed "Euro-X," does indeed function as an economic government, complementing the logic of the new European Central Bank.
9 Various recommendations for strengthening the powers of the EP were considered in the IGC, especially those aimed at expanding the realm of co-decision.

Bibliography

Abélès, M. (1995) "La fonction politique européenne: acteurs et enjeux," in Y. Mény, P. Muller and J.-L. Quermonne (eds) *Politiques Publiques en Europe*, Paris: Harmattan.

Andersen, S. S. and Eliassen, K. A. (1993) *Making Policy in Europe: The Europeification of National Policy-making*, London: Sage.

Anderson, C. and Kaltenthaler, K. (1996) "The Dynamics of Public Opinion toward European Integration, 1973–1993," *European Journal of International Relations* 2, 2: 175–200.

Beetham, D. and Lord, C. (1996) "Legitimacy and the European Union," paper presented at the ECPR Workshop, Oslo.

Betz, H.-G. (1994) *Radical Right-wing Populism in Western Europe*, New York: St. Martin's Press.

Dehousse, R. (1995) "Constitutional Reform in the European Community. Are There Alternatives to the Majoritarian Avenue?" in J. Hayward (ed.) *The Crisis of Representation in Europe*, London: Frank Cass.

Eichenberg, R. and Dalton, R. (1993) "Europeans and the European Community: The Dynamics of Public Support for European Integration," *International Organization* 47, 4: 507–34.

EPP Congress (1995) *Basic Document. Ability to Act, Democracy and Transparency: The European Union – the Road to European Integration. Proposals and Objectives for the 1996 Intergovernmental Conference*, XIth EPP Congress.

Gallagher, M., Laver, M. and Mair, P. (1995) *Representative Government in Modern Europe*, 2nd edn, New York: McGraw-Hill.

Haahr, J. (1993) *Looking to Europe: The EC Policies of the British Labour Party and the Danish Social Democrats*, Aarhus: Aarhus University Press.

Haas, E. (1958) *The Uniting of Europe: Political, Social and Economic Forces, 1950-1957*, Stanford, CA: Stanford University Press.

Hanley, D. (1994) *Christian Democracy in Europe: A Comparative Perspective*, London: Pinter.

Hix, S. (1995) "Parties at the European Level and the Legitimacy of EU Socio-economic Policy," *Journal of Common Market Studies* 33, 4: 527–55.

Katz, R. and Mair, P. (1995) "Changing Models of Party Organisation and Party Democracy: The Emergence of the Cartel Party," *Party Politics* 1, 1: 5–28.

Ladrech, R. (1993) "Social Democratic Parties and EC Integration: Transnational Party Responses to Europe 1992," *European Journal of Political Research* 24, 3: 195–210.

—— (1994) "The Europeanization of Domestic Politics and Institutions: The Case of France," *Journal of Common Market Studies*, 32, 1: 69–88.

—— (1997) "Partisanship and Party Formation in European Union Politics," *Comparative Politics* 29, 2: 167–86.

Lindberg, L. and Scheingold, S. (1970) *Europe's Would-be Polity: Patterns of Change in the European Community*, Englewood Cliffs, NJ: Prentice-Hall.

Lodge, J. (1993) "EC Policymaking: Institutional Dynamics," in J. Lodge (ed.) *The European Community and the Challenge of the Future*, 2nd edn, New York: St. Martin's Press.

Mair, P. (1995) "Political Parties, Popular Legitimacy and Public Privilege," in J. Hayward (ed.) *The Crisis of Representation in Europe*, London: Frank Cass.

Mény, Y., Muller, P. and Quermonne, J.-L. (1996) "Introduction," in Y. Mény, P. Muller and J.-L. Quermonne (eds) *Adjusting to Europe: The Impact of the European Union on National Institutions and Policies*, London: Routledge.

Milward, A. (1992) *The European Rescue of the Nation State*, Berkeley, CA: University of California Press.

Moravcsik, A. (1994) "Why the European Community Strengthens the State: Domestic Politics and International Cooperation," Center for European Studies Working Paper Series 52, Harvard University.

Panebianco, A. (1988) *Political Parties: Organization and Power*, Cambridge, UK: Cambridge University Press.

Peters, B. G. (1994) "Agenda-setting in the European Community," *Journal of European Public Policy* 1, 1: 9–26.

Peterson, J. (1995) "Decision-making in the European Union: Towards a Framework for Analysis," *Journal of European Public Policy* 2, 1: 69–93.

PES Bureau, appendix to the working programme 1996/7: evaluation of the Activity Programme as adopted by the PES Barcelona Congress.

PES Leaders' Declaration, Madrid, 1990.

PES Leaders' Declaration, Madrid, 1995.

Poguntke, T. (1996) "Anti-party Sentiment – Conceptual Thoughts and Empirical Evidence: Explorations into a Minefield," *European Journal of Political Research* 29, 3: 319–44.

Scharpf, F. (1996) "Negative and Positive Integration in the Political Economy of European Welfare States," in G. Marks, F. Scharpf, P. Schmitter and W. Streck (eds) *Governance in the European Union*, London: Sage.

Shackleton, M. (1994) "The Internal Legitimacy Crisis of the European Union," Europa Institute Occasional Paper no. 1, University of Edinburgh.

Sinnott, R. (1995) "Policy, Subsidiarity, and Legitimacy," in O. Niedermayer and R. Sinnott (eds) *Public Opinion and Internationalized Governance*, Oxford, UK: Oxford University Press.

Smith, M. (1997) "The Commission Made Me Do It: The European Commssion as a Strategic Asset in Domestic Politics," in N. Nugent (ed.) *At the Heart of the EU: Studies of the European Commission*, London: Macmillan.

Teague, P. (1994) "Between New Keynesianism and Deregulation: Employment Policy in the European Union," *Journal of European Public Policy* 1, 3: 315–46.

Wallace, H. (1996) "Politics and Policy in the EU: The Challenge of Governance," in H. Wallace and W. Wallace (eds) *Policy-making in the European Union*, Oxford, UK: Oxford University Press.

Wessels, W. (1996) "The Modern West European State and the European Union: Democratic Erosion or a New Kind of Polity?" in S. Andersen and K. Eliassen (eds) *The European Union: How Democratic Is It?*, London: Sage.

6

NATIONAL PARTIES AND THE CONTESTATION OF EUROPE

Gary Marks and Carole Wilson[1]

Analyses of multi-level governance in Europe have drawn attention to the diffusion of authority away from national governments to the supranational and subnational level, and the multi-lateral relationships that result (Hooghe, 1996; Ansell, Parsons and Darden, 1997). The emphasis understandably has been on explaining politics in emerging supranational and subnational arenas, yet there are signs that politics in national arenas is being transformed in the process. If a European polity is in the making (this volume, Introduction; Hooghe and Marks, forthcoming), then it would be surprising if this did not have profound consequences at the national level. At this point in time, however, we have very little idea about how multi-level governance in the EU affects democratic politics at the national level. Attention to domestic politics in member states illuminates important, but little-understood patterns of contestation and representation within the EU. These patterns have critical implications for EU legitimacy, because they reflect an increasing tendency of major party families to pursue national political projects through European means.

Contestation about the institutional shape and policies of the Euro-polity has drawn diverse national interests to Brussels and diverse European issues into national arenas. While it has been true for some time that one cannot understand the institutional path of European integration without examining national political parties, it is now the case that one cannot understand European political parties without examining European integration. As the chief aggregators of interests in Europe, political parties are at the interface of national and European arenas. In this chapter we explore how European integration shapes contestation among political parties at the national level.

This topic, which we explore with newly available cross-national data, places the problem of EU legitimacy in a new light. Where national parties – and cross-national party families – take consistent stands on European problems, they create a new link between EU governance and European citizens. A focus solely on formal EU representative institutions, such as the party groups represented in the European Parliament, ignores the implications of national patterns of representation for EU legitimacy. Much of the scholarly literature focuses on lack of identification with Europe or the persistence of a "democratic deficit." Our research suggests that national parties across the political spectrum encompass the EU as an arena for the contestation of policies. The traditional left–right cleavage refracts European issues through a familiar lens. Moreover, the increasing salience of the European issue in national politics makes national parties more important representative institutions within the Euro-polity.

We proceed in three parts. Part one sets out data on party orientations toward European integration and discusses their overall significance. This portion of the chapter demonstrates the existence of cross-national party families and suggests the emergence of socio-economic cleavages around EU issues. Part two compares and contrasts party families. The discussion underscores the centrality of clashing social democratic and conservative approaches to European Monetary Union as an axis of contestation in European domestic politics. Part three addresses competing explanations for these patterns of contestation. This section contends that the embeddedness of the left–right spectrum in national institutions best explains contestation of EU issues. The conclusion suggests that this extension of national political cleavages to the European level fosters the legitimation of the integration project.

New patterns of contestation

How do national political parties orient themselves to European integration? How do party political orientations vary across countries and through time? And how can one explain these variations? To begin to answer these questions one needs to have reliable longitudinal data on the orientations of parties to European integration. Until very recently, however, there has been no good cross-national data. In place of direct evaluations of party orientations, researchers have had to rely on indirect indicators derived from Eurobarometer surveys. These ask individual respondents what party they support and ask questions about attitudes toward European integration. By combining these, one can measure the orientations of party supporters as a proxy for party positions. But this measure is poor. While supporters' orientations and party positions presumably influence each other, they are far from the same thing. Surveys across Europe have indicated that political elites tend to be more pro-EU than the public as a whole, and in most countries the difference is considerable.

Leonard Ray, a doctoral student in political science at UNC–Chapel Hill, has created a data set on party orientations toward European integration that provides the basis for this chapter. Ray asked eight to ten experts from each EU country to evaluate different party positions on European integration on a seven-point scale, from very anti- to very pro-European.[2] Statistical tests indicate that these judgments are reliable and reasonably consistent with data derived from party manifestos and public opinion surveys (Ray, 1998). The data allow us to cross a fault line in political research between the established study of national political parties and research on European integration.

The nexus between these areas may prove to be extraordinarily fruitful given the substantive importance of the topic and the accumulated knowledge on either side of the divide. In recent years, two literatures have been in the vanguard in exploiting this intellectual seam. A handful of researchers have turned their attention to the creation and activities of party federations in the European Parliament (Hix, 1995; Hix and Lord, 1997; Ladrech, 1993, 1997; Schmitt and Thomassen, 1997), while a larger group of scholars has examined the European orientations of certain national parties and their representatives in one or more countries (Baker *et al.*, 1997; Christensen, 1996; Clarke and Curtice, 1997; Sciarini and Listhaug, 1997). But no one has provided a systematic cross-national analysis of party stances on integration.

Our analysis centers on the ideological groupings, or "party families," that dominate politics across the EU – extreme right, conservative, liberal, Christian democratic, social democratic, green, and extreme left. How cohesive are these groupings in terms of orientations toward European integration? Have party families become more, or less, cohesive over time? A first, striking, finding is that variation of party position on European integration within party families tends to be much lower than variation within individual countries. On the seven-point scale we use to measure positions of individual parties toward integration, the average standard deviation for party families is 0.87, while the average standard deviation for parties grouped by country is 1.20. Hence, party family tells us more about the position of a party on European integration than national location. This suggests that any effort to distinguish "nationalist" from "European" countries is empirically suspect.

Still, it is worth noting the absence of any overall trend toward greater cohesiveness within party families. Simon Hix and others have provided detailed evidence that interaction within party groupings has intensified at the European level (Hix and Lord, 1997). In cross-national terms, however, EU enlargement to include Sweden, Finland, and Austria has undermined party family cohesiveness. With the addition of former agrarian parties less favorably inclined toward the EU than liberal parties, the standard deviation within the liberal party family increased from 0.65 in 1984 to 0.80 in 1996. Over the same period, the addition of Euroskeptic Protestant parties increased the standard deviation within the Christian democratic party family from just 0.17 to 1.3. Conservative parties remained relatively incohesive at both junctures, with a deviation of 1.2. Only the social democratic party family grew more cohesive (0.95 to 0.53) despite the addition of new EU members.[3]

A comparison of the average scores for party families for 1984 and 1996 on a conventional ten-point left–right dimension and our nationalism/pro-European integration dimension reveals an interesting pattern. Figures 6.1 and 6.2, which include parties receiving at least 5 percent of the vote and party families made up of at least two parties, feature ellipses that demarcate the entire range of individual party positions within each party family.

The pattern in 1984 is the horseshoe described in most accounts (Hix and Lord,

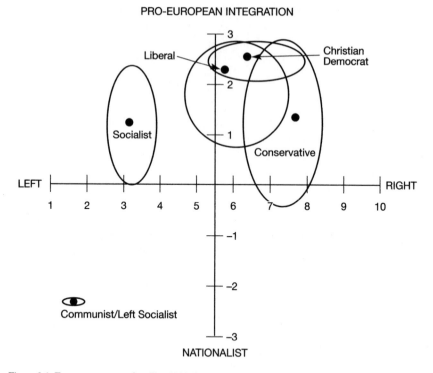

Figure 6.1 European party families (1984)

1997). There is no linear relation between left–right position and position on European integration either among the big four party families or among all party families. Once extreme right parties break into the figure, as they do in 1988, we can speak of a double horseshoe – a large horseshoe describing all party families and a smaller one representing the subset of the four big party families. But this changes as we move toward the present, as is clear in Figure 6.2. Among all parties the horseshoe remains – an artifact of the Euroskepticism of the minor families – but among the big four there is a downward slope from social democrats on the left to conservatives on the right. This is consistent with a hypothesis put forward by Liesbet Hooghe and Gary Marks before these data were available, namely, that contestation within the EU is structured by a socio-economic cleavage pitting a diverse center-left coalition which wishes to create a capacity for regulating capitalism at the European level against an equally diverse right-wing coalition in favor of regime competition and reduced state intervention in the economy (Hooghe and Marks, forthcoming). In order to evaluate the plausibility of this hypothesis, we turn to a detailed analysis of variations in EU orientation within and across the four major party families.

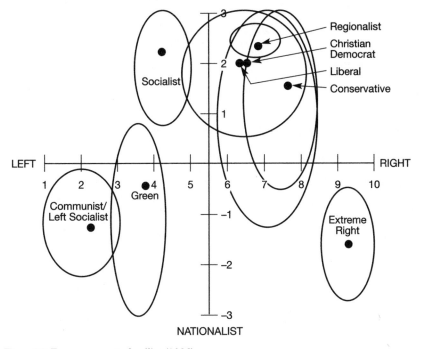

Figure 6.2 European party families (1996)

Comparing party families

Social democratic parties

Table 6.1 presents data on social democratic parties in the fifteen EU member states plus Norway.

These data reveal a marked shift toward a more pro-EU stance since the 1980s. Traditionally, social democratic parties have been sharply divided along a national/European dimension. During the period before the First World War, a European – or, more accurately, international – orientation prevailed. While they campaigned in national elections and gained the support of national union movements, most socialist parties considered themselves an integral part of the First and Second Socialist Internationals. Marxist parties looked to an international transformation of capitalism to achieve their goals. In the post- Second World War era, by contrast, the national state became the chief instrument of social democratic reform. Welfare states, neocorporatist bargaining, and government planning – these and other policies pursued at the national level were prized achievements of postwar social democratic government. Not surprisingly, then, social democratic parties were deeply divided in their response to the onset of the integration process

117

Table 6.1 Social democratic parties in the EU

		Party position					
		European integration				Left–right	
Country	Party	1984	1988	1992	1996	1984	1996
Austria	SPÖ	−1.60	0.60	2.40	3.00	3.00	4.80
Belgium	PS	1.80	1.80	2.00	2.20	2.50	4.20
Belgium	SP	2.17	2.33	2.50	2.33	2.90	4.00
Denmark	S	0.67	0.89	1.44	1.89	3.80	4.20
Finland	SDEM	−0.57	−1.40	2.00	2.50	3.00	4.40
France	PS	1.89	2.11	2.44	2.00	2.60	4.10
Germany	SPD	2.29	2.29	2.14	1.71	3.30	3.80
Greece	PASOK	0.00	1.60	2.30	2.70	4.66	4.60
Ireland	LAB	0.00	0.67	0.57	0.88	3.60	4.10
Italy	PDS	1.80	2.00	2.25	2.50	5.40	3.50
Italy	PSI	2.38	2.38	2.38	2.25	3.10	5.00
Netherlands	PVDA	1.78	1.78	1.67	1.78	2.60	4.20
Norway	NAP	0.67	1.00	2.43	2.17	–	–
Portugal	PS	2.86	2.86	2.86	2.71	–	4.90
Spain	PSOE	2.77	2.85	2.62	2.62	3.60	4.00
Sweden	SD	−1.86	−1.71	2.00	2.14	2.90	4.10
UK	LAB	0.50	1.50	2.00	2.00	2.30	4.40
		1.35	1.92	2.09	2.20	3.14	4.22

in the 1950s (Griffiths, 1993). On the one hand, socialists could support supranational federalism as a means to tame nationalism and to democratize international capitalism. But on the other hand, they realized that free trade advantaged employers in bargaining with trade unions and socialists wished to defend their capacity to regulate capitalism within national states. National social democracy rested upon the insulation of national economies from international economic forces and upon the exclusive authority of national governments to legislate and implement socio-economic policy. The speeches of socialist leaders in the 1950s in response to plans for European integration are full of concern that hard-won capacity for regulation at the national level would be diluted by economic internationalization and supranational empowerment (Griffiths, 1993). The sharp divisions within the social democratic family can be traced into the early 1980s, when the British Labour Party advocated withdrawal from the Community and the French Socialists under François Mitterrand flirted with an anti-European, national economic stance.

The data in Table 6.1 point to a historic transformation since the mid-1980s: at that juncture, the overwhelming majority of social democrats in established EU member states came to recognize that the European Union was the "only game in town," and adjusted their policies accordingly. The causes for this are to be found at the national level and in the EU. To the extent that social democratic parties were able to achieve their goals (national Keynesianism, strong welfare states, neo-corporatism) within the national state, they tended to oppose the integration process (Geyer, 1997). Since the 1980s, however, the political foundations for national economic policies have eroded. The bases of national Keynesianism and neocorporatism have been progressively weakened by economic changes (e.g. inter-nationalization of capital and goods markets, decline of traditional manufacturing and resource extraction); political changes (e.g. intensified employer demands for labor market flexibility, increased influence of neoliberalism, elimination of con-sensual incomes policies); and social changes (e.g. growing heterogeneity of the workforce and of labor unions, declining salience of social class) (Kitschelt *et al.*, forthcoming). As a result, social democratic parties have moved to the right on socio-economic issues – a trend also evident in Table 6.1. They have also become more sympathetic to efforts to create a single European market and move toward monetary union (Haahr, 1993).

The increasing attractiveness of the EU for social democratic parties is not only a function of changes at the national level; it also reflects the increasing salience of the EU as a context for economic and social policy in Europe. The EU has come to wield authoritative competences in a range of policy areas relevant to social democrats, including social policy, cohesion policy, environmental policy, and com-munications. There is the expectation that monetary integration will give rise to serious pressures for the creation of a fiscal policy to counter asymmetries of response to exogenous economic shocks within the Union. Decision-making in the European Union has become more open to democratic (and, therefore, social democratic) pressures. The European Parliament, in which social democrats form the largest party fraction, has come to play a decisively larger role in decision-making since the introduction of the cooperation (1986) and codecision (1993) procedures. Interest groups, including trade unions and a range of social move-ments, have mobilized at the European level. The European Union is no longer a preserve of conservatively oriented national governments operating in a business-dominated climate. It has become a highly contested polity in which the social democratic project for organized capitalism competes with neoliberal and nation-alist projects (Hooghe and Marks, forthcoming).

For both national and European reasons, then, it has become infeasible for social democratic parties to propose to pull out in order to sustain or resuscitate national Keynesianism. In this respect the 1990s are very different from the early 1980s. Our conception of the underlying relationship between social democracy and European integration is set out in Figure 6.3. Minimal European integration is consistent with the Keynesian policies that underpinned national social democ-racy. But social democratic goals of welfare, equality, and regulated capitalism become harder to achieve as increased integration undermines national Keynesianism and intensifies competition among governments to attract mobile capital. What socialists do at this point cannot be inferred from their absolute preference for national social democracy over European organized space. What matters is the choice set that confronts socialists in the valley of single market

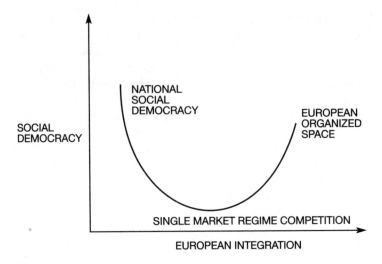

Figure 6.3 The social democratic valley

regime competition, and this, we hypothesize, has led socialists to prefer further European integration over the status quo.

While the overall pattern has been toward a more favorable stance toward integration, there is still considerable variation across social democratic parties. The most powerful factor differentiating socialist parties in this pooled data set is the interaction of party–union links and state welfare commitment. Social democratic parties that have weak or medium ties with trade unions and a weak or medium level of welfare state spending – that is, parties that do not defend entrenched national social democracy and are not dominated by the constituency most prone to economic nationalism – are distinguished by their very high level of support for European integration. Nationally based opposition is now strongest among those social democratic parties with the strongest constituency ties to blue-collar workers and trade unions, particularly where these are in protected economic sectors.

Among countries with strong union–party links, variation in orientations toward the EU appears related to the timing of membership. The first cut here is between social democratic parties in the original Six and social democratic parties in countries that joined later. By 1984, the European Community had been in existence for a quarter of a century and had deep political, economic, and cultural roots in the original member countries. The debate between national social democrats and supporters of European organized capitalism had turned decisively in favor of the latter, and, under Jacques Delors's leadership of the European Commission, social democratic parties in these countries sought to deepen and extend the Single Market program. Among countries that joined later – after longer periods of nationally oriented social democracy – lukewarm attitudes toward integration through the mid-1980s gave way to a pro-European stance by the mid-1990s. These overall patterns are set out in Figure 6.4.

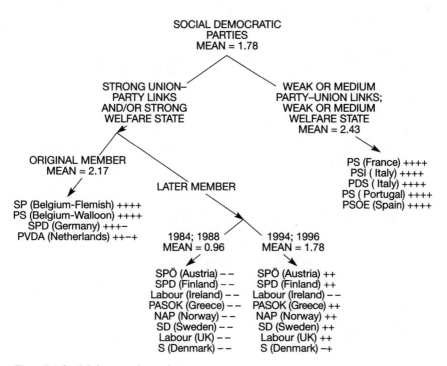

Figure 6.4 Social democratic parties
Notes:
The +/– symbols refer to the parties' position on European integration for the years 1984, 1988, 1992, 1996. + indicates a position greater than the social democratic mean, and – indicates a position less than the mean.

Liberal parties

Liberal parties form the most ideologically diverse of the major party families when viewed on the conventional left/right dimension. They are center parties that share a diffuse commitment to individual rights and freedoms, but the substantive content of their programs varies considerably (Kirchner, 1988; Smith, 1972; 1988; Von Beyme, 1985). Political liberals, such as the Danish Radicale Venstre and the Dutch D66, favor substantial state intervention in the economy on the grounds that this is necessary to achieve social justice and protect individuals from the vagaries of the market. Economic liberals, such as the Danish Venstre, the Dutch VVD, and the Belgian liberal parties, adopt an economically conservative or neoliberal agenda advocating a minimal role for the state in the economy.

With the enlargement of the EU first to Denmark and most recently to northern Scandinavia, these liberal parties have been joined by center parties which are distinguished by their agrarian roots. Some scholars of parties place agrarian liberal parties in a separate category. We lump them together with liberal parties because this reflects their self-perception: each of these parties is a member of the European Liberal, Democratic and Reform Party at the European level.

While they differ in left/right terms, there is good reason to expect that political and economic liberals will be similarly oriented to European integration. While political liberal parties have long supported national self-determination, they have opposed the communal presumptions underlying nationalism. They have sought to minimize the constraints that national borders exert over the lives of individuals, and they have been strong supporters of European integration as a means both to extend individual freedom and contain aggressive nationalism (Clarke and Curtice, 1997). Economic liberals, by contrast, support European integration mainly as a means to lower international trade barriers and institutionalize free markets. Support for European integration is in tune with basic liberal predispositions, but it is not absolute. Liberal-radicals also value decentralized decision-making on the grounds that it enhances the political influence of individuals, and this can lead them to criticize centralization and the lack of direct democracy in the EU. Liberal-conservatives are wary of the potential for a Fortress Europe to develop behind regional tariff barriers and oppose the social democratic project for organized capitalism at the European level. These are real concerns for liberal parties, but they are not front-line issues. The demand for more direct democracy in the EU is a demand for greater, not less, integration, and the prospect of European social democracy is yet distant. The overall picture, then, is one of support for deeper integration, as Table 6.2 indicates.

Table 6.2 Liberal parties in the EU

		Party position					
		European integration				Left–right	
Country	Party	1984	1988	1992	1996	1984	1996
Belgium	VLD	2.67	2.67	2.67	2.50	–	–
Belgium	PRL	2.80	2.80	2.80	2.60	–	–
Denmark	RV	0.78	1.00	1.22	1.33	4.80	5.70
Denmark	V	2.89	2.67	2.89	2.89	6.70	8.10
Denmark	CD	3.00	2.67	2.89	2.67	5.70	6.00
Finland	KESK	−1.86	−1.71	0.25	0.50	5.20	7.00
France	UDF-RAD	2.11	2.11	2.11	2.11	–	6.70
Germany	FDP	2.71	2.71	2.71	2.71	5.10	5.60
Italy	PRI	2.50	2.50	2.50	3.00	4.80	5.60
Netherlands	VVD	2.11	2.22	1.44	1.11	7.40	7.20
Netherlands	D66	2.44	2.33	2.33	2.22	4.40	4.80
Portugal	PSD	2.00	2.29	2.57	2.43	–	6.40
Spain	CDS	2.46	2.54	2.58	2.83	–	5.40
Sweden	CP	−2.14	−2.00	0.86	1.00	5.90	5.90
Sweden	FPL	0.86	1.71	3.00	3.00	5.50	5.90
UK	Liberals	2.50	2.50	2.42	2.24	5.00	5.20
		2.34	2.35	2.49	2.11	5.63	6.46

The main rift within the liberal party family separates political and economic liberals, on the one hand, from agrarian liberals, on the other. Farmers are one of the least mobile factors of production and are often highly vulnerable to international competition. This is particularly true of relatively inefficient, small-scale peasant-farmers.[4] Given the political power of farmers based in tightly knit communities and their likely opposition to market integration, it is no accident that they have been the beneficiaries of the chief distributional policy of the European Union. Whether the EU's agricultural policy makes farmers content with European integration depends on their standards for comparison. There is plenty of evidence that where national subsidies are higher than European subsidies (as they were in Sweden and are in Norway and Switzerland), farmers are deeply opposed to European integration. Figure 6.5 indicates variations in support for integration across the three liberal sub-groupings.

Three parties stand apart from their respective groupings: the Danish Venstre, which is far more supportive of European integration than the other liberal-agrarian parties, and the Danish Radicale Venstre and Dutch VVD, which are more Euroskeptic than their respective party types. The orientation of the Venstre is indicative of the competitive strength of Danish farming (the party proposes to dismantle EU agricultural subsidies) and the shift of the party away from its agrarian roots towards a liberal-conservative position.[5] The Radicale Venstre and VVD compete in party systems where there are at least two liberal parties, and this may induce

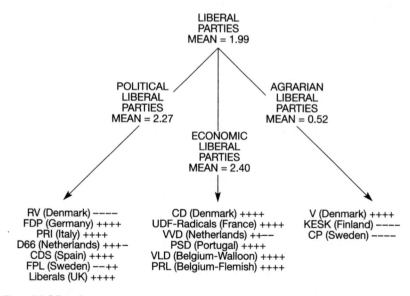

Figure 6.5 Liberal parties
Notes:
The +/− symbols refer to the parties' position on European integration for the years 1984, 1988, 1992, 1996. + indicates a position greater than the liberal mean, and − indicates a position less than the mean.

"product differentiation" on European integration. Overall, though, the standard deviation in liberal approaches to European integration is fairly low, as noted earlier. The diversity of liberal party orientations to European integration did grow from 1984 to 1996. At the later date, however, the liberal party family was unique in that the range of party positions on the European integration dimension was less than the range along the left/right dimension. In other words, liberals across Europe had more in common on EU issues than on domestic economic and social ones.

Christian democratic parties

Christian democratic parties have been more closely associated with the founding of the European Union than any other party family. Each of the countries that joined the European Coal and Steel Community and the European Economic Community in the 1950s had influential or governing Christian democratic parties, and all but one of the countries where such parties were strong (Austria) were part of the integration process. In sharp contrast to their conservative, socialist, and communist counterparts, not a single Christian democratic deputy abstained or voted against either of the EC's founding treaties (Irving, 1979: 239; Papini, 1997: ch. 2). This support has traditionally reflected both a determination to break with the disastrous nationalism which spawned two world wars, and the tenets of Catholic social teaching, which focus on individual human worth, and transcend the framework of the nation state. The first program of the European Peoples' Party (1977), for example, grounds its pro-European stance in the principle that "human rights and fundamental liberties have priority everywhere in the world over national sovereignty" (quoted in Papini, 1997: 110).

The affinity of Christian democratic parties for European integration is moderated in two respects. First, the basic characteristics described above are not shared by all Christian democratic parties. Scandinavian Christian democratic parties are Lutheran Protestant parties with roots in Churches organized on a national, not an international, basis. Norwegian, Finnish, Swedish, and Danish Christian parties have been based on some combination of Christian fundamentalist opposition to liberalism and permissiveness, defense of rural values (with the exception of the Finnish SKL), and association with distinctly national Churches (Karvonen, 1994; Madeley, 1994). These characteristics place them on the right within the Christian democratic family and give them a distinctly less favorable orientation to European integration. Second, the influence of both secularism and national conservatism has eroded some of Christian democracy's traditional pro-European fervor. Moves away from any emphasis on social Catholicism, with its themes of transnational solidarity, may have dampened that fervor. In addition, competition with more nationally oriented conservative parties – or the effort to prevent such parties from bursting on to the political scene – has created an incentive for some Christian democratic leaders to moderate their traditionally strong pro-EU stances. Table 6.3 supports this overall trend: strong, but somewhat diminished, support for European integration within the party family.

Table 6.3 Christian democratic parties in the EU

Country	Party	European integration				Left–right	
		1984	*1988*	*1992*	*1996*	*1984*	*1996*
Austria	ÖVP	0.20	2.00	2.60	3.00	5.80	6.30
Belgium	PSC	2.60	2.60	2.60	2.40	6.30	6.00
Belgium	CVP	2.50	2.50	2.67	2.67	5.80	5.70
Denmark	KRF	1.00	0.89	1.22	1.13	–	–
Finland	SKL	−2.43	−2.43	−2.87	−2.62	–	–
France	UDF–CDS	2.56	2.67	2.78	2.67	–	5.80
Germany	CDU	2.86	2.86	3.00	2.86	6.70	6.40
Germany	CSU	2.50	2.29	1.43	1.43	7.90	7.00
Ireland	Fine Gael	2.29	2.29	2.57	2.38	6.80	–
Italy	DC/PP	2.38	2.38	2.38	2.38	5.40	6.30
Netherlands	CDA	2.44	2.56	2.44	2.33	5.70	6.30
Norway	KFP	−1.00	−1.14	−1.71	−1.43	6.10	–
Portugal	CDS	2.86	2.57	0.57	−1.29	–	8.40
Sweden	KDS	−1.17	−1.17	2.17	2.50	–	–
		2.52	2.52	2.45	2.08	6.37	6.47

These data reveal considerable deviation across Christian democratic orientations towards European integration in the mid-1990s, and a marked increase from the previous decade. It is clear that enlargement of the EU to northern Scandinavia significantly increased the heterogeneity of this party family. But these Protestant parties have rarely received more than 5 percent of the vote in national elections, and so are mostly excluded from our calculation of average party family positions in Figure 6.2. Hence, the addition of Protestant parties to the EU's Christian democratic party family cannot account for the drop in Christian democratic mean score on European integration between 1984 and 1996. Two parties, the CSU and the Portuguese CDS – the most right wing among Catholic Christian democratic parties – are more influential sources of this decline. Both have switched from being strongly supportive of European integration to Euroskepticism, or in the case of the CDS, Europhobia. Figure 6.6 sets out three overall groups within the party family: it distinguishes among social Catholic parties which remain extremely pro-European integration, more right-wing Catholic parties, and the more Euroskeptical Protestant parties.

Conservative parties

The conservative party family, like its Christian democratic counterpart, is marked by considerable internal diversity. The enlargement of the EU to the north and the south has added conservative parties from Spain, Finland, and Sweden that are supportive of European integration, with the result that average support has increased

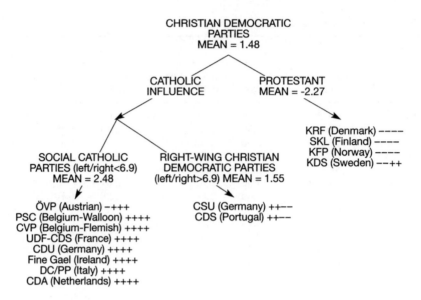

CHRISTIAN DEMOCRATIC
PARTIES
MEAN = 1.48

CATHOLIC
INFLUENCE

PROTESTANT
MEAN = -2.27

KRF (Denmark) ----
SKL (Finland) ----
KFP (Norway) ----
KDS (Sweden) --++

SOCIAL CATHOLIC
PARTIES (left/right<6.9)
MEAN = 2.48

RIGHT-WING CHRISTIAN
DEMOCRATIC PARTIES
(left/right>6.9) MEAN = 1.55

ÖVP (Austrian) -+++
PSC (Belgium-Walloon) ++++
CVP (Belgium-Flemish) ++++
UDF-CDS (France) ++++
CDU (Germany) ++++
Fine Gael (Ireland) ++++
DC/PP (Italy) ++++
CDA (Netherlands) ++++

CSU (Germany) ++--
CDS (Portugal) ++--

Figure 6.6 Christian democratic parties
Notes:
The +/– symbols refer to the parties' position on European integration for the years 1984, 1988, 1992, 1996. + indicates a position greater than the Christian democratic mean, and – indicates a position less than the mean.

Table 6.4 Conservative parties in the EU

Country	Party	Party position					
		European integration				Left–right	
		1984	1988	1992	1996	1984	1996
Denmark	KF	1.67	1.56	1.89	1.63	7.30	7.60
Finland	NC	0.86	1.26	2.88	3.00	7.20	7.40
France	UDF-PR	2.11	2.00	1.89	1.78	–	–
France	RPR	0.11	0.67	1.00	1.25	8.20	7.90
Greece	ND	2.90	3.00	3.00	3.00	8.33	8.30
Ireland	FF	1.00	1.29	1.71	1.25	6.30	6.80
Italy	FORZA	–	–	–	0.00	–	–
Norway	HOYRE	2.43	2.86	3.00	2.86	7.70	–
Spain	AP/PP	1.85	1.92	2.15	2.31	8.40	7.50
Sweden	MOD	1.14	1.71	2.86	2.71	7.70	8.30
UK	Conserv	–0.62	–0.50	–0.12	–0.50	7.80	7.70
		1.41	1.42	1.65	1.64	7.63	7.69

slightly since the mid-1980s. A closer look at the data (Table 6.4) reveals a threefold distinction: national conservative parties; less national Scandinavian parties; and post-authoritarian conservative parties with a European orientation. Nationalists are most concentrated on the extreme right, in parties like the Front National and Austrian FPÖ, which are distinguished by their Europhobia, but they are also present to varying degrees in conservative parties. Among conservative parties in the European Union, three stand out as "national" parties – the Irish Fianna Fáil, the French Rassemblement pour la République, and the British Conservative Party. Fianna Fáil and the RPR have, from their founding, been expressly nationalist parties in which neoliberalism has been relatively weak. The Conservative Party has been far more neoliberal than either of these parties. Edward Heath privileged the market-oriented Whig tradition of the party, and the party's neoliberal wing became dominant under Margaret Thatcher. From the mid-1980s onward, however, overt nationalism gained considerable force within the party. In 1994, almost half of Conservative MPs believed that the establishment of a single EU currency would signal the end of the UK as a sovereign nation (Baker *et al.*, 1997).

The remaining conservative parties have been far less nationalist. Traditional conservative parties in Scandinavia have defined themselves as opposing national social democracy in these countries rather than as nationalist parties (Ljunggren, 1988). In these countries the left, rather than the right, has been more successful in appropriating the claim to represent the nation. In Spain and Greece, nationalism evokes negative associations with a legacy of authoritarianism which still weighs upon conservative parties. In Spain, the Alianza Popular struggled to escape the shadow of Franco (Montero, 1988), and established itself as a moderate right party only after its relaunching as the Partido Popular in 1989. The Greek Nea Dimokratia (ND) has been closer to the Gaullist model of a party of the nation. ND has been centrist or even statist on economic issues, including nationalization, but has drawn on a rhetoric of national independence, emphasizing the "true" interests of the nation (Clogg, 1987: ch. 5). However, "national" considerations, in particular a vulnerable geopolitical position vis-à-vis Turkey, have led ND leaders strongly to support the integration of Greece into the European Union (Verney, 1987). Figure 6.7 illustrates the threefold organization of conservative party orientations toward Europe.

How might we account for relatively stable conservative stances toward Europe in the face of deepening integration? Since the 1980s, a growing number of policy-making competences have shifted to the European level, and Maastricht envisioned further transfers in areas of traditional national symbolic value – monetary and foreign policy. Still, conservative parties remained, on the whole, favorable to further integration. Elsewhere, Hooghe and Marks argue that the orientation of conservative parties to European integration is a function of the relative strength of neoliberal and nationalist tendencies within these parties. Neoliberals support European integration insofar as this leads to regime competition within an integrated market. For neoliberals, European integration is essentially market integration, though they realize that market integration demands some form of political suprastructure, that is, supranational institutions that can induce compliance to market-making agreements, constrain monopolies, and adjudicate on

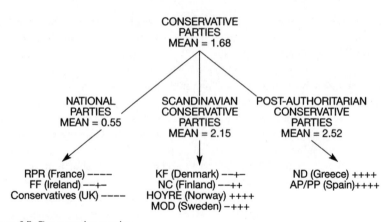

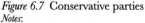

Figure 6.7 Conservative parties
Notes:
The +/− symbols refer to the parties' position on European integration for the years 1984, 1988, 1992, 1996. + indicates a position greater than the conservative mean, and − indicates a position less than the mean.

conflicts arising from incomplete contracting. But such supranational institutions should not compromise regime competition, that is, competition among governments to attract mobile factors of production to their territory. Neoliberals acknowledge the necessity of some supranational authority in the EU, but they are minimalists in this regard. The institutional architecture of Europe should, they believe, sustain competition among individuals and firms and competition among governments. Their chief concern is to constrain the ability of any individual, firm, or government to determine prices, and this requires that the scope of market activity be as large as possible and the scope of political control be as small as possible.

From a neoliberal perspective, EMU represents not the sacrifice of national sovereignty but, rather, an extension of the logic of the single market. Nationalists, in contrast, are deeply opposed to EMU because it threatens national sovereignty. For nationalists, the purported economic benefits of EMU are secondary – they wish above all to defend national particularities (i.e. culture, language, community) and national sovereignty (i.e. the unlimited right of the nation state to govern those in its territory). However, the differences between nationalists and neoliberals should not be exaggerated. Neoliberals, too, are deeply opposed to further political integration, whether it is to democratize the Euro-polity or to shift authoritative competences to the European level. In particular, they oppose social democratic efforts to move from economic and monetary to social policy coordination. The social democratic valley set out in Figure 6.4 – market integration with little capacity for authoritative regulation – is the preferred outcome for neoliberalism. The consequences of European integration for neoliberals are set out in Figure 6.8.

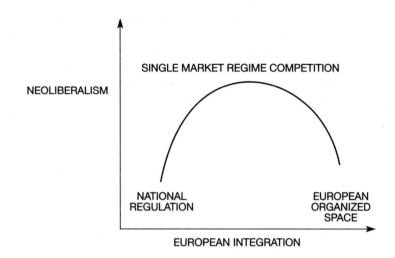

Figure 6.8 The neoliberal peak

The shifting axis of national political contestation: competing explanations

A first possible explanation for the findings detailed above focuses on the shifting economic interests of actors and their aggregation at the level of party politics. The view that political parties represent particular constituencies with particular economic interests provides a straightforward point of departure for analyzing party positions on a range of issues. This model applies the economic logic of interest group politics developed by Jeffry Frieden to political parties (Frieden, 1991). Political parties are channels through which economically driven interests influence government policy. From this standpoint, party orientations to European integration are a function of the economic effects of the creation of Europe-wide markets. Market deepening has had transparent distributional consequences which favor the most mobile factors of production (international capital) at the expense of immobile factors (labor and sheltered capital), and those sectors that are able to compete effectively in Europe-wide markets at the expense of uncompetitive sectors.

Any effort to draw strong analytical links between societal groupings and patterns of party orientations is problematic. Survey research suggests that the relationship between an individual's socio-economic location and orientation to European integration is weak (Gabel and Palmer, 1995; Franklin and van der Eijk, 1996). The weakness of economic interest explanations is due to: the volatility of individual orientations to the EU; the difficulty individuals have in specifying their economic interests on European integration; and the influence of factors not captured in economic models. While surveys have shown that individuals have a reasonably clear conception of their socio-economic position along the class divide, the sectoral distinctions that feature in hypotheses relating political orientations to economic internationalization are less deeply rooted. Distinctions based on sectoral location are not reinforced by organizational experiences, as are class distinctions. The latter reflect the experience of a century of economic and political mobilization in Western Europe. Given the ambiguous nature of voter attitudes toward Europe, parties should not be viewed simply as aggregators of interests. The volatility of societal orientations opens up a strategic terrain upon which party leaders frame competitive appeals to disparate and fluctuating sets of individual voters around particular elections.

These considerations do not mean that one should ignore constituency economic interests in explaining party orientations, but it makes it plausible that party orientations represent efforts to shape – as well as respond to – the interests of constituencies. Political parties are not empty vessels into which issue positions are poured in response to constituency pressures, but are organizations with historically rooted orientations that guide their response to new issues. Parties may shift their stances in response to electoral failure (or success), coalitional pressures, leadership change, government performance, or the decline of certain constituencies and the rise of others. But one would expect them to encompass new issues into existing frames of reference (Kitschelt, 1994: ch. 6). The larger a party's stake in existing issue cleavages, the more it has built a reputation for particular policy stands, and the less fixed the views of the electorate on an issue are, the greater the inducement for that party to encapsulate the issue into its existing ideological framework. This may be precisely what we are seeing within the EU. As the integration process proceeds, parties are increasingly defining their appeals mainly around the basic economic left/right cleavage characteristic of Western European party systems – that is, social democratic, liberal, Christian democratic, and conservative parties – in an attempt to assimilate European issues into the existing political spectrum (Hooghe and Marks, forthcoming).

Conclusion

Simon Hix and Chris Lord have suggested that contestation over European integration raises new territorial issues that could generate another in a series of cleavages that have shaped party systems in Western Europe over the past five centuries (Lipset and Rokkan, 1967; Hix and Lord, 1997). The nationalist backlash to Maastricht also points to the salience of tension between national and European orientations in the politics of integration. Our examination of party orientations towards integration, however, suggests another possible trajectory: the emergence of the traditional left–right spectrum as the major axis of contestation over Europe. Political parties that have long competed with one another along that spectrum have an interest in sustaining its predominance against efforts to introduce a new dimension of contestation. Familiar patterns in new circumstances are particularly evident in the context of the EMU debate, which pits a center-left coalition committed to deeper social and political integration against a center-right one in pursuit of neoliberal policies.

The assimilation of new policy controversies into established political and ideological frameworks has important implications for EU legitimacy. Critics of a "democratic deficit" have underscored the absence of strong, centralized representative institutions at the European level. In a multi-level polity, however, national institutions also constitute an important site for the democratic contestation of EU policies. By conceiving European policies as a means for realizing their visions of domestic society, national political parties effectively incorporate the EU into domestic political debate.

Notes

1 We thank Liesbet Hooghe, Thomas Banchoff, Mitchell Smith, and Marco Steenbergen for comments and advice.
2 Our data for each party are the means of these expert judgments. Ray currently is writing a dissertation on the interaction of national parties and electorates, which explicates how party orientations influence and are influenced by voters' attitudes.
3 We use the terms "socialist" and "social democratic" interchangeably.
4 The Euroskepticism of small-scale farmers is reinforced by low levels of education and their rural, frequently anti-cosmopolitan, values.
5 This is very clear in the Venstre's Proposals for the Intergovernmental Conference of the EU in 1996 (http://www.venstre.dk/english/default.htm).

Bibliography

Ansell, C. K., Parsons, C. A. and Darden, K. A. (1997) "Dual Networks in European Regional Development Policy," *Journal of Common Market Studies* 35, 3: 347–75.

Baker, D., Gamble, A., Ludlam, S. and Seawright, D. (1997) "The 1994/96 Conservative and Labour Members of Parliament Surveys on Europe: The Data Compared," presented at the APSA Meeting, Washington, DC.

Christensen, D. A. (1996) "The Left-wing Opposition in Denmark, Norway and Sweden; Cases of Euro-phobia?" *West European Politics* 19, 3: 525–46.

Clarke, S. and Curtice, J. (1997) "Why Have the Liberals Been so Keen on Europe? An Analysis of the Attitudes Held by the British Liberals towards European Integration 1945–1996," paper presented at the American Political Science Association Meeting, Washington, DC.

Clogg, R. (1987) *Parties and Elections in Greece: The Search for Legitimacy*, Durham, NC: Duke University Press.

Franklin, M. and van der Eijk, C. (1996) *Choosing Europe? The European Electorate and National Politics in the Face of Union*, Ann Arbor: University of Michigan Press.

Frieden, J. A. (1991) "Invested Interests: The Politics of National Economic Policies in a World of Global Finance," *International Organization* 45: 425–51.

Gabel, M. and Palmer, H. (1995) "Understanding Variation in Public Support for European Integration," *European Journal of Political Research* 27: 3–19.

Geyer, R. (1997) *The Uncertain Union: British and Norwegian Social Democrats in an Integrating Europe*, Aldershot, UK: Avebury.

Geyer, R. and Swank, D. (1997) "Rejecting the European Union: Norwegian Social Democratic Opposition to the EU in the 1990s," *Party Politics* 3, 4: 1–21.

Griffiths, R. T. (ed.) (1993) *Socialist Parties and the Question of Europe in the 1950s*, Leiden: E. J. Brill.

Haahr, J. H. (1993) *Looking to Europe: The EC Policies of the British Labour Party and the Danish Social Democrats*, Aarhus: Aarhus University Press.

Hix, S. (1995) "Political Parties in the European Union System: A 'Comparative Politics Approach' to the Development of Party Federations," Ph.D. thesis, European University Institute.

Hix, S. and Lord, C. (1997) *Political Parties in the European Union*, New York: St. Martin's Press.

Hooghe, L. (1996) *Cohesion Policy and European Integration: Building Multi-level Governance*, Oxford, UK: Oxford University Press.

Hooghe, L. and Marks, G. (forthcoming) "Making of a Polity: European Integration from the 1980s," in H. Kitschelt, P. Lange, G. Marks, and J. Stephens (eds) *Continuity and Change in Contemporary Capitalism*, Cambridge, UK: Cambridge University Press.

Irving, R. E. M. (1979) *The Christian Democratic Parties of Western Europe*, London: George Allen & Unwin.

Karvonen, L. (1994) "Christian Parties in Scandinavia: Victory over the Windmills?" in D. Hanley (ed.) *Christian Democracy in Europe: A Comparative Perspective*, London: Pinter.

Kirchner, E. J. (ed.) (1988) *Liberal Parties in Western Europe*, Cambridge, UK: Cambridge University Press.

Kitschelt, H. (1994) *The Transformation of European Social Democracy*, Cambridge, UK: Cambridge University Press.

Kitschelt, H., Lange P., Marks, G. and Stephens, J. (eds) (forthcoming) *Continuity and Change in Contemporary Capitalism*, Cambridge, UK: Cambridge University Press.

Ladrech, R. (1993) "Social Democratic Parties and EC Integration: Transnational Party Responses to Europe 1992," *European Journal of Political Research* 24, 2: 195–210.

—— (1997) "Partisanship and Party Formation in European Union Politics," *Comparative Politics* 29, 2: 167–86.

Lipset, S. M. and Rokkan, S. (1967) "Cleavage Structures, Party Systems and Voter Alignments: An Introduction," in S. M. Lipset and S. Rokkan (eds) *Party Systems and Voter Alignments: Crossnational Perspectives*, New York: Free Press.

Ljunggren, S.-B. (1988) "Conservatism in Norway and Sweden," in B. Girvin (ed.) *The Transformation of Contemporary Conservatism*, London: Sage.

Madeley, J. (1994) "The Antimonies of Lutheran Politics: The Case of Norway's Christian People's Party," in D. Hanley (ed.) *Christian Democracy in Europe: A Comparative Perspective*, London: Pinter.

Montero, J. R. (1988) "More than Conservative, Less than Neoconservative: Alianza Popular in Spain," in B. Girvin (ed.) *The Transformation of Contemporary Conservatism*, London: Sage.

Papini, R. (1997) *The Christian Democratic International*, trans. R. Royal, London: Rowman and Littlefield.

Ray, L. (1998) "Politicizing Europe: Political Parties and the Changing Nature of Public Opinion about the EU," Ph.D. dissertation, University of North Carolina, Chapel Hill.

Schmitt, H. and Thomassen, J. (1997) "European Parliament Party Groups: An Emerging Party System?" paper presented at the ECPR Workshop, Bern.

Sciarini, P. and Listhaug, O. (1997) "Single Cases or a Unique Pair? The Swiss and Norwegian 'No' to Europe," *Journal of Common Market Studies* 35, 3: 407–38.

Smith, G. (1972) *Politics in Western Europe*, London: Heinemann.

—— (1988) "Between Left and Right: The Ambivalence of European Liberalism," in E. J. Kirchner (ed.) *Liberal Parties in Western Europe*, Cambridge, UK: Cambridge University Press.

Verney, S. (1987) "Greece and the European Community," in K. Featherstone and D. K. Katsoudas (eds) *Political Change in Greece: Before and After the Colonels*, London: Croom Helm.

Von Beyme, K. (1985) *Political Parties in Western Democracies*, Aldershot, UK: Gower.

7

THE EUROPEAN PARLIAMENT
AND EU LEGITIMACY

Wolfgang Wessels and Udo Diedrichs

The issue of legitimacy, long controversial in the context of national political systems, is now the object of heated debate among politicians and scholars in the context of the European Union (EU). This chapter contributes to that debate as it pertains to the European Parliament (EP). In all national democratic systems, parliaments are considered strongholds and symbols of legitimacy. As directly elected bodies, they represent national citizens and act on their behalf. In terms of form and function, the EP differs sharply from its national counterparts. Nevertheless, it also has central significance with respect to the legitimacy issue. In this context legitimacy is about representation, the existence or non-existence of political communication linking governing institutions and elites, on the one hand, with citizens and intermediary groups, on the other. In this essay, we argue that a proper understanding of the EP and the legitimacy issue requires attention to the EU "fusion" process in which national, subnational and supranational actors merge their instruments of governance to produce policy outcomes (Wessels, 1992, 1997; Risse-Kappen, 1996).

The EP's capacity to deliver a kind of "European legitimacy" depends to a large extent upon the character of the EU system as a whole and the special role the EP plays within it. This special character is highlighted in this volume by the notion of a "contested polity." On the one hand, the structure of the EU, more than national political systems, is the object of ongoing fundamental public and political debate. The EP itself is a highly *contested institution*; like the EU as a whole, its role, importance, and status are subject to varying political interpretations, guided by different strategies and interests. On the other hand, the EU is increasingly recognized by political actors as an arena in which a discourse is emerging and arguments are exchanged. Within this broader context, the European Parliament is becoming an important *forum of contestation*, by providing a stage for the expression and exchange of diverging views on institutional and policy issues, and fostering debate among the political families represented at the European level. The concept of "fusion," we argue, illuminates both dimensions of contestation and their relevance for legitimacy.

We proceed in three parts. Part one contrasts and critiques federalist and realist views of the EP, its role within the EU, and its relevance for the problem of legitimacy. This part of the chapter argues that established perspectives cannot capture the dynamics of the EU – and of the EP within it – and suggests some alternative theoretical approaches. Part two sets out the concept of "fusion" and contends that it better captures the evolution of the EP as a contested institution within the EU political system. This portion of the chapter illustrates the fusion concept through an exploration of the EP's policy-making functions in the wake of the Maastricht and Amsterdam treaties. Part three explores links between the fusion thesis and the problem of legitimacy. Fusion implies an evolution towards a new kind of European democracy creating a complex and highly differentiated entity, a "mixed polity" combining several levels of governance and a wide range of actors (Wessels, 1996, 1997). Our analysis revolves around the EP's system-development and inter-action functions, that is, the role of the EP in the evolution of the EU system and its links with European society. A concluding section situates the role of the European Parliament in the institutional context of the EU polity and addresses the prospects for the EP to contribute to legitimation of the EU in this setting.

The European Parliament and legitimacy: traditional approaches

Assessments of the role of the EP within the EU are shaped by conceptions of the EU as a system. The schools of thought sketched below represent ideal-type constructs that orient us toward different approaches to the legitimacy of the EU. They link basic beliefs with theoretical assumptions about integration. Though rarely defended in their pure version, these ideal types nonetheless represent useful points of reference for the ongoing debate about the place of the EP within the EU as a whole and its importance for the problem of legitimacy.

A European state-centered approach: federalism

From the federalist perspective, legitimacy rests upon links between the EU and European citizens, citizen involvement in policy-making at the European level, and identification with the institutions of European governance. Central to this configuration is the importance of the citizens of Europe, or "the European people" (Spinelli, 1958), who already possess a kind of European identity that complements their national, regional, and local orientations. Through the election of a parliament they freely express their will and contribute directly to decision-making in the EU (Schneider, 1986). For federalists, this process gradually generates a state-like polity, a "parliamentary Europe" (Duff, 1995) or even a "supranational parliamentary democracy" (Laming, 1995: 117). The role of the EP could evolve in accordance with the Westminster model; its functions might in the long run resemble those of national parliaments.

In the field of policy-making, this evolution of a parliamentary Europe would entail the election and control of the Commission as a type of European government, full legislative powers for the EP shared with the Council as a second chamber representing the member states, and the representation and articulation of political currents organized through and within European parties (Schneider, 1986; Spinelli, 1958). The European Parliament would also, by giving its assent to all important constitutional matters, become one of the engines of system-development in the EU; its interaction with the citizens would gradually replace connections with national parliaments. In a virtuous circle, these powers and capabilities would reinforce each other (see Figure 7.1).

The federalist view holds that citizens increasingly see their interests satisfied at the European level, generating increased support for integration and, in neo-functionalist terms, a "shift of loyalties" (Haas, 1968). The EP is regarded as the main legitimating factor of the EU system. For this shift of loyalties to occur, the EP's role in EU policies must be enhanced, thus attracting people's interest in the Parliament and the EU as a whole. Direct elections, introduced in 1979, are considered an essential but not sufficient step toward molding the EP in the image of its national counterparts; this must be followed by an increase in the EP's power and competencies.

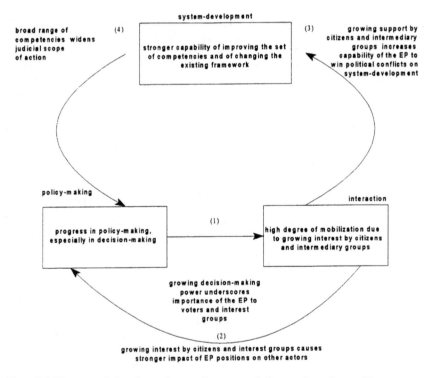

Figure 7.1 Virtuous circle of growing parliamentary influence in policy-making, system-development, and interaction with the citizens
Sources: Grabitz *et al.*, 1988: 641; Wessels, 1995: 889, translated and adjusted

According to this perspective, the democratic deficit of the existing EU is caused by an undervalued role of the EP as a directly elected, democratic element of representation. As the EU assumes competencies, Parliament should correspondingly be endowed with relevant powers (Naßmacher, 1972: 76f.). The "democratic deficit" of the EU can thus precisely be defined as "the shift in decision-making powers from the national to the EU level, without accompanying strengthening of parliamentary control of executive bodies" (Archer and Butler, 1996: 58). In this sense, the lack of control over European governance – first at the national and then at the European level – creates a "double democratic deficit" (Lodge, 1996: 190f.).

Furthermore, the lack of transparency in policy-making inhibits citizens from identifying with the Union. Here, too, the European Parliament has a fundamental role. As Lodge argues, the EP, the sole institution "capable of engendering popular belief in its own and the EC/EU's democratic legitimacy," has from the inception of the Community been a "marginal player." Direct election alone "is not enough to generate the democratic consent needed to give EC authority structures legitimacy yet" (Lodge, 1996: 189f.). From the federalist standpoint, a European constitution would supplement direct election of the EP and serve as a fundamental political charter and a focus of identification (Läufer, 1995; Weidenfeld, 1996). European values and interests would gain force and strengthen the emotional links between the citizens and the EU system. Ultimately the individual nation states that comprise the EU's membership would play a minor role in the hierarchy of preferences of the citizens and organized political forces.

A nation state-centered approach: realism

The realist view ascribes only a minor role to the European Parliament. As the German Constitutional Court puts it, legitimacy is mainly secured by the peoples of the member states via their nationally elected representative bodies, and only in a supplementary manner by the European Parliament (Bundesverfassungsgericht, 1993). The basic assumption is that there is no single European people on whom a European statehood could be founded (Weiler, 1997: 255–58), nor a European public space that would shape the will and opinion of the population (European Constitutional Group, 1993; Kielmansegg, 1996; Lübbe, 1994). From this perspective, the EP is a marginal institution, lacking the quality and attributes of national representative assemblies considered as parliaments in the "full" sense of the term (Schröder, 1994; Lübbe, 1994).

Since member-state preferences are the driving forces behind the integration process according to the realist view, and decision-making therefore rests primarily with the Council, system-development is initiated by the European Council, which also secures the links of interaction between the national and the European levels. Realism therefore suggests a very different kind of democratic dilemma from that proposed by federalism. According to realist analysis, the EU is mired in a "legitimacy trap": the more it is endowed with new competencies and exerts them through supranational structures and procedures of decision-making, the less it can be regarded as legitimate, simply because it is moving away from the source of legitimacy – the nation state (Kielmansegg, 1996). Citizens will always cling to familiar values and symbols, making it nearly impossible to develop a European identity.

Even where scholars in this tradition acknowledge the existence of a "democratic deficit" at the European level, they insist that efforts to close it may have negative consequences in terms of efficiency. As Rolf Gustavsson puts it, "there is this fundamental dilemma: a choice between a quasi-federalist option which probably provides more efficiency but weaker formal democratic legitimacy and a confederalist option with less efficiency but stronger formal legitimacy" (Gustavsson, 1996: 226).

In contrast to the assumptions of the federalist school, then, this approach supposes a relationship between the different parliamentary functions of policy-making, system-development and interaction that can be expressed as a vicious circle. Lacking political power, the EP is unable to change the rules of the game; this deficiency is reinforced by a lack of public support, further weakening the position of the Parliament relative to other institutions in the European arena.

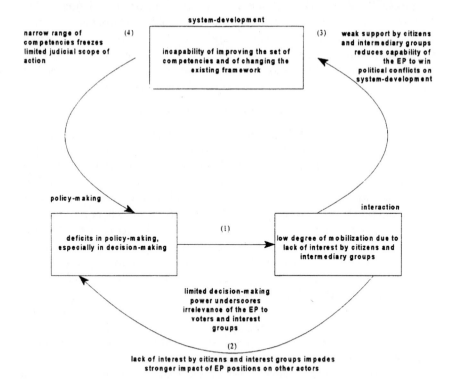

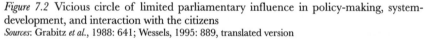

Figure 7.2 Vicious circle of limited parliamentary influence in policy-making, system-development, and interaction with the citizens
Sources: Grabitz *et al.*, 1988: 641; Wessels, 1995: 889, translated version

Shortcomings of established approaches

Both federalist and realist conceptualizations of the European polity are state-centric and cling to classical patterns of direct accountability between the electorate and Parliament. The two alternatives seem to be those of either building up a state on the European level or preserving nation states. However, the process of integration cannot be explained according to concepts taken from (national) statehood. What is needed is an innovative conception of the EU and the European Parliament that takes account of the peculiar nature of this political system. For example, some authors favor the ideas of "governance without government" (Rosenau and Czempiel, 1992) or "governance beyond the state" (Jachtenfuchs and Kohler-Koch, 1996) in order to characterize the declining role of the state in decision-making in both the domestic and international spheres.

The analysis of the role of the Parliament and its contribution to the legitimacy of the EU presented here departs from the federalist and realist perspectives on two fundamental points. First, the development of the EP cannot be explained by static or state-centric concepts but must be situated in a dynamic model formulated here as a new kind of polity characterized by fusion. The polity emerging from the fusion process implies a particular role for a European Parliament that departs from national models and essentially renders the EU a new kind of parliamentary system. Second, this fusion process, characterized by the merging of instruments of governance from several levels, suggests a more nuanced understanding of the legitimacy problem within the EU. In the following two sections, we develop our conceptualization of the Parliament's role through an empirical survey of its functions in the EU policy process, and then explore the implications of that emergent role for the problem of legitimacy.

Reconceptualizing the role of the EP

Neither federalist nor realist concepts are adequate to describe, analyze, and explain the process of integration in the EU. West European states are increasingly merging their instruments of government in order to cope with the problems of interdependence and cooperation, thus creating a new kind of political system. This fusion process involves more than merely a horizontal "pooling of sovereignties"; it implies a merger of public resources from several levels of governance and a diffusion of responsibilities across these units that renders conventional conceptions of accountability unviable (Wessels, 1997). National governments and administrations are not replaced or absorbed by a European mega-bureaucracy; instead they form part of a complex and differentiated mix of political and institutional arrangements and actors. EU institutions become "agents for efficient and effective policy-making," developing their own "institutional ambitions" (Wessels, 1997: 274). These institutions are driven by the dynamics of growing participation by an increasing number of actors, leading in turn to a high degree of complexity and differentiation in decision-making procedures. In the competition for power between EU institutions that ensues, success for each institution depends upon its ability to act as a reliable and constructive partner.

This overall constellation contrasts sharply with federalist and realist visions of the EU. It suggests a dynamic, evolving role for the EP within that constellation. The particular competencies of the European Parliament contrast sharply with those of its national counterparts. And its complex, evolving relations with other EU institutions correspondingly do not fit analytical categories of federalism and realism.

The Maastricht Treaty introduced several important changes in the role and position of the EP (Jacobs, Corbett and Shackleton, 1992: 10):

- co-decision procedure (Article 189b TEC);
- extension of application of assent procedure to a wider range of international agreements (Article 228 (3) TEC) and other sectors;
- approval of the newly elected Commission (Article 158 (2));
- election of an Ombudsman (Article 138e TEC);
- installation of Committees of Inquiry (Article 138c TEC);
- only minor powers in the Second (Common Foreign and Security Policy) and Third (Cooperation in Justice and Home Affairs) Pillars (Articles J and K TEU); and
- no competence on Treaty amendments or modifications (Article N TEU).

The Amsterdam Treaty of October 1997 added new rights and competencies and reinforced existing Treaty provisions. These included:

- extension of the co-decison procedure, especially in fourteen cases previously governed by cooperation;
- stronger role when electing the new Commission (Article 158 (2));
- simplification of the co-decision procedure in a manner that provides for greater equality between Council and Parliament (Article 189);
- enhanced rights of information and consultation ("avis") in the Third Pillar (Title VI, Article K.11); and
- communitarization of matters hitherto dealt with in the Third Pillar (chapter on free movement of persons, asylum, and immigration).

How have the changes adopted in Maastricht and envisioned in Amsterdam altered the position of the EP within the EU political system? And what are the implications of those changes for legitimacy? In order to capture the role of the EP in this dynamic and evolving political system, we distinguish and trace its different functions. Drawing on Bourguignon-Wittke (1985), Grabitz et al. (1988), and Wessels (1995), we define these functions as policy-making, system-development, and interaction. The analysis of the policy-making function that follows illustrates how the EP resists conceptualization according to either federalist or realist categories. The ensuing discussion of the system-development and interaction functions addresses the role of popular representation in the process of institutional reform and the potential development of the EP as a forum for partisan political exchange more familiar to European publics.

Policy-making function: considerable progress

The policy-making function refers to the influence exerted by the EP in the EU-policy cycle in relation with the Council and the Commission, that is, its ability to participate in the preparation, making, and implementation and control of decisions produced by the EC/EU system. It also includes the elective function with regard to the investiture of the Commission and the competencies relating to the treaty-making powers of the EU. The EP has increased its role in EU decision-making considerably, especially since the introduction of the co-decision procedure specified in Article 189b TEU introduced at Maastricht and extended and revised at Amsterdam. The procedure gives the European Parliament the ability finally to block any decision by the Council, that is, it has a nearly equal say at least in veto-ing proposed legislation, without being able, however, to secure legislation against resistance by the Council. In the case of divergent positions, a conciliation committee composed of members of the Council and the EP tries to find a compromise. As Jacobs, Corbett and Shackleton put it, "the right to say 'no' gives Parliament a bargaining position which it has hitherto lacked regarding Community legislation, and is of fundamental importance to public perception of Parliament's role – it can no longer be accused of lacking teeth" (Jacobs, Corbett and Shackleton, 1992: 191).

The enhanced role of the EP has not paralyzed or even delayed policy-making; on the contrary, interaction with the Council has proved rather successful. From the entry into force of the Treaty on European Union (TEU) in November 1993 until December 1996, there were 179 proposals submitted by the Commission based upon the co-decision procedure, of which sixty-nine were finally adopted. While the Council requested that the Conciliation Committee be convoked in twenty cases, in only one of these was the final proposal rejected by the EP. Parliament is intensively using its new rights of co-decision and increasingly is regarded as a reliable and serious partner by both the Council and the Commission (Maurer, 1996; Schmuck, 1995, 1996; Smith and Kelemen, 1997).

Furthermore, at Amsterdam, cooperation (Article 189c TEC) was replaced by co-decision in eleven cases, leaving only some questions concerning economic and monetary union to the cooperation procedure. Additionally, the realm of co-decision has been broadened to include cases involving employment, social, and health issues. The co-decision procedure also covers the creation of a uniform electoral procedure and adoption of provisions under Union Citizenship residency rights or the use of structural funds. Within five years the procedure also will cover matters like asylum, refugees, and immigration, forming part of an area of freedom, security, and justice. Generally, this set of rules, which was simplified and streamlined at Amsterdam, has been upgraded to the status of "normal" legislative pattern in the EU.

In the field of external relations, the EP has nearly acquired treaty-enabling powers. The Single European Act already introduced parliamentary assent for all association agreements, including the subsequent conclusion of financial protocols, excluding commercial agreements according to Article 113. The European Parliament has used these rights to promote its political preferences, as demonstrated by its hesitation to approve the Customs Union with Turkey in 1996. In recent years the European Parliament has blocked the conclusion of financial protocols with Turkey, Israel, Morocco, and Syria in order to promote human rights. Furthermore, at Maastricht the assent procedure was extended to all important international agreements establishing a specific institutional framework, having important implications for the Union budget, or requiring the amendment of Union legislation pursuant to co-decision (Article 228 (3) TEC). This can be interpreted as the expression of a treaty-enabling power which provides Parliament with a considerable influence on external relations of the European Union.

A first step in the direction of an elective function came with the assent of the EP to the new Commission according to Article 158 (2). The EP's approval cannot be regarded as a merely formal act, a kind of *"nihil obstat,"* but was designed as a genuinely political decision. The EP sent a clear signal that it insists on this right and regards it as an essential part of its competencies. Even where the European Parliament does not have the formal right to approve a candidate – as in the case of the President-designate of the Commission – but is only consulted, it tries to offer a public forum for discussion and political debate that can hardly be ignored by the member states, as suggested by the investiture of Jacques Santer in 1995. Parliament is also consulted when appointing the President of the European Monetary Institute and the President, the Vice-Presidents and the other members of the board of the European Central Bank (Article 109f, 109l TEC and Article 50 of the Statute of the European Central Bank). Here again, the Amsterdam Treaty enhanced Parliament's influence in a two-track procedure. The revised Article 158 (2) stipulates that the President-designate of the Commission requires confirmation by the EP before this person can, in close cooperation with the governments of the member states, name the single candidates for the Commission posts. After that the whole Commission needs the approval of the EP.

It remains to be seen if the deputies will be able to add a political dimension to these decisions and thereby serve as a controlling authority. Jacobs, Corbett and Shackleton argue that this political dimension is likely to follow formal changes in the EP's powers, for "when it comes to a public vote in an elected parliament on an individual, it would be surprising if that individual wished to take office should Parliament reject his or her candidacy." Even without formal veto powers, parliamentary consultation "will amount, in practice, to a vote of confirmation in which Parliament enjoys a virtual right of veto" (Jacobs, Corbett and Shackleton, 1992: 228).

While the EP's influence in the legislative process has grown since Maastricht and been bolstered by Amsterdam, there are some Union policy areas, including the decision on the coming into force and the shaping of an economic and mone-tary union, and the Maastricht Treaty's Second and Third Pillars, in which the EP's role and impact are rather limited. On the other hand, it is in the Second and Third Pillars that Parliament enjoys a judicially fixed right to be informed by the Council, and its decision to set up a foreign and security affairs committee docu-ments the political will of the deputies to tackle those issues seriously and to make their voices heard in the policy-making process.

The EP's Third Pillar rights were extended and consolidated at Amsterdam according to the new Article K.11, which established parliamentary consultation before the Council can act in important areas and conferred on the EP the right to be informed, to ask questions and to make recommendations on justice and home affairs issues. This can be regarded as a relative gain which does not imply a qual-itative leap for the EP in decision-making, but leaves no doubt that parliamentary participation – even if in a "soft" form – is necessary and shall not be ignored by the member states. Moreover, if we consider that critical policy matters like asylum and immigration have been transferred from the Third Pillar into the EC, there is evidence of substantial advances for the Parliament as an institution in the policy-making function.

Ultimately the Amsterdam Treaty has confirmed the long-run evolution of the European Parliament into a real co-decision-maker in the European Union, approaching a more equal status with the Council (Maurer, 1996) as part of a sort of bicameral system. Overall, the SEA, the Treaty of Maastricht, the Summit of Amsterdam and the informal adjustments that have followed these punctuations of formal change have made the European Parliament one of the winners in the development of policy-making in the EC/EU. However, its emergent role is only poorly captured by federalist and realist perspectives. The EP is neither the emer-gent legislature of a European super-state in the making nor a powerless institution at the center of an intergovernmental system. It is instead an increasingly impor-tant, if still-contested, institution within an increasingly fused EU polity.

System-development and interaction functions: implications for legitimacy

How does the position of the EP within the EU system illuminate the problem of legitimacy? In particular, to what degree has the EP emerged as a locus of politi-cal representation, linking European governance with European society? Two further functions of the EU shed light on these questions. The system-development function refers to the EP's ability to participate in constitutive decisions (constitution-building) and in shaping the functional, sectoral, and geographical scope of the political system. To the extent that the EP, the only directly account-able EU institution, shapes the evolution of the EU as a whole, it constitutes a means for European citizens to influence European governance. The interaction function refers to the ability to attract the attention, interaction, and support of citizens. To the extent that the EP increases its interaction with European publics by serving as a locus of partisan exchange and a site of interest articulation, it constitutes a more effective representative institution.

System-development function: halting progress

In the case of constitution-building, the essence of the system-development function, the influence of the EP appears quite limited. In 1994 the draft report coordinated by Belgian MEP Fernand Herman (Herman Report), intended to serve as a basis for a European constitution, was not taken up by the EP's plenary but referred back to the committee in order to be reconsidered in a broad public debate (Hilf, 1994). This de facto failure of the report reveals that a constitutional solution currently is not on the agenda of the EP itself, let alone any federalist-inspired blueprints for a European polity. However, it is important to recall that though a decade earlier the Draft Treaty on European Union submitted by the European Parliament – the so-called Spinelli Draft – was not taken up as a political strategy, it nevertheless inspired the proceedings and preparations leading to the conclusion of the Single European Act (Archer and Butler, 1996: 49). Moreover, as Derek Urwin points out, the Spinelli Draft "reconfirmed the EP's role as the conscience of the original EC ideal, worrying away around the edges of the existing system" (Urwin, 1995: 224).

In a clear contrast to the proceedings in 1991, the preparation of the 1996 IGC revealed considerable progress for the European Parliament. Though still lacking the critical right of assenting to Treaty revisions and amendments, the EP took a step closer to full integration into the negotiation framework. Before, during, and after the 1991 IGC, Parliament followed up the Martin and Colombo reports with several resolutions in which it expressed its opinion on the process of Treaty revision and made clear what kind of reform it preferred. The impact of these resolutions was limited (Corbett 1993: 17ff.); neither report generated decisive pressure for compliance with the Parliament's preferences. However, these reports served as supporting elements for those governments – like the German and Belgian – and institutions that wished substantial reforms to be concluded. By 1995, the situation was different (Dankert, 1997). The Reflection Group installed in Messina to prepare the ground for the 1996 IGC included two members of Parliament, a Christian democrat and a socialist. Based upon reports by Jean-Louis Bourlanges and David Martin, the European Parliament issued an assessment of the functioning of the TEU and its basic demands for the IGC, later adding a resolution on its fundamental priorities for the conference (European Parliament, 1995, 1996a, 1996b).

The EP's impact on the IGC itself proved modest. Its representatives to the Reflection Group closely followed the different stages of negotiations on the revision of Maastricht. Due to French and British pressure, however, no member of Parliament participated at the conference itself. Rather, through its representatives a close association developed with some member-state governments in which the Parliament was kept closely informed of developments. While they were largely excluded from the IGC's deliberations, most EP deputies reacted positively to its outcome. Although its members identified some deficiencies and drawbacks, the European Parliament was generally satisfied with the results of Amsterdam. In a first resolution, the deputies voiced their intention to accept the Treaty revision (European Parliament, 1997).

The future evolution of the EP as an effective actor at the level of system-development will depend in no small part on the evolution of its party groups. Since the very inception of European integration, the members of the Assembly of the European Communities have organized themselves into groups along party lines rather than national delegations. The parliamentary parties have therefore developed largely independently from the co-existing Europe-wide party federations. Throughout this process, partisan conflict has been overshadowed by a common understanding among the main groups in the EP, leading to a "Grand Coalition" of European People's Party (Christian democrats and conservatives) and social democrats. The multinational composition of the Parliament has led to overlapping cleavages in which the "national factor" has become diminished as a source of division within the larger group. This contrasts with the case of national parliaments, in which policy differences between those parties in government and those in opposition typically are exaggerated by the political process. The Parliament's institutional need to strive for the expansion of its competencies and enhanced political influence in a coherent way has a significant impact on the structure and organization of decision-making within Parliament. Constitutionally induced constraints have, to a great extent, kept the centrist "Grand Coalition" together.

The absence of partisan cleavages within the EP has arguably hampered its effectiveness as a forum for Europe-wide democratic representation. But this cohesiveness has also contributed to the EP's strength within the overall EU system. Only with an absolute majority of its members has Parliament been able to fight effectively for its interests and positions in the co-decision and assent procedures, and to be perceived as a single actor by the public. In recent years, however, this situation has begun to change, giving way to a more pronounced political and even ideological profile of the different parties on the European level. Ever more cleavages familiar from the national scene emerge in the Brussels and Strasbourg arenas. Recent investigation of the confirmation of Jacques Santer as Commission President in 1994 reveals traces of a "soft" cleavage between center-right and center-left groups in the plenary, as well as between parties in government and those in opposition in their home countries (Hix and Lord, 1996). Additionally, scholars have identified a growing left–right split concerning socio-economic policy within the EP that is likely to become more pronounced in the future as social policy occupies a more central place on the policy agenda (Hix and Lord, 1997).

Ultimately, then, the Parliament faces a conundrum. Until recently, the strategic institutional requirements of the Parliament have hindered the emergence of political and ideological discussion, conflict and debate among the party groups. Intensified political contestation within the EP seems to be a necessary condition for greater public visibility and support for the Parliament. To the extent that Europeans identify familiar left–right cleavages at the EU level, European governance might come to seem less alien and more familiar. At the same time, however, greater partisan contestation could make it even more difficult for the EP to act coherently and effectively in its interactions with other EU institutions. There appears to be a trade-off between the EP as a representative institution, on the one hand, and as an effective institutional actor, on the other.

Interaction with citizens: a weak link

It is the interaction function of the EP which addresses the problem of legitimacy most directly. This function includes communications with citizens and intermediary groups that creates support for the EU as a political system as a whole. Interaction between the Parliament and European citizens remains thin; popular attention devoted to the EP is low, rising when elections are held, but even then overshadowed by national issues in the member states. Some innovations introduced by the Maastricht Treaty were designed to bridge the gap between the citizens and the European Parliament. The Ombudsman elected according to Article 138e TEC was put in charge of receiving complaints from any citizen or any natural or legal person residing in the member states concerning instances of maladministration in the activities of the Union institutions or bodies other than the Court. This official has the right to conduct inquiries, except where court cases are under way (Jacobs, Corbett and Shackleton, 1992: 266). In July 1995, Parliament elected the Finnish politician Jacob Söderman as Ombudsman. His first report of activities in March 1996 noted that the Ombudsman's office had received 537 complaints, of which 81 had been admitted, reflecting the fact that most citizens were not clearly informed about the precise functions and competencies of the Ombudsman (Schmuck, 1995).

Perhaps the strongest prospect for an enhanced public profile for the Parliament emerges from its right, given legal standing by Article 138c of the Maastricht Treaty, to set up a temporary committee of inquiry into an area of suspected "contravention or maladministration" of Union law (Smith and Kelemen, 1997). Parliament's use of this power enjoyed widespread public attention in the BSE ("mad cow") case, when members and civil servants of the Commission responsible for agriculture had to face the deputies in order to clarify their personal performance and responsibility in that affair.

Despite post-Maastricht changes, there remains little strong evidence of public consciousness of the work of the EP, let alone a clear knowledge of its role and function within the EU (Schmuck, 1995). At the same time, according to results of Eurobarometer surveys, European publics are more aware of the activities of the European Parliament than of other EU institutions. The percentage of surveyed citizens reporting that they had heard or read about the EP in the media was 63 percent in early 1995, as against 52 percent in 1994 and 57 percent in 1993. Compared with this, the Commission reached some 59 percent in 1995, the

Council 47 percent and the Court of Justice 45 percent (Eurobarometer, 1993, 1995). In 1995, 56 percent of those questioned indicated that they considered the European Parliament important; 49 percent desired an enhanced role for the Parliament, a substantial falloff from the 62 percent recorded in 1991 (ibid.).

Evidence on the issues of trust in Parliament and interest mediation further complicates the ambiguous picture generated by survey data. Only 41 percent of respondents declared that they rely on the European Parliament, and only 35 percent were convinced that it defended their interests. But here, also, comparison is important: only 45 percent held trust in their national parliaments (ibid.). Furthermore, 47 percent described themselves as dissatisfied with the way democracy works in the EU, with 41 percent in favor. But still more people showed dissatisfaction with the way democracy works in their home countries: 55 percent expressed dissatisfaction and only 42 percent were satisfied (ibid.).

As the introductory chapter in this volume by Banchoff and Smith points out, the results of the opinion polls must be analyzed carefully; they cannot simply be translated into a reflection of political reality. On the one hand, many citizens appear to desire an enhanced role for Parliament, yet, on the other hand, both the level of information they possess and their degree of trust are quite limited. A similar ambivalence is typical of attitudes toward national institutions, suggesting that citizen perceptions of the European Parliament are consistent with the broader current of Western political systems. Overall, the data do not tell us much about the quality, depth, and consistency of such attitudes. They provide the outlines of a general trend, and a seismographic warning on changes and shifts in public perception, which in any case must be supplemented and accompanied by broader and more detailed research on political activity.

A great deal of work on political interactions with the Parliament remains to be done. Of particular significance is the increased importance of the EP for intermediary groups, lobbies, and interest organizations. Enhanced importance in policy-making renders Parliament more of a magnet for intermediary groups (Mazey and Richardson, 1996: 209), hitherto an almost exclusive domain of the Commission and national administrations (Wallace, 1996: 64; Kohler-Koch, 1997). Beate Kohler-Koch emphasizes that as a consequence of the strengthened institutional role of the EP in the decision-making process, "the Parliamentarians are becoming a decisive target group for lobbyists and lobbyists have to cope with the institutional structure, the procedures, and the policy style within the Parliament" (Kohler-Koch, 1997: 7). So far there has been relatively little empirical research on lobbying activities, though there have been some case studies of this interaction. Recently, the EP has set up a Code of Conduct for lobbyists and intermediary groups, establishing rules of behavior on the one hand, and recognizing those actors as "legitimate" players in shaping political decisions in Parliament on the other.

Neither of these developments – recognition of the EP as a relevant actor in opinion polls and the emergence of new representative links – suggests that the EU is gaining in legitimacy at the expense of other institutions. Within the political community generated by the process of fusion, national and subnational institutions keep their legitimacy while at the same time the EP might acquire a share of basic acceptance and identification by the citizens. Complementary and mutually reinforcing processes of legitimacy-building are possible (Schneider, 1994; Laffan, 1996). This implies that, in contrast with the classical patterns familiar from national experience, the EP is neither the sole nor the central stronghold of legitimacy in the European Union, but only one of several loci of legitimacy in the fused polity.

A fundamental feature of this new kind of polity is that its legitimacy is neither based on a collective personality called "the people," as federalists might argue, nor on the single peoples of the member states, as in the realist vision. Instead, its legitimacy derives from a pluralistic "citizenship." This "multinational civitas" is not only a community of the states, but also of the citizens in a "unity-in-diversity" (Schneider, 1994; Hassner, 1995; Laffan, 1996). As Wessels suggests, "From the highest political authorities in the European Council to the sectoral interest groups, the actors within the EC/EU system bring in their respective legitimacy into the new polity. Without replacing one level, several functional, legal and political sources of legitimacy are merged" (Wessels, 1997: 291). The criterion for citizenship is therefore not ethnic or cultural, religious or historical, but in a modern sense political, that is, oriented towards new loci of decision-making, their rules and principles. Citizenship as a political concept includes participation, either direct or indirect, in decision-making and the political community generally.

Conclusion: a new kind of parliament in a new kind of polity

The European Parliament is an increasingly important component of the EU political system. On balance there remain significant gaps in the EP's capacities to contest policy choices. It cannot be denied, however, that the EP has grown in importance – in some fields considerably (especially in policy-making in the First Pillar of the EU, with the exception of EMU), in others only slightly. Archer and Butler describe the changes after Maastricht as "the contrast between the 'bicephalous' Community political system of the 1960s, and the emerging outlines of a triumvirate, where power is increasingly shared between Commission, Council and Parliament" (Archer and Butler, 1996: 50; see also Smith and Kelemen, 1997).

To a growing degree Parliament is assuming the role of an agenda-setter, shaping the political debate and behavior of other actors (governments and EU institutions), without dominating decision-preparation, making, and implementation. A principal vehicle of expanded EP influence in the future might be public debate, which by entering the plenary in a more substantial way could create a political forum providing citizens with closer contact to EU policy-making than secretive bargaining in the Council or technocratic administration within the Commission. Although this forum has not yet developed sufficiently to enter into public consciousness, Parliament is not as far from being a main actor in the game as it was before Maastricht. As the results of Amsterdam show, the EP's role and influence continue to increase, leading potentially to a kind of bicameral system for legislation in the EC Pillar. Even in the Second and Third Pillars, EP influence has grown in concert with strengthened rights of information, consultation, and discussion. Viewed from a medium-term perspective, especially since the SEA, the EP has steadily gained political importance that extends beyond the increase in its formal powers.

At the same time, as an actor with substantial powers of co-decision, the EP must balance this interaction with its decision-making responsibilities. Furthermore, as we have seen in this chapter, the EP's institutional need for coherence and internal discipline will complicate its efforts to offer a forum where partisan conflict can take place. The EP may be able to resolve this problem by differentiating between constitutional issues and questions of daily policy-making. While presenting a united front on the former, the latter could become the subject of further debate and contestation. Of course, such an approach to resolving the fundamental dilemma of forum of contestation vs. institutional power facing the EP presupposes a great deal of flexibility among the political groups in the EP. It is possible that, to the extent that partisan contestation develops, the EP as an institution will become less able to pursue coherently a more formative role in the EU decision-making process.

Neither the reconstruction of a parliamentary democracy on the supranational level nor a "Union of the States" is a model for future orientations. The EU will remain a multi-level system of governance (Jachtenfuchs and Kohler-Koch, 1996; Wallace, 1996), consisting of "complex multitiered, geographically overlapping structures of governmental and non-governmental elites" (Wessels, 1997: 291). The EP's relative strength lies in providing a public arena of debate and political discussion, in which different political and social currents and actors can identify their positions and interests. The EP's direct representative capacity will continue to play an important role in this system, potentially bolstering a European legitimacy complementary to the national and functional ones. However, as the process of fusion progressively blurs the boundaries between the different actors and makes their roles functionally less distinguishable, the ability of the public to identify outcomes with their sponsors and assign responsibility accordingly will diminish. It is therefore more critical than ever before that the EP deepen its links with the electorate, social and political organizations, and interest groups. The EP will likely never become a central representative institution comparable to national parliaments. Nonetheless, the Parliament's further development will continue to have far-reaching implications for EU legitimacy.

Bibliography

Andersen, S. S. and Burns, T. (1996) "The European Union and the Erosion of Parliamentary Democracy: A Study of Post-parliamentary Governance," in S. Andersen and K. A. Eliassen (eds) *The European Union: How Democratic Is It?*, London: Sage.

Archer, C. and Butler, F. (1996) *The European Union, Structure and Process*, 2nd edn, London: Pinter.

Bourguignon-Wittke, R. (1985) "Five Years of the Directly Elected European Parliament: Performance and Prospects," *Journal of Common Market Studies* 24, 1: 39–59.

Bundesverfassungsgericht (1993) "Maastricht–Urteil," *Juristische Zeitschrift* 22: 1100–12.

Corbett, R. (1993) *The Treaty of Maastricht*, Harlow, UK: Longman.

Dankert, P. (1997) "Pressure from the European Parliament," in G. Edwards and A. Pijpers (eds) *The Politics of European Treaty Reform*, London: Pinter.

Dinan, D. (1994) *Ever Closer Union? An Introduction to the European Community*, Boulder, CO: Lynne Rienner.

Duff, A. (1995) "Building a Parliamentary Europe," in M. Teló (ed.) *Démocratie et Construction Européenne*, Brussels: Edition de l'Université de Bruxelles.

Eurobarometer (1993) "Public Opinion in the European Community," no. 39, June, Brussels.

—— (1995) "Public Opinion in the European Community," no. 43, April–May, Brussels.

European Constitutional Group (1993) "A Proposal for a European Constitution," London.

European Parliament (1995) "Resolution from 17 May 1995 on the functioning of the Treaty on European Union with a view to the Intergovernmental Conference 1996," OJ C 151, June 19.

—— (1996a) "Resolution from 14 December 1995 on the agenda of the IGC 1996 with a view to the meeting of the European Council at Madrid," OJ C 17, January 1.

—— (1996b) "Resolution on the Opinion of the European Parliament on the calling of the IGC 1996 and on the assessment of the work by the Reflection Group and on the establishment of the political priorities of the European Parliament with a view to the IGC 1996," March 13, Brussels.

—— (1997) "Resolution on the Conclusion of the European Council at Amsterdam of 16 and 17 June 1997," PE 260.914, June 26.

Grabitz, E. *et al.* (1988) *Direktwahl und Demokratisierung, eine Funktionenbilanz des Europäischen Parlaments nach der ersten Direktwahl*, Bonn: Europa Union Verlag.

Gustavsson, R. (1996) "The European Union: 1996 and Beyond – A Personal View from the Side-line," in S. Andersen and K. A. Eliassen (eds) *The European Union: How Democratic Is It?*, London: Sage.

Haas, E. B. (1968) *The Uniting of Europe*, 2nd edn, Stanford, CA: Stanford University Press.

Hassner, P. (1995) "Nationalstaat – Nationalismus – Selbstbestimmung," in K. Kaiser and H.-P. Schwarz (eds) *Die Neue Weltpolitik*, Bonn: Europa Union Verlag.

Hilf, M. (1994) "Eine Verfassung für die Europäische Union: Zum Entwurf des Institutionellen Ausschusses des Europäischen Parlamentes," *Integration* 2: 68–78.

Hix, S. and Lord, C. (1996) "The Making of a President: The European Parliament and the Confirmation of Jacques Santer as the President of the Commission," *Government and Opposition* 31, 1: 62–76.

—— (1997) *Political Parties in the European Union*, New York: St. Martin's Press.

Jachtenfuchs, M. and Kohler-Koch, B. (1996) "Regieren im Dynamischen Mehrebenensystem," in M. Jachtenfuchs and B. Kohler-Koch (eds) *Europäische Integration*, Opladen: Leske und Budrich.

Jacobs, F., Corbett, R. and Shackleton, M. (1992) *The European Parliament*, 2nd edn, Harlow, UK: Longman.

Kielmansegg, P. G. (1996) "Integration und Demokratie," in M. Jachtenfuchs and B. Kohler-Koch (eds) *Europäische Integration*, Opladen: Leske und Budrich.

Kohler-Koch, B. (1996) "Die Gestaltungsmacht organisierter Interessen," in M. Jachtenfuchs and B. Kohler-Koch (eds) *Europäische Integration*, Opladen: Leske und Budrich.

——— (1997) "Organized Interests and the European Parliament," paper prepared for presentation, Panel 38.2, "Bringing Order to a Conflictual World: Business Collective Action at the Transnational Level," at the International Political Science Association XVII World Congress, Seoul, August 17–21.

Laffan, B. (1996) "The Politics of Identity and Political Order in Europe," *Journal of Common Market Studies* 34, 1: 81–102.

Laming, R. (1995) "Is the European Union Legitimate?" *The Federalist: A Political Review* 2: 114–19.

Läufer, T. (1995) "Zum Stand der Verfassungsdiskussion in der Europäischen Union," in A. Randelzhofer, R. Scholz and D. Wilke (eds) *Gedächtnisschrift für Eberhard Grabitz*, München: Beck.

Lodge, J. (1996) "The European Parliament," in S. Andersen and K. A. Eliassen (eds) *The European Union: How Democratic Is It?*, London: Sage.

Lübbe, H. (1994) *Abschied vom Superstaat, die Vereinigten Staaten von Europa Wird es nicht Geben*, Berlin: Siedler.

Maurer, A. (1996) "Demokratisierung der Europäischen Union: Möglichkeiten für das Europäische Parlament," in A. Maurer and B. Thiele (eds) *Legitimitätsprobleme und Demokratisierung der Europäischen Union*, Marburg: Schuren.

Mazey, S. and Richardson, J. (1996) "The Logic of Organisation," in J. Richardson (ed.) *European Union: Power and Policy-making*, London and New York: Routledge.

Naßmacher, K.-H. (1972) *Demokratisierung der Europäischen Gemeinschaften*, Bonn: Europa Union Verlag.

Neunreither, K. (1994) "The Democratic Deficit of the European Union: Towards Closer Cooperation between the European Parliament and the National Parliaments," *Government and Opposition* 29, 3: 299–314.

Risse-Kappen, T. (1996) "Exploring the Nature of the Beast: International Relations Theory and Comparative Policy Analysis Meet the European Union," *Journal of Common Market Studies* 34, 1: 53–80.

Rosenau, J. N. and Czempiel, E.-O. (eds) (1992) *Governance without Government: Order and Change in World Politics*, Cambridge, UK: Cambridge University Press.

Schmuck, O. (1994) "Europäisches Parlament," in W. Weidenfeld and W. Wessels (eds) *Jahrbuch der europäischen Integration 1993/94*, Bonn: Europa Union Verlag.

——— (1995) "Europäisches Parlament," in W. Weidenfeld and W. Wessels (eds) *Jahrbuch der europäischen Integration 1994/95*, Bonn: Europa Union Verlag.

——— (1996) "Europäisches Parlament," in W. Weidenfeld and W. Wessels (eds) *Jahrbuch der europäischen Integration 1995/96*, Bonn: Europa Union Verlag.

Schneider, H. (1986) *Rückblick für die Zukunft, Konzeptionelle Weichenstellungen für die europäische Einigung*, Bonn: Europa Union Verlag.

——— (1992) "Europäische Integration – die Leitbilder und die Politik," in M. Kreile (ed.) *Die Integration Europas*, PVS-Sonderheft 23, Opladen: Westdeutscher Verlag.

——— (1994) "Föderale Verfassungspolitik für eine Europäische Union," in H. Schneider and W. Wessels (eds) *Föderale Union – Europas Zukunft?*, München: Beck.

Schröder, M. (1994) "Das Bundesverfassungsgericht als Hüter des Staates im Prozeß der europäischen Integration," *Deutsches Verwaltungsblatt* 6: 316–25.

Smith, M. P. and Kelemen, R.D. (1997) "The Institutional Balance: Formal and Informal Change," Brussels: Centre for European Policy Studies Working Document No. 111.

Spinelli, A. (1958) *Manifest der Europäischen Föderalisten*, Frankfurt-am-Main: Europäis che Verlags Anstalt.

Teló, M. (1995) "Démocratie internationale et démocratie supranationale," *Démocratie et Construction Européenne*, Brussels: Edition de l'Université de Bruxelles.

Urwin, D. (1995) *The Community of Europe*, 2nd edn, Harlow, UK: Longman.

Wallace, H. (1996) "Politics and Policy in the EU: The Challenge of Governance," in H. Wallace and W. Wallace (eds) *Policy-making in the European Union*, Oxford, UK: Oxford University Press.

Weidenfeld, W. (ed.) (1995) *Reform der Europäischen Union, Materialien zur Revision der Maastrichter Vertrages 1996*, Gutersloh: Bertelsmann-Stiftung.

Weiler, J. H. H. (1997) "Legitimacy and Democracy of Union Governance," in G. Edwards and A. Pijpers (eds) *The Politics of European Treaty Reform, the 1996 Intergovernmental Conference and Beyond*, London and Washington: Pinter.

Wessels, W. (1992) "Staat und (westeuropäische) Integration," in Michael Kreile (ed.) *Die Integration Europas, PVS-Sonderheft* 23: 35–61.

—— (1995) "Wird das Europäische Parlament zum Parlament?, Ein dynamischer Funktionenansatz," in A. Randelzhofer, R. Scholz and D. Wilke (eds) *Gedächtnisschrift für Eberhard Grabitz*, München: Beck.

—— (1996) "The Modern West European State and the European Union: Democratic Erosion or a New Kind of Polity?" in S. Andersen and K. A. Eliassen (eds) *The European Union: How Democratic Is It?*, London: Sage.

—— (1997) "An Ever Closer Fusion? A Dynamic Macropolitical View on Integration Processes," *Journal of Common Market Studies* 35, 2: 267–99.

Part 3

LEGITIMACY AND IDENTITY

8

EU CITIZENSHIP: IMPLICATIONS FOR IDENTITY AND LEGITIMACY[1]

Rey Koslowski

European Union citizenship is one of the least understood and most important aspects of the integration process. After decades of incremental policy-making bearing on the free movement of persons within the EU, Article 8 of the 1992 Maastricht Treaty made "every person holding the nationality of a Member State" a "citizen of the Union" and gave rights to nationals of one EU member state living in another to participate in the local and European elections of the member state of residence. EU citizenship differs fundamentally from previous forms of political citizenship – membership in city-states and then, after the French and American Revolutions, much larger nation states and federal states[2] because the EU is not a state and it may never become one. Therefore, the significance of European citizenship cannot be captured within established statist categories. What, then, are the characteristics of this novel form of citizenship and what are its implications for questions of identity and legitimacy?

Revisions of the Maastricht Treaty agreed to during the 1996–97 Intergovernmental Conference (IGC) provide a clue. The Amsterdam Treaty of June 1997 states that "Citizenship of the Union shall complement and not replace national citizenship" (see Appendix I). A European citizenship designed to complement member-state nationality sets out bundles of rights in distinct areas of public life. This extension of rights creates a divergence between nationality and citizenship – categories that traditionally coincide in the context of nation states. This divergence corresponds with the co-existence of multiple political identities, national and European. Moreover, by extending democratic participation, EU citizenship represents a potential source of legitimacy for the integration process as a whole; it is therefore more than empty symbolism. Ultimately EU citizenship represents a new form of political membership with important implications for the future evolution of the European polity.

I set out this argument in three parts. First, I establish the uniqueness of EU citizenship through a review of its historical development and an analysis of its various dimensions. Second, I discuss links between citizenship, identity and

155

legitimacy through an examination of the Maastricht ratification controversies. Third, I examine the discussion of citizenship at the 1996–97 IGC and its broader implications for the problem of legitimacy within the EU.

The emergence of EU citizenship

EU citizenship can be understood only in reference to previously existing forms of political membership. Aristotle pointed out long ago that citizenship is constitutive of the state.[3] Likewise, the innovation of national citizenship during the French Revolution was constitutive of the nation state (Hammar, 1990: 41–49). At the end of the eighteenth century, the terms "subject," "national," and "citizen" were used indiscriminately (Plender, 1988: 8). With popular sovereignty eventually becoming a norm of state legitimation, the distinction between citizen and subject became clear. Then as polities became more inclusive through the spread of universal suffrage, nationality and citizenship increasingly overlapped. Nationality refers to the status of being subject to a state's laws, its taxes, and military conscription, while enjoying the right of protection by the state even when abroad. Citizenship refers to a bundle of civil, political, and social rights possessed by individuals (Marshall, 1964). As Paul Weis notes, "Every citizen is a national, but not every national is necessarily a citizen of the State concerned" (Weis, 1979: 5–6). Within most nation states, however, both categories have converged in practice as most nationals are citizens and few non-nationals enjoy the rights of citizenship.

The institutional and political make-up of the EU rules out the establishment of citizenship on the model of the traditional nation state. From its inception, the EU has consisted of institutions alongside and above states – not as their replacement. The creation of a larger territorial entity has not produced a superstate; it has left existing nation states in place. In contrast to previous forms of citizenship associated with nation states, then, EU citizenship is not and cannot be a form of state citizenship (Wiener, 1997). EU citizenship is meant to complement member-state nationality rather than to be a proto-European nationality. Nevertheless, EU citizenship is a novel form of multiple political membership that violates the logic of the classical system of nation states which is based on the principle that everyone belongs to a state and preferably only one state.

Working within the traditional statist logic, Raymond Aron considered such multiple citizenship a "contradiction in terms" and he argued that EC member states might have been willing to extend economic rights to non-nationals, but "(N)either in theory nor in fact do any properly *political* rights – the vote, freedom of speech, freedom to hold office, etc. – now extend beyond the borders of the old states. Perhaps, on the day that a European Assembly is elected by universal suffrage, a Frenchman will be able to be nominated for office in West Germany or a German in France. Yet how many people would avail themselves of such a right?" (Aron, 1974: 638, 647). Five years after Aron's words were published, Europeans directly elected the European Parliament and twenty years later Germans living in France voted for MEPs from the French delegation and, something Aron did not foresee, French nationals living in Germany voted in local German elections. In fact, Europeans are availing themselves of these political rights and they are increasingly supporting the concept of EU citizenship. Although only codified in the Maastricht Treaty, EU citizenship developed out of decades of European practice. The following section explores this evolution of EU citizenship in more detail.

The evolution of EU citizenship

The evolution of citizenship within the EU context took place in connection with steps toward deeper economic integration.[4] In conjunction with the principle of free movement of goods, capital, and services, the Treaty of Rome enunciated the freedom of movement of economic agents. Freedom of movement within the Community was not conferred on individuals as citizens of member states, but rather as "workers" and recipients of services.[5] Subsequent regulations realized the principle of free movement of workers in terms that were generally applicable and binding on the member states. A 1961 regulation enabled workers from one EC member state to take a position in another member state if a suitable worker from that state could not be found within three weeks; a 1964 regulation removed the need to search for local workers and augmented rights of family reunification; and a 1968 regulation stipulated that workers from another member state had "the right to take up available employment in the territory of another Member State with the same priority as a national of that State."[6] The 1986 Single European Act (SEA) enshrined the free movement of persons as one of the core principles of the single market. Throughout this entire period, the European Court of Justice rigorously applied prohibitions against discrimination based on nationality and secured the Treaty of Rome's guarantees through decisions on civil and social rights (Johnson and O'Keefe, 1994).

The issue of free movement within the European Community, then, spurred the de facto development of European citizenship conceived as a bundle of social and economic rights. Member states, however, were reluctant to consider the elimination of border controls within the framework of EU citizenship; such control was considered more central to state sovereignty than work and residence rights. A 1975 Commission report, "Towards European Citizenship," called for the elimination of controls, and the topic became the subject of intergovernmental negotiations among justice and interior ministers during the 1980s (Commission, 1975). Reluctance by the United Kingdom to lift border controls and conflict between the UK and Spain over Gibraltar, however, sidetracked any agreement. While the prospects for EC-wide cooperation appeared dim, a protest by truck drivers tired of long lines at internal borders prompted France and Germany to lift controls between them. A year later, the Benelux countries (which had lifted border controls among themselves in 1960) joined France and Germany at Schengen to sign an agreement to allow unimpeded travel and erect common external border controls. Parties to the 1985 Agreement signed a Convention in 1990 to which

Italy, Spain, Portugal, Greece, and Austria subsequently joined. As members of the Nordic Passport Union, Denmark, Sweden, Finland, Norway, and Iceland (the latter two EU non-member states), joined Schengen in 1996. The 1997 Amsterdam Treaty incorporated the Schengen Convention into the EU, while permitting the United Kingdom and Ireland, as island nations, to remain outside.

Economic integration not only raised questions about free movement across borders, it also introduced citizenship issues that went beyond economic and social rights for those living abroad. As increasing numbers of member-state nationals took advantage of the right to work and live in fellow member states – over 4 million by 1988 – a particular kind of "democratic deficit" emerged from the absence of political rights for these Europeans. In the wake of the Single European Act, the European Commission drew attention to the irony of the situation. "In a Community of Member States whose basic common characteristic is that they are all democracies," a 1988 Commission report noted, "the implementation of one of the four fundamental freedoms provided by the Treaty has . . . led indirectly to the loss of certain political rights." The report continued: "This paradox in the building of Europe cannot be allowed to continue if the principles underlying the democratic political systems of the Member States are to be respected" (Commission, 1988: 26).

The drive for political rights to remedy this "democratic deficit" began with the European Parliament's (EP) 1960 draft convention on direct elections to the Parliament (van den Berghe, 1982; Magiera, 1988). The draft called for a uniform electoral system across member states that enabled member-state nationals to vote and run in elections in the member state in which they resided. The proposal did not garner sufficient support in the Council and progress on political rights was postponed until the 1970s. Member states first considered extending voting rights to EC nationals at the 1974 Paris Summit and instructed the Commission to prepare a report on the subject. While the report stated that full political rights at all levels of member-state government would be "desirable in the long-term" (Commission, 1975), the Commission advocated local voting rights and participation in EP elections as an interim solution. Yet even this limited proposal died. In the first parliamentary election in 1979, some states allowed resident aliens from fellow member states to vote in their place of residence and some states did not. Some provided consular voting facilities for their nationals in other member states, some did not (van den Berghe, 1982: 133).

The issue of political rights arose again in the context of the relaunching of European integration in the 1980s. Anticipating that the SEA's goal of eliminating barriers to movement would eventually increase international population mobility within the EU, the Commission's Committee on a People's Europe, chaired by Pietro Adonnino, called for expanding political rights for resident aliens in both EP and local elections (Commission, 1985, 1986, 1988). Members of the Council did not act on the Commission's initiative until 1990, when Helmut Kohl and François Mitterrand led the drive to convene an intergovernmental conference on political union.[7] The Spanish government drafted the language on citizenship that was ultimately incorporated into the Maastricht Treaty.[8] Article 8 (see Appendix I) establishes the existence of European citizenship and sets out its various dimensions. Citizenship entails: the right to move and reside within the Union; the right to vote and stand for election in local and European parliamentary elections in the citizen's place of residence; the right to diplomatic and consular protection of fellow member states in countries in which the citizen's member state is not represented; the right to petition the European Parliament; and the right to register complaints about Union institutions (except the Court) with an Ombudsman.

Dimensions of EU citizenship

Each of these dimensions of European citizenship took on clear contours during the early and mid-1990s. With the codification of rights to move and reside, member states, for the most part, ceded sovereignty with respect to the migration of fellow member-state nationals within the Union. Strictly speaking, one can argue that the delayed implementation of Schengen and the incomplete removal of border checks throughout the entire EU indicates a lack of free movement and a retention of sovereignty by member states (Anderson, den Boer and Miller, 1994: 104–06). However, defining free movement in terms of an absence of border checks and defining sovereignty in terms of border control is misleading. A passport check at an internal EU border may slow a properly documented, law-abiding EU national crossing the border. However, it does not stop that person from entering another member state or residing there (Koslowski, 1998).

When a Council Directive issued shortly after the Maastricht Treaty went into effect in November 1993, resident aliens from fellow member states were able to vote in the June 1994 European elections in their member state of residence.[9] The December 1994 Council Directive on local voting rights, which included a controversial derogation for Belgium, began the process of realizing local voting rights for resident aliens from fellow member states through transposing the directive into member-state law.[10] As of January 1, 1997 only eight member states had fully done so and the Commission decided to take action against France, Greece, Belgium, Spain, Sweden, Austria, and Finland. (Austria and Finland have partially implemented the directive and all foreign residents have been able to vote in Swedish local elections.) Participation of non-national EU citizens in EP elections was low, with an average turnout of 11.81 percent, and only one non-national candidate, a Dutch citizen, Wilmya Zimmermann, was elected in her member state of residence, Germany. Non-national EU citizens have participated in local elections in Luxembourg, Italy, Germany, Austria, Finland, and the UK. At this point, assessing participation in local elections is difficult because turnout rates are incomplete and not systematically gathered, but in Bavarian elections non-national voter turnout was between 21 and 25 percent and in Vienna it was 35.5 percent.[11] Low participation has primarily been attributed to the fact that EU citizens lacked knowledge of their political rights at the time.[12]

Maastricht also extended the right of diplomatic and consular protection to nationals of one member state from any of the fourteen other member states when traveling or residing in a third country in which their member state is not represented.[13] This represented a clear break with the traditional convergence of nationality and citizenship (O'Leary, 1995: 523). The EU's extension of a right of citizenship impinges on traditional member-state obligations in terms of extra-territorial protection. As the practice of reciprocal protection among EU member states becomes established, it reduces the need for member states to open new consulates in states in which other member states already have consulates. It also increases the incentives for states with dwindling foreign ministry budgets to close consulates in more peripheral areas because their nationals will still be protected by fellow EU member states. If member states do reduce their overall diplomatic presence around the world, it would decrease the number of classic signifiers of sovereign statehood maintained by member states while at the same time increasing the practical importance of EU citizenship in the lives of member-state nationals.

Article 8 also anchored the right of citizens to petition the EP within the Treaty and established the office of Ombudsman. Although petitions cannot initiate legislation, they offer remedies to individuals seeking legal assistance and represent an additional venue for interest articulation at the European level. According to Astrid Thors, a member of the EP's petition committee, social issues and the environment are the primary subjects of petitions. The number of petitions more than doubled from 484 in 1987 to 1,051 in 1993 when the Maastricht Treaty went into effect, and reached over 1,250 in 1994 and 1995. Petitions dropped back to 1,067 in 1996, largely due to the establishment of the Ombudsman's office,[14] which is designed to deal with specific cases of maladministration, to promote effective implementation of citizens' rights and transparency in EU institutions, as well as to improve relations between the EU and its citizens in general. While elected by the EP, the Ombudsman is independent of the Parliament and has a separate budget. Jacob Söderman was elected in July 1995, and received more than 500 complaints in his first year in office (European Ombudsman, 1995).

By extending partial political rights to resident aliens from fellow member states, EU citizenship supplements the civil and social rights that were established by the Treaty of Rome, expanded by the Single European Act, and enforced by the European Court of Justice. For some, Maastricht's citizenship provisions do not go far enough. Hans Ulrich Jessurn d'Oliveria, for example, called EU citizenship "nearly exclusively a symbolic plaything without substantive content" and argued that Maastricht added little "to the existing status of nationals of Member States" (Jessurn d'Oliveria, 1995: 82–83). The Commission essentially concurred with d'Oliveria (although in more diplomatic language). It concluded its 1995 assessment of Union citizenship by noting that it had "immense potential" but had not yet lived up to expectations, mainly as evidenced by slow progress toward the abolition of border controls (Commission, 1995: 21–22).

These criticisms, whatever their particular merits, deflect attention from the historical shift represented by the creation of European citizenship. The extension of civil and social rights within the EU, and even of partial political rights to resid   dent aliens from fellow member states, demonstrates a gradual separation of nationality status and citizenship rights – categories which had previously coincided. This growing disjunction between nationality and citizenship blurs the boundaries of European nation states and is indicative of a transformation of Europe into a new form of political organization. Attention to citizenship reveals a little-understood aspect of the multi-level, contested European polity – one with important implications for questions of both identity and legitimacy.

Citizenship, legitimacy, and identity

The establishment of European citizenship has been central to the Commission's efforts to build EU legitimacy. In 1985, for example, Carlo Ripa di Meana, a member of the Adonnino Committee, singled out the establishment of local voting rights as a "decisive step toward involving the Community's ordinary citizens in their common destiny" (Commission, 1985: 5). In its efforts to address the legitimacy issue in the run-up to the Maastricht Treaty, the Commission combined support for a stronger European Parliament with suggestions for stronger European citizenship. "Further democratization of the running of the Community," it argued in a 1991 report, "must be seen from the twin standpoint of its institutions and its citizens" (Commission, 1991: 78). Several years later, the Commission Report for the Reflection Group preparing the 1996–97 IGC included a chapter entitled "Heightening the Sense of Belonging to the Union and Enhancing its Legitimacy." The purpose of Union citizenship, it argued, was to "deepen European citizens' sense of belonging to the European Union and make that sense more tangible by conferring on them the rights associated with it" (Commission, 1995: 21).

To what extent has European citizenship successfully addressed the legitimacy issue? If legitimacy is conceived in normative terms as the presence of democratic and representative institutions, that impact has been rather limited. To the extent that EU citizenship extends the political rights of Europeans living abroad – and allows them to participate in EP elections – it addresses the European Union's "democratic deficit." Given the modest numbers of Europeans residing abroad within the EU (approximately 5.5 million)[15] and the still circumscribed competencies of the European Parliament, the impact of EU citizenship on democratic legitimation should not be overestimated. If legitimacy is conceived not just in terms of representation, however, but also in terms of recognition – as support for and identification with the EU – the effects of EU citizenship appear more extensive. To the degree that the extension of citizenship leads more Europeans to recognize the EU as a legitimate framework for political contestation, it promotes the legitimation of the integration project. This section explores the legitimacy-building potential of citizenship through an analysis of public attitudes and political controversies during the 1990s.

Public attitudes toward European citizenship

Assessing the contribution of EU citizenship to legitimacy through opinion polls is fraught with difficulty. Even though many of the rights associated with EU citizenship existed in various forms since the Treaty of Rome, EU citizenship was only formally established with the Maastricht Treaty. Moreover, many of the provisions of European Union citizenship are not yet fully incorporated into member-state law and policies. As a result, many Europeans seem to know little of EU citizenship itself. For example, in 1996, while 77 percent of EU citizens surveyed knew that they had the right to live anywhere in the Union, only 46 percent knew that non-nationals had the right to vote in EP elections in their state of residence and only 38 percent knew that non-nationals had the right to vote in the local elections of their state of residence (Eurobarometer, 1996: 92). Furthermore, little systematic study of the influence of EU citizenship on changing attitudes has taken place. However, two kinds of evidence illuminate actual and potential implications of EU citizenship for legitimacy. The first concerns levels of public support for the different dimensions of European citizenship, while the second concerns the compatibility of different kinds of identity, European and national, within the European Union.

Public opinion reveals growing support for EU citizenship and each of its dimensions – an indication of its promise as a legitimacy-building strategy. One of the most controversial provisions of European citizenship concerns the lowering of borders to the free movement of EU citizens. While the free movement provisions of the Maastricht Treaty and the removal of border controls for signatories of the Schengen convention have compromised a major aspect of member-state sovereignty, proponents of European integration argued that free movement within the EU was one of the practical benefits that citizens would experience and anticipated that it would lead to greater popular support for integration. Polls taken shortly after the implementation of the Schengen Convention in March 1995 reflected, on balance, negative public opinion, with 46 percent considering removal of border controls a "bad thing" and 41 percent calling it a "good thing" (Europinion, 1995). Within a year, however, only 40 percent thought removing border controls was a bad thing and 43 percent considered it a good thing (Europinion, 1996). When EU citizens were asked in an April–May 1996 survey if they thought it was important to be able to travel anywhere in the EU without border formalities, 74 percent said it was important and 19 percent said it was unimportant (Eurobarometer, 1996: 93).

A similar pattern of growing support is evident in the context of voting rights. Although the extension of local voting rights generated some opposition during the Maastricht ratification debates in several member states, opposition faded in years after the Treaty took effect. In 1993, only 47 percent of a sample of member-state nationals said they were prepared to give local voting rights to nationals of fellow EU member states. In a spring 1996 survey, 56 percent thought it was important that EU citizens from fellow member states have the right to vote in local elections

Table 8.1 Popular support for giving the right to vote and to be a candidate in local elections to nationals from fellow member states

	Fall 93 (EU 12)	Spring 94 (EU 12)	Dec. 94 (EU 12)	Spring 95 (EU 15)	Fall 95 (EU 15)	Spring 96 (EU 15)
Support for						
Vote	47%	53%	56%	54%	54%	56%
Candidate	39%	42%	46%	45%	45%	n/a

Sources: Eurobarometer 42 (released spring 1995), p. 75 (includes figures for fall 93, spring 94); Eurobarometer 43 (released autumn 1995), p. 36; Eurobarometer 44 (released April 1996), p. 71; Eurobarometer 45 (released December 1996).

and 30 percent thought it was unimportant (Eurobarometer, 1996: 93; see Table 8.1).

The establishment of the Ombudsman is an attempt to address directly the problem of the legitimacy of EU institutions by providing an additional channel of access for individual citizens. The statistics from its first year of operation depict neither a very wide channel of access nor one that is overutilized. This may demonstrate the lack of public awareness of the rights of European citizenship more than the Ombudsman's potential contribution to the legitimacy of European institutions. This potential is evident in the fact that of all of the dimensions of European citizenship, the Ombudsman received the highest ratings in public opinion surveys. In a 1995 Eurobarometer survey, 81 percent said that having a European Ombudsman is "a good idea," while 9 percent think it is a "bad idea," and 4 percent think it is neither good nor bad. The Ombudsman may also contribute to citizens' sense of political efficacy, with 69 percent believing that the Ombudsman could "improve things" and only 12 percent saying that the Ombudsman would not (Europinion, 1995).

Overall, then, these figures point to growing support for the different dimensions of EU citizenship. Europeans appear increasingly willing to accept a level of citizenship above the level of the nation state. Moreover, many not only accept EU citizenship but also think that it is necessary. In a 1996 Eurobarometer survey, respondents were asked, "Do you think that, to make progress in building Europe, it is necessary to have a European citizenship in addition to your (national) citizenship?" In response, 50 percent said that European citizenship was necessary, 37 percent said it was not necessary and 14 percent said that they did not know (Eurobarometer, 1996: 87).

A parallel pattern is evident at the level of identities. Here, as in the case of citizenship, the national level takes precedence over the European – but both exist side by side. In a 1990 Eurobarometer survey, 48 percent of respondents felt attached to the European Community and 47 percent to Europe as a whole, while 46 percent said they did not feel attached to the EC or Europe as a whole. In contrast, 88 percent felt attached to their country, 87 percent to their region, 85 percent to their locality. Growing numbers of Europeans have little trouble identifying with Europe, their nation states, and their subnational regions and localities. Although the co-existence of political identities, one "nested" in the other, appears at first glance to be a new phenomenon, it is perhaps better understood as a return to patterns of political identification characteristic of premodern European polities and premodern polities in general (Ferguson and Mansbach, 1996). While Eurobarometer surveys suggest the extent of national and European identification has fluctuated, and did so especially in the year after Maastricht took effect, a minority of this sample of Europeans have consistently identified themselves only as nationals or Europeans (between 40 and 45 percent), while 52 to 56 percent identify themselves as some combination of both (see Table 8.2).

Recently, Eurobarometer has changed the question to prioritize responses and asked respondents if in the near future they see themselves above all as citizens of the EU or citizens of their member states or citizens of their regions, and then asked for second and third preferences (see Table 8.3).

This survey also demonstrates the persuasiveness of multiple identities, including European identity among them. Only 6 percent of respondents did not express a second or third preference (i.e. multiple identification). If we assume that those without second and third preferences gave citizen of country as their first preference and that those without a third preference gave citizen of country or citizen of region for their first and second preferences, then at least 89 percent of those asked saw themselves to some degree as EU citizens.

There is no clear causal link between EU citizenship and shifting conceptions of identity. It is striking, though, that efforts to construe European and national citizenships as compatible find parallels at the level of identity. EU citizenship constitutes a new layer of political identity alongside existing national ones. It seems plausible that the introduction of EU citizenship has reinforced the trend toward multiple, compatible identities in Europe. Not only does EU citizenship

Table 8.2 National identity/European identity

	Fall 1993 EU 12	Dec. 1994 EU 12	Spring 1995 EU 12	Spring 1995 EU 15	Oct.–Dec. 1995 EU 12	Oct.–Dec. 1995 EU 15
"In the near future do you see yourself as . . .?"						
(Nationality) only	40%	33%	36%	37%	39%	40%
(Nationality) and European	45%	46%	46%	45%	46%	46%
European and (Nationality)	7%	10%	9%	9%	6%	6%
European only	4%	7%	6%	6%	5%	5%
Don't know	4%	4%	3%	3%	3%	3%

Sources: Eurobarometer 42 (released spring 1995) appendix 9.5 (includes figures for fall 93f); Eurobarometer 43 (released autumn 1995), B14; Eurobarometer 44 (released April 1996), pp. B22–23.

Table 8.3 Feelings toward citizenship

	First preference	*Second preference*	*Third preference*
Citizen of EU	16%	21%	56%
Citizen of (country)	61%	32%	4%
Citizen of region	22%	42%	30%
Don't know	–	6%	11%

Source: Eurobarometer 45 (December 1996), p. 86.

provide an institutional object of identification at the European level, but the acceptance of a form of multiple state membership by EU member states legitimates the expression of multiple identities possessed by individual nationals of those member states. The existence of such multiple identities, the evidence suggests, constitutes a reservoir of legitimacy for the EU – not a legitimacy crisis. To construct the EU on the model of a state, and to impose a more unified EU citizenship at the expense of its national counterparts, would almost certainly generate fierce societal opposition and undermine the legitimacy of the integration project as a whole. In a sense, then, the "incomplete and fragmented" European citizenship criticized by the Commission is simply a reflection of the fragmented identities of European citizens who do not accept political identification as an either/or proposition. Public toleration of such political complexity represents a source of legitimacy for a multi-level EU and an evolving European polity.

Ratification controversies

The interplay between citizenship, identity, and legitimacy was also evident in the struggle over Maastricht ratification. In most of the member states, ratification of the Treaty, particularly its citizenship provisions, occasioned little controversy. An examination of the three states where the ratification battle was most divisive – Denmark, Britain, and France – reveals both the salience of the citizenship issue and some of its implications for legitimacy. In all three states, Maastricht's opponents construed European citizenship as a threat to national sovereignty and identity. In the British and Danish debates, EU citizenship's symbolic infringement on national sovereignty and identity proved most salient. In France, by contrast, the issue of extending political rights to non-nationals became a highly contentious constitutional issue as well. By giving nationals of one member state who are permanent resident aliens in another the right to vote and stand for office in local and EP elections, Maastricht challenged received notions of popular sovereignty. It called into question the delineation of the demos that is to be sovereign, traditionally defined in terms of nationality (Koslowski, 1994).

British and Danish Euroskeptics seized upon the symbolic implications of

European citizenship in their efforts to defeat Maastricht. Perceived threats to national identity and British sovereignty figured prominently in the rebellion of members of the Conservative Party against the government's efforts to ratify the Treaty signed by John Major (Baker, Gamble and Ludlam, 1994). Early in the campaign against Maastricht, Margaret Thatcher directly linked sovereignty to citizenship in her criticism of the Maastricht Treaty.

> We should cooperate more closely together as nation-states. I don't think it does anyone any good to try to dissolve 12 countries, 12 different languages into something called European citizenship. We do it better (when) confident in our own nationhood, confident in our own parliament, confident in our own nationality.[16]

During the House of Lords debate on ratification of Maastricht, Thatcher argued that EU citizenship was unprecedented, created a legal and political entity toward which citizens may shift their loyalties and gave the EU a fundamental attribute of a sovereign state.

> If there is a citizenship, you would all owe a duty of allegiance to the new Union. What else is citizenship about? There will be a duty to uphold its laws. What will happen if the allegiance to the Union comes into conflict with the allegiance to our own country? How would the European Court find then? The Maastricht Treaty gives this new European Union all the attributes of a sovereign state.[17]

The first vote in the House of Lords on Maastricht was on an amendment to remove aspects of EU citizenship from the Ratification Bill. As the government beat back the Euro-rebels by 242 to 48, it became clear that the Euroskeptics' last stand would fail.[18] After the House of Lords motion for a referendum on ratification was defeated by a majority of 269, it cleared the way for the Maastricht Bill to become law in July 1993.

Much of the Danish electorate echoed Thatcher's assessment; opposition to EU citizenship proved one of the main reasons that most Danes voted against ratification in a first May 1992 referendum. Ironically, Denmark had already extended local voting rights to resident aliens from fellow member states – and non-member states! Moreover, the Danish government had been among the strongest supporters of efforts to introduce European citizenship into the Maastricht Treaty.[19] During the ratification debate, however, many Danes apparently viewed EU citizenship as a replacement for Danish citizenship, while others simply considered it an affront to national sovereignty which grated against the Danish sense of national identity. In response to the referendum, the other eleven member-state governments addressed the concerns of the Danish government at the Edinburgh Summit and agreed to opt-outs for Denmark on monetary union and common defense policy as well as the recognition of a Danish "Unilateral Declaration on

Citizenship of the Union." Although Denmark accepted voting rights for nationals of other member states in EP and local elections (which they already had), the Declaration states

> Citizenship of the Union is a political and legal concept which is entirely different from the concept of citizenship within the meaning of the Constitution of the Kingdom of Denmark and of the Danish legal system. Nothing in the Treaty on European Union implies or foresees an undertaking to create a citizenship of the Union in the sense of citizenship of a nation-state. The question of Denmark participating in any such development does, therefore, not arise.[20]

Only after receiving the opt-outs and recognition of the Danish interpretation of EU citizenship at Edinburgh did the Danish government submit the Treaty to a second referendum in which it was ratified.

The symbolism of European citizenship also played a key role in the French referendum debate. During the campaign leading up to the September 1992 vote, some resident aliens in France voiced their demands for political rights, while French center-right and right-wing parties opposed extension of voting rights as a threat to French sovereignty and identity. Prompted by the interpretations of anti-Maastricht politicians, many came to associate European citizenship's reduction of barriers to free movement with migration of undesirables rather than that of professionals, students, and retirees (Buchan, 1992; Laxer, 1992). Michel Poniatowski, interior minister from 1974 to 1977 and a close associate of Valery Giscard d'Estaing, warned of "a free market in immigration, drugs and crime" (Criddle, 1993: 232). A National Front candidate even argued against EU citizenship by calling attention to the threat posed by the British who had moved to France's Dordogne region, one of the most contested regions during the Hundred Years War (Pfaff, 1992)! While the Maastricht referendum passed by a slim margin, exit polling showed "loss of French sovereignty" to be the number-one reason for voting "no" (Criddle, 1993: 238).

In the French case, Maastricht's citizenship provisions also raised sensitive constitutional questions. Since the French parliament had to approve an amendment to the French constitution allowing resident aliens from fellow member states voting rights, European citizenship became a pivotal issue in the ratification process (Hoffmann, 1993: 71). When the Treaty on European Union was signed, the Gaullist Rally for the Republic (RPR) Party's general secretary, Alain Juppé, said that EU citizenship was "unacceptable" and that his party would oppose changing the constitution to give non-citizens the vote.[21] Another Gaullist, Charles Pasqua, even charged that such constitutional revision amounted to "treason."[22] The party sponsored an amendment in the Senate that denied resident aliens from fellow member states the right to vote, but it was rejected. In order to avoid an impasse, the Socialist prime minister, Pierre Bérégovoy, eager to secure the necessary constitutional changes, endorsed a compromise bill stating that "eligibility and the right to vote *may* be granted to citizens of the Union residing in France" (emphasis added) and that "the citizens cannot exercise the function of mayor or deputy mayor, nor take part in the appointment of senatorial electors or the elections of senators."[23]

On the face of it, the degree of public controversy surrounding Maastricht ratification in all three states undermines any link between EU citizenship and legitimacy. The controversies demonstrate the potential for EU citizenship to arouse opposition and actually detract from the legitimacy of the integration project. However, Maastricht did eventually pass in all three countries, and opposition to its citizenship provisions was often based on a misunderstanding of their content. Subsequent developments suggest that to the extent that Europeans learn about what EU citizenship actually entails, they may become more supportive of the integration process. Ultimately the French ratification process demonstrated the successful, if contested, incorporation of EU citizenship provisions into a national constitution. It is difficult to imagine a clearer demonstration of the compatibility of European and national citizenship in practice.

Controversy surrounding European citizenship parallels other areas of EU politics. While Europeans increasingly acknowledge the EU as a framework for politics, they differ over its institutional make-up and appropriate policy competences. Given the fluid, unfolding nature of the EU polity, such contestation is inevitable. But a focus on conflict obscures broad recognition of – and identification with – the reality of the European polity. In the case of citizenship, Europeans increasingly recognize the existence of political rights in their possession as members of a European political community. Many are ready to embrace a European identity alongside national and subnational ones. As the ratification controversies demonstrated, political conflicts over European citizenship are more about its content than its existence. While such conflicts will continue, they do not indicate an intractable legitimacy problem.

The future of EU citizenship: Amsterdam and beyond

What are the implications of citizenship for the future development of the European polity, and the legitimacy question in particular? To what degree might the further development of EU citizenship generate additional support for the integration process? At what point might it generate opposition and have the opposite effect? This section addresses these questions in two parts. It first examines the discussion of citizenship at the 1996–97 IGC. Controversy over the issue, and the modest provisions of the Amsterdam Treaty, reveal possible future directions for European citizenship, and the political opposition that they may well engender. The section then discusses the broader implications of the citizenship issue for the evolution of a European polity characterized by the divergence of nationality and citizenship.

The 1996–97 IGC

At the top of the Italian presidency's agenda for the Intergovernmental Conference (IGC) after the March 1996 Florence European Council was "strengthening European citizenship, without replacing national citizenship and while respecting the national identity and traditions of the Member States."[24] In October 1996, Italy and Austria submitted a joint proposal for revisions of EU citizenship to be incorporated into a draft treaty intended to form the basis for negotiations at the IGC. The proposal called for granting citizens who are residents of a member state other than their own: the right to take part in local referenda in that state; a right affirming that EU citizens may, by means of a proposal drafted in the form of Articles and signed by at least a tenth of the electorate in each of at least three member states, "demand the adoption of normative European instruments;" rights to associate freely within political parties acting at the European level and to participate in trade unions and other associations at the European level; the right of access to documents held or issued by Union institutions for both physical or legal persons (within well-defined limits); and the right to receive an education taking account of the common heritage of European civilization, and to learn in school another EU language than one's own.[25]

These proposed revisions of the Maastricht Treaty represented direct efforts to infuse EU citizenship with meaningful content and thereby enhance EU legitimacy. The right of member-state nationals to "demand the adoption of normative instruments" contingent on a sufficient number of signatures would represent nothing less than the establishment of citizens' initiative as a procedure of EU legislation. Together with the right for resident aliens from fellow member states to participate in local referenda, the right of citizens' initiative represented the expansion of direct democracy in the process of European integration. At the same time, however, they appeared at odds with the Italian agenda of "strengthening European citizenship, without replacing national citizenship and while respecting the national identity and traditions of the Member States" in that they extend the scope of European institutions in political life at the expense of corresponding member-state institutions and promote a type of "European nationalism" through history and culture to support European institutions.[26] Both the content and the fate of these proposals point to the limits of European citizenship as a legitimacy-building strategy.

While, on the face of it, such revisions would seem to enhance legitimacy by bringing citizens more directly into the legislative process, they presented serious pitfalls. The right to participate in local referenda would increase the political rights of resident aliens from fellow member states. However, given that some member states utilize referenda and others do not, such a revision would lead to inequalities of political rights among EU member-state nationals.[27] Similarly, the right to initiate EU referenda could produce political inequalities across member states favoring the smaller members. The effort necessary for an initiative requiring the signatures of 10 percent of the electorate of three member states would vary depending on which member states were included. Fewer than a million citizens from Denmark, Ireland, and Luxembourg, for example, could initiate legislation for more than 350 million other EU citizens. Moreover, as the experience of American states demonstrates, sophisticated interest groups could use professional signature gatherers, public opinion polling, and major advertising campaigns to further their causes through initiatives and referenda. Smaller member states would most likely become the focus of such activity.

The right to access Union documents and the right to education emphasizing the common European heritage refer to the information citizens have at their disposal when they participate politically. The lack of transparency in the EU legislative process has been roundly criticized as a large part of the "democratic deficit" (Lodge, 1994) and citizen access to documents would no doubt reduce this gap. Given that education, particularly in history, literature, and language, has been the means by which national identities have been inculcated into successive generations of citizens, the right to a Europe-oriented education would most likely foster European identity formation in the long term. In the immediate future, however, such a right could well provoke pitched battles, given that the required incorporation of a European dimension into the curriculum would most likely reduce the amount of time and effort that could be devoted to national themes, while simultaneously increasing costs. Efforts to legislate the cultivation of a European heritage have the potential to generate a political backlash against the EU and actually decrease popular support.

Soon after Italy and Austria put forward these proposals, it became clear that these dramatic extensions of rights would not be incorporated into the Union citizenship provisions of the Amsterdam Treaty. Such provisions could not plausibly be squared with Denmark's interpretation of EU citizenship that had been recognized by the other member states at the Edinburgh Summit. Given the difficulties EU citizenship raised in the first Danish referendum, most negotiators sent by member states to the IGC were, not surprisingly, loath to introduce any citizenship provisions into the Treaty that might produce another failed ratification referendum. Expanding EU citizenship became a low priority, even among member states that might have favored it in principle, and the most ambitious proposals were quickly abandoned in negotiations for a final deal.[28] Moreover, it was not imperative for those member states who favored expanding the rights of EU citizenship to do so during the IGC, because, according to Article 8e TEU, rights could be added to EU citizenship via normal legislative procedures (see Appendix II).

Ultimately, the only significant revision to Union citizenship proposed by the Italian presidency that survived the Irish Draft Treaty of December 1996[29] and found its way into the Amsterdam Treaty was the stipulation that "Citizenship of the Union shall complement and not replace national citizenship" (see Appendix I). A cynic may easily interpret this amendment as a rearguard action by the member states to reclaim their sovereign prerogatives and insure that Union citizenship does not become the foundation for some sort of supranational European state. Indeed, this provision obviously is intended to insure that voters in a referendum do not mistake EU citizenship for something it is not. But it also reflects the reality of EU citizenship as it evolved over the postwar decades and found concrete expression in Maastricht. Member states remain committed to the extension of economic, social, and some political rights to Europeans residing abroad within the EU. At the same time they do not consider European citizenship a step towards the constitution of a state-like polity.

Implications of citizenship for the European polity

While EU citizenship is not analogous to member-state nationality, it nevertheless is an institution that sets out legal relationships which together constitute a novel form of membership in an equally novel form of polity. What are the broader implications for the future evolution of that polity, and the question of its political legitimacy in particular? Over two hundred years ago the United States constitution likewise introduced a national citizenship alongside and in tension with the citizenship of its constituent member states. The US Constitution says precious little about citizenship except, "The Citizens of each State shall be entitled to all the Privileges and Immunities of Citizens in the Several States (Article 6)." It was not until the ratification of the 14th Amendment in 1868 that an unambiguous form of US citizenship emerged: "All persons born or naturalized in the United States, and subject to the jurisdiction thereof, are citizens of the United States and of the State in which they reside" (Kettner, 1978: ch. 6). Generally speaking, the Maastricht Treaty's concept of citizenship articulated in Article 8 is more developed than that found in the pre-civil war US constitution but not as developed as that of the 14th Amendment.

The parallel with the United States suggests that we consider EU citizenship as an aspect of the development of the EU into a traditional federation. A quintessential characteristic of a federation is dual state/suprastate citizenship, which makes it fundamentally different from a confederation. In a federation, Kenneth Wheare has argued, "general and regional governments both operate directly upon the people; each citizen is subject to both governments" (Wheare, 1963: 2). Drawing on this definition, Richard Nathan views the European citizenship that developed out of the right of free movement and the direct effect of European legislation as a primary reason to consider the EU a federation (Nathan, 1991). However, EU citizenship renders the emerging European polity rather different from the traditional models of federalism followed in the United States or Germany. EU citizenship bounds political units so that the composition of European parliamentary and local electorates does not necessarily overlap with national and regional electorates. For example, a German national from Frankfurt living in London for more than five years may vote in elections for the London city council, the Hesse Landtag, the German Bundestag and the Member of the European Parliament from the London district in which he or she lives. Someday Europeans may establish a form of EU citizenship that gives full political rights to residents of one EU member state who move to another. The German who moved to London could then also vote for a member of the British Parliament. As mentioned above, granting such full political rights would, practically speaking, extend citizenship to non-nationals. Hence the European demos would more closely resemble traditional federal models and its complexity would be reduced. However, the 1996–97 IGC and the agreement forged at the Amsterdam Summit indicate that such an outcome is not likely anytime soon.

Elsewhere, I have argued that the restructuring of EU citizenship may lead the European demos toward a type of non-territorial federalism or European consociationalism analogous to the politics of the Netherlands, Belgium, and Switzerland (Koslowski, 1994: 394–96). Not only have member states demonstrated a willingness to accept the constitutional and electoral complications inherent in Maastricht's version of EU citizenship; the Amsterdam Summit reaffirms their toleration of such constitutional and political complexity. This toleration is indicative of a further ad hoc evolution of the European polity towards some sort of European consociationalism, in which there are multiple overlapping demoi and multiple access points of interest articulation at all levels of governance. For the foreseeable future, EU citizenship is likely to remain in a permanent state of tension with member-state nationality.

This tension may well be sustainable, consistent with the continued evolution of the EU along lines different from traditional nation states. Joseph Weiler has suggested the constitutive dimension of a Union citizenship that separates citizenship from nationality outside of a state-centric constitutionalism, in which "the Union belongs to, is composed of, citizens who by definition do not share the same nationality." From this perspective, "The substance of membership (and thus of the demos) is in a commitment to the shared values of the Union as expressed in its constituent documents, a commitment, inter alia, to the duties and rights of a civic society covering discrete areas of public life, a commitment to membership in a polity which privileges exactly the opposites of nationalism – those human features which transcend the differences of organic ethno-culturalism" (Weiler, 1997: 119). In this frame of view, EU citizenship embodies a type of general European "constitutional patriotism" (Habermas, 1992) as well as the delineation of rights and duties in the discrete jurisdictional spaces allocated between member states and the EU by treaty. Political identification with the values embodied in the EU's constituent documents represents one potential source of legitimacy while another source is found in the practical realization of the rights and duties of citizens within the jurisdictional spaces created.

Rather than conceiving democracy as only possible within nation states, the emerging European polity can be better thought of as a site for the practice of democracy on several levels by overlapping demoi as constituted by the combination of member-state nationality and European citizenship. To the extent that Europeans view the EU as a diverse polity with a common democratic foundation, the EU can perhaps dispense with projects to develop a common identity defined in cultural terms – on the model of the nation state. As Weiler proposes, "On this reading, the conceptualization of a European demos should neither be based on real or imaginary trans-European cultural affinities or shared histories, nor on the construction of European 'national' myth of the type which constitutes the identity of the organic nation. The decoupling of nationality and citizenship opens the possibility, instead, of thinking of co-existing multiple demoi" (Weiler, 1997: 119). While the institutional framework for such co-existing multiple demoi to practice democracy may still be inchoate, it is important to remember that democracy originated in city-states; it was only the invention of representation that permitted the practice of democracy in much larger nation states – the kind of democracy we now consider normal – and it is quite possible that new institutions of transnational democracy are currently developing (Dahl, 1994: 23–24). Much as citizenship was constitutive of the state known to Aristotle and national citizenship was constitutive of democratic nation states, the emergence of EU citizenship marks the contemporary transformation of democracy in Europe.

From such a perspective, the future evolution of EU citizenship as a set of economic, social, and political rights that complements and does not replace those proffered by national citizenship has the potential to reinforce the legitimacy of the integration project. The freedom of movement sanctioned by European citizenship, the political rights it engenders, and the compatible identities it has encouraged may well help to sustain support for the EU in the future. Moreover, EU citizenship provides a potential foundation for new forms of legitimate democratic representation outside of the established framework of the nation state. Much will depend on whether the traditional statist association between nationality and citizenship can be overcome in practice.

Conclusion

EU citizenship is constitutive of the emerging European polity. Because it complements rather than replaces member-state nationality, European citizenship renders the European polity and its form of political membership unique. In practice, European citizenship has encouraged the articulation of compatible identities within Europe and has become the object of growing societal acceptance. It has furthered recognition of the EU as a legitimate framework for politics, and extended democratic representation to a growing number of Europeans living in fellow member states. Efforts to extend EU citizenship at the expense of national prerogatives – like those presented at the 1996–97 IGC – could potentially undermine support for the integration project. As the Maastricht ratification controversies demonstrated, European publics are wary of any EU citizenship that threatens established national identities. As it happened, the original IGC proposals were abandoned in favor of a reiteration of a preference for the complex, fragmented European demos constituted at Maastricht. Popular toleration of such complexity – of a new relationship between nationality and citizenship – reflects a broad recognition and acceptance of the EU as an evolving polity without precedent.

APPENDIX I

Draft Treaty of Amsterdam amending the Treaty on European Union, the Treaties establishing the European Communities and certain related acts

9) Article 8 (1) shall be replaced by the following:

"1. Citizenship of the Union is hereby established. Every person holding the nationality of a Member State shall be a citizen of the Union. Citizenship of the Union shall complement and not replace national citizenship."

10) Article 8a (2) shall be replaced by the following:

"2. The Council may adopt provisions with a view to facilitating the exercise of the rights referred to in paragraph 1; save as otherwise provided in this Treaty, the Council shall act in accordance with the procedure referred to in Article 189b. The Council shall act unanimously throughout this procedure."

11) In Article 8d, the following paragraph shall be added:

"Every citizen of the Union may write to any of the institutions or bodies referred to in this Article or in Article 4 in one of the languages mentioned in Article 248 and have an answer in the same language."

(Europa, http://ue.eu.int/Amsterdam/en/treaty/treaty.htm)

APPENDIX II

Part Two
Citizenship of the Union

Article 8

1. Citizenship of the Union is hereby established. Every person holding the nationality of a Member State shall be a citizen of the Union.
2. Citizens of the Union shall enjoy the rights conferred by this Treaty and shall be subject to the duties imposed thereby.

Article 8a

1. Every citizen of the Union shall have the right to move and reside freely within the territory of the Member States, subject to the limitations and conditions laid down in this Treaty and by the measures adopted to give it effect.
2. The Council may adopt provisions with a view to facilitating the exercise of the rights referred to in paragraph 1; save as otherwise provided in this Treaty, the Council shall act unanimously on a proposal from the Commission after obtaining the assent of the European Parliament.

Article 8b

1. Every citizen of the Union residing in a Member State of which he is not a national shall have the right to vote and to stand as a candidate at municipal elections in the Member State in which he resides, under the same conditions as nationals of that State. This right shall be exercised subject to detailed arrangements to be adopted before 31 December 1994 by the Council, acting unanimously, on a proposal from the Commission and after consulting the European Parliament; these arrangements may provide for derogations where warranted by problems specific to a Member State.

2. Without prejudice to Article 1 38 (3) and to the provisions adopted for its implementation, every citizen of the Union residing in a Member State of which he is not a national shall have the right to vote and to stand as a candidate in elections to the European Parliament in the Member State in which he resides, under the same conditions as nationals of that State. This right shall be exercised subject to detailed arrangements to be adopted before 31 December 1993 by the Council, acting unanimously on a proposal from the Commission and after consulting the European Parliament; these arrangements may provide for derogations where warranted by problems specific to a Member State.

Article 8c

Every citizen of the Union shall, in the territory of a third country in which the Member State of which he is a national is not represented, be entitled to protection by the diplomatic or consular authorities of any Member State, on the same conditions as the nationals of that State. Before 31 December 1993, Member States shall establish the necessary rules among themselves and start the international negotiations required to secure this protection.

Article 8d

Every citizen of the Union shall have the right to petition the European Parliament in accordance with Article 138d. Every citizen of the Union may apply to the Ombudsman established in accordance with Article 138e.

Article 8e

The Commission shall report to the European Parliament, to the Council and to the Economic and Social Committee before 31 December 1993 and then every three years on the application of the provisions of this Part. This report shall take account of the development of the Union. On this basis, and without prejudice to the other provisions of this Treaty, the Council, acting unanimously on a proposal from the Commission and after consulting the European Parliament, may adopt provisions to strengthen or to add to the rights laid down in this Part, which it shall recommend to the Member States for adoption in accordance with their respective constitutional requirements.

(Council and Commission of the European Communities, *Treaty on European Union* (Luxembourg: Office for the Official Publications of the European Communities 1992))

Notes

1 This chapter was written while I was a Research Associate of the Center for German and European Studies at Georgetown University's School of Foreign Service. I am very grateful for both the Center's financial support and its dynamic intellectual community.
2 For a good historical overview, see Riesenberg (1992).
3 " 'What is a state?' . . . [A] state is composite, like any other whole made up of its parts; — these are the citizens, who compose it. It is evident, therefore, that we must begin by asking, who is the citizen, and what is the meaning of the term?" Aristotle, *Politics*, Book III, chs 1 and 2, in Richard McKeon (ed.) *The Basic Works of Aristotle*, New York: Random House, 1941, pp. 1176–78.
4 For a review, see Plender (1988), ch. 6, Magiera (1991), and Meehan (1993), chs 3 and 7.
5 Treaty of Rome, Articles 48–59.
6 Regulation 1612/68 of the Council of October 15, 1968 on freedom of movement for workers within the Community, OJ, No. L257/2. See also Regulation No. 15/61 of the Council of August 16, 1961 and Regulation No. 38/64 of the Council of March 15, 1964 on the freedom of movement for workers within the Community (*Official Journal of the European Communities* (OJ) No. 965/64 as well as discussion by Boehning (1972), pp. 11–19).
7 "Belgian Memorandum, 19 March 1990," in Laursen and Vanhoonacker (1992).
8 "Spanish Delegation, Intergovernmental Conference on Political Union, European Citizenship (21 February 1991)," in Laursen and Vanhoonacker (1992).
9 See Council Directive 93/109 of December 6, 1993 in OJ L329/34 of December 30, 1993.
10 Council Directive 94/80 of December 19, 1994 in OJ L 368 of December 31, 1994.
11 See Second Report of the European Commission on Citizenship of the Union, at http://www.europa.eu.int/comm/dg15/en/update/report/citen.htm.
12 For EP elections, see Eurobarometer No. 41 (July 1994).
13 For implementing legislation, see "Decision of the Representatives of the Governments of the Member States Meeting within the Council of 19 December 1995 Protection for Citizens of the European Union by Diplomatic and Consular Representations," OJ, L314/73.
14 Statistics presented by Astrid Thors, MEP, at the conference, "EU Citizenship – Current State and Future Perspectives," European Parliament, Brussels, May 5–6, 1997.
15 See "Non-nationals make up less than 5% of the population of the European Union on 1.1.1993," Statistics in Focus, Population and Social Conditions, no. 2/1996.
16 "Thatcher Sees Advantages in European Currency Crises," Reuter Library Report, September 19, 1992.
17 Speech of June 7, 1993, Parliamentary Debates, House of Lords, vol. 546, p. 564.
18 "Euro-rebels Crushed in Lords Vote," *Herald* (Glasgow), June 23, 1993.
19 See "Memorandum from the Danish Government (4 October 1990)," in Laursen and Vanhoonacker (1992).
20 European Council 11 and 12 December 1992 Conclusions of the Presidency, Annex 3.

21 "Maastricht Prepares Europe as 'Greatest World Power,' France Says," Agence France Presse, December 11, 1991.
22 "French Senate Waters Down Maastricht," Reuters, June 16, 1992.
23 "France: Senate Approves Constitutional Revision Needed for Ratification of the Maastricht Treaty," Agence Europe, June 18, 1992.
24 "Presidency Conclusions," Florence European Council, June 21–22, 1996.
25 See "EU: IGC/Italy/Austria, Proposals on Fundamental Rights (with Mechanisms for Sanctions) and on Citizenship (with a Legislative Right of Initiative for Citizens)," Agence Europe, October 2, 1996.
26 Obradovic (1996) offers a representative sample of this approach to EU legitimacy.
27 For a general discussion of the problem of political rights for resident aliens from fellow member states and inequality among member states, see Koslowski (1994).
28 Points made by Georg Birgelen, Consultant of MEP Brok for the IGC, in his presentation at the conference, "EU Citizenship – Current State and Future Prospects," European Parliament, Brussels, May 5–6, 1997.
29 Conference of the Representatives of the Governments of the Member States, "The European Union Today and Tomorrow, Adapting the European Union for the Benefit of its Peoples: A General Outline for a Draft Revision of the Treaties, Dublin II," Brussels, December 5, 1996, p. 37.

Bibliography

Anderson, M., den Boer, M. and Miller, G. (1994) "European Citizenship and Cooperation in Justice and Home Affairs," in A. Duff, J. Pinder and R. Price (eds) *Maastricht and Beyond*, London: Routledge.

Aron, R. (1974) "Is Multinational Citizenship Possible?" *Social Research* 41: 638–56.

Baker, D., Gamble, A. and Ludlam, S. (1994) "The Parliamentary Siege of Maastricht 1993: Conservative Divisions and British Ratification," *Parliamentary Affairs* 47, 1: 37–60.

Boehning, W. R. (1972) *The Migration of Workers in the United Kingdom and the European Community*, London: Oxford University Press.

Buchan, D. (1992) "The French Referendum: Wrong End of the Maastricht Stick — Campaigners are Misinterpreting the Treaty for Their Own Ends," *Financial Times* September 3, p. 2.

Commission of the European Communities (1975) "Towards European Citizenship: Implementation of Point 10 of the Final Communiqué Issued at the European Summit Held in Paris on 9 and 10 December 1974," *Bulletin of the European Communities* Supplement 7/75.

—— (1985) "A People's Europe: Reports from the ad hoc Committee," *Bulletin of the European Communities* Supplement 7/85.

—— (1986) "Voting Rights in Local Elections for Community Nationals: A Report from the Commission to the European Parliament," *Bulletin of the European Communities* Supplement 7/86.

—— (1988) "A People's Europe: Proposal for a Council Directive on Voting Rights for Community Nationals in Local Elections in their Member State of Residence," *Bulletin of the European Communities*, Supplement 2/88.

—— (1991) "Intergovernmental Conferences: Contributions by the Commission," *Bulletin of the European Communities* Supplement 2/91.

—— (1995) *Commission Report for the Reflection Group*, Luxembourg: Office for Official Publications of the European Communities.

Criddle, B. (1993) "The French Referendum on the Maastricht Treaty, September 1992," *Parliamentary Affairs* 46, 2: 228–38.

Dahl, R. (1994) "A Democratic Dilemma: System Effectiveness vs Citizen Participation," *Political Science Quarterly* 109, 1: 23–34.

Eurobarometer (1996) No. 45, December release, Commission of the European Communities.

European Ombudsman, *Report of the Year 1995*, Europa, http://www.europarl.eu.int/ombud/report/en/default.htm.

Europinion (1995) "Results of Monthly Surveys of European Opinion," No. 6 (July, September, October).

—— (1996) "Results of Monthly Surveys of European Opinion," No. 9 (May, June, July).

Ferguson, Y. H. and Mansbach, R. W. (1996) *Polities, Identities and Change*, Columbia, SC: University of South Carolina Press.

Habermas, J. (1992) "Citizenship and National Identity: Some Reflections on the Future of Europe," *Praxis International* 12, 1: 1–19.

Hammar, T. (1990) *Democracy and the Nation-State: Aliens, Denizens and Citizens in a World of International Migration*, Aldershot, UK: Avebury.

Hoffmann, S. (1993) "Thoughts on the French Nation Today," *Daedalus* 122, 3: 63–79.

Jessurn d'Oliveria, H. U. (1995) "Union Citizenship: Pie in the Sky?" in A. Rosas and E. Antola, *A Citizens' Europe: In Search of a New Order*, London: Sage.

Johnson, E. and O'Keefe, D. (1994) "From Discrimination to Obstacles to Free Movement: Recent Developments Concerning the Free Movement of Workers 1989–1994," *Common Market Law Review* 31: 1313–46.

Kettner, J. H. (1978) *The Development of American Citizenship, 1608–1870*, Chapel Hill, NC: University of North Carolina Press.

Koslowski, R. (1994) "Intra-EU Migration, Citizenship, and Political Union," *Journal of Common Market Studies* 32, 3: 369–402.

—— (1998) "EU Migration Regimes: Established and Emergent," in C. Joppke (ed.) *Challenge to the Nation-state: Immigration in Western Europe and the United States*, Oxford, UK: Oxford University Press.

Laursen, F. and Vanhoonacker, S. (eds) (1992) *The Intergovernmental Conference on Political Union: Institutional Reforms, New Policies and International Identity of the European Community*, Dordrecht: Martinus Nijhoff.

Laxer, J. (1992) "As Mitterrand Found, a Referendum's Fraught with Peril," *The Toronto Star* September 22, p. A19.

Lodge, J. (1994) "Transparency and Democratic Legitimacy," *Journal of Common Market Studies* 32, 3: 343–68.

Magiera, S. (1988) "Kommunalwahlrecht in den EG-Mitgliedstaaten," *Europa-Archiv*, Folge 16: 475–80.

—— (1991) "A Citizens' Europe: Personal, Political, and Cultural Rights," in L. Hurwitz and C. Lequesne (eds) *The State of the European Community*, Boulder, CO: Lynne Rienner.

Marshall, T. H. (1964) "Citizenship and Social Class," in T. H. Marshall, *Class, Citizenship and Social Development*, Chicago, IL: University of Chicago Press.

Meehan, E. (1993) *Citizenship and the European Community*, London: Sage.

Nathan, R. (1991) "Implications for Federalism of European Integration," in N. J. Ornstein and M. Perlman (eds) *Political Power and Social Change: The United States Faces a United Europe*, Washington, DC: AEI Press.

Obradovic, D. (1996) "Policy Legitimacy and the European Union," *Journal of Common Market Studies* 34, 2: 191–221.

O'Leary, S. (1995) "The Relationship between Community Citizenship and the Protection of Fundamental Rights in Community Law," *Common Market Law Review* 32: 519–54.

Pfaff, W. (1992) "Unity Agreement Causing Wave of Anxiety in Europe," *Chicago Tribune*, May 17.

Plender, R. (1988) *International Migration Law*, Dordrecht: Martinus Nijhoff.

Reif, K. (1993) "Cultural Convergence and Cultural Diversity as Factors in European Identity," in S. Garcia (ed.) *European Identity and the Search for Legitimacy*, London: Pinter.

Riesenberg, P. (1992) *Citizenship in the Western Tradition*, Chapel Hill, NC: University of North Carolina Press.

van den Berghe, G. (1982) *Political Rights for European Citizens*, Aldershot, UK: Gower.

Weiler, J. H. H. (1997) "The Reformation of European Constitutionalism," *Journal of Common Market Studies* 35, 1: 97–131.

Weis, P. (1979) *Nationality and Statelessness in International Law*, Alpen aan den Rijn: Sijthoff & Noordhoff.

Wheare, K. (1963) *Federal Government*, 4th edn, Oxford, UK: Oxford University Press.

Wiener, A. (1997) *European Citizenship Practice – Building Institutions of a Non-state*, Boulder, CO: Westview.

9

NATIONAL IDENTITY AND EU LEGITIMACY IN FRANCE AND GERMANY

Thomas Banchoff

From the outset of the integration process, European leaders have struggled to justify the creation of supranational institutions in tension with established national identities. In order to legitimate the integration process at home, they have sought, in part, to construct an overarching European identity based on shared historical experience, culture, and political values. More important, and less understood, they have also endeavored to redefine established national identities in ways compatible with membership in the European Union (EU). Through the depiction of integration as an extension of *national* history, culture, and political values, EU supporters have redescribed the nation state as inextricably embedded within European institutions. Efforts to Europeanize national identity – to construe the nation state as part of an evolving supranational community – have provoked different kinds of resistance at different junctures. A comparison of French and German controversies in the 1950s and the 1990s illuminates the character of those efforts in two key cases, the nature of resistance to them, and their degree of success over time.

A focus on the redefinition of national identities runs counter to established approaches to identity and EU legitimacy. Most observers have focused on the absence of a European identity – of common history, culture, and political values that might bind Europeans to one another and legitimate European governance (Smith, 1992; Obradovic, 1996). This chapter argues that the continued salience of national identity does not represent an insurmountable problem for EU legitimacy. Given the EU's character as a multi-level, contested polity in which nation states persist alongside supranational institutions, European identity is unlikely to supersede national identity in the foreseeable future. In the context of the legitimacy problem, this makes it crucial whether Europeans perceive their nation states as irreversibly anchored within the EU; whether they conceive of national identity as compatible with the integration process. Such an approach shifts the analytical focus from the presence or absence of European identity toward the changing content of national identity.

How have pro-integration leaders sought to rework received national identities in ways compatible with integration? How successful have they been over time? This chapter addresses these questions through an analysis of French and German controversies surrounding the ratification of the European Coal and Steel Community (ECSC) in the early 1950s and the Maastricht Treaty exactly four decades later. This relatively narrow approach to broad questions can be justified on several grounds. A focus on France and Germany makes sense given the central role of both states in the integration process. Partisan controversies reveal the distribution of views about national identity and European integration across the political spectrum in both countries. And the ECSC and Maastricht challenged existing conceptions of national identity, explicitly raising the legitimacy problem. This focus on partisan controversies in Germany and France at two key historical junctures obviously cannot provide a comprehensive overview of links between national identity and EU legitimacy. However, the comparison of both cases sheds light on important – if often overlooked – efforts to build EU legitimacy, and the extent of their success over time.

The chapter is divided into three parts. Part one defines the approaches to national identity and EU legitimacy that inform the analysis. It distinguishes between external and internal dimensions of identity, and shows how the integration process challenged both of them in the French and German cases. Parts two and three examine the construction of national identity in the ECSC and Maastricht debates, respectively. They outline leaders' efforts to rework national identity in ways compatible with the integration project – and the opposition they encountered at the level of partisan discourse. A concluding section compares the debates in France and Germany over both periods and draws out some of their broader implications. The comparison suggests some Europeanization of national identity over time, but also points to ongoing tensions between national identity and integration and the problems that they pose for EU legitimacy.

National identity and EU legitimacy

European leaders at the turn of the twentieth century bequeathed their successors a difficult legacy. They constructed identities which proved useful in the context of one political project, the consolidation of the nation state, but came to complicate another, European integration. During the nineteenth and early twentieth centuries, European leaders successfully asserted the sovereign supremacy of the nation state at home and abroad. This involved not only the concentration of state power, but also the construction of national identities – the invention of national traditions and the invocation of shared values designed to bind citizens to one another and foster their identification with state authority (Anderson, 1991; Hobsbawm and Ranger, 1983). During the second half of the twentieth century, the resilience of those national identities has engendered an ongoing legitimacy problem for European leaders committed to deeper economic and political integration: how to justify the transfer of sovereignty away from national institutions that remain an object of broad identification.

Two dimensions of national identity

Conceptualizing the nature of this legitimacy problem – and the efforts to address it – requires a definition of national identity. Scholars have developed numerous approaches to national identity, including well-known distinctions between its ethnic and civic, and objective and subjective dimensions (Greenfield, 1992; Kupchan, 1995; Eley and Sung, 1996). In the context of the legitimacy issue, the distinction between the external and internal dimensions of national identity is most useful – between what situates the state with respect to the outside world, and what unites state and society at home.[1] While external identity consists of relations with other states and international institutions, internal identity is constituted by a sense of "we-ness" through time. A nation state, for example, can have an identity as a sovereign power or as part of a supranational community (external identity), or as a community linked by shared culture or political values (internal identity). The internal/external distinction is not clear cut. For example, a conception of national identity in terms of democratic values can both situate a state abroad (as a member of a democratic international community) and bind state and society at home (through a shared identification with a democratic constitution). Nevertheless, the distinction captures different, important aspects of the historical development of national identity in Europe.

The national identities constructed during the late nineteenth and early twentieth centuries were *sovereign* identities in a dual sense. Externally, the breakdown of the Ottoman and Austro-Hungarian empires and the unification of Germany and Italy made nation states the key actors in European international politics. National identity became defined in terms of the national sovereignty that constituted states as participants in a shifting balance of power system (Dehio, 1962). Internally, the spread of constitutional and democratic norms made nation states – and, more particularly, their accountable governments – the key actors in European domestic politics. National identity became defined in terms of the popular sovereignty that joined state and society, and the historical and cultural bonds that united society internally. Nation states, then, assumed an identity as sovereign actors in both realms, the international and the domestic – as masters of their own fate abroad and at home. These identities did not fit empirical reality: complete external and internal autonomy never existed. But they constituted the dominant view of the nation state in political discourse, public education, and popular culture.

The French and German cases reveal different patterns in the evolution of national identity before the onset of European integration. Externally, national identities in both countries developed in similar directions from the nineteenth century onward. With Napoleon's final defeat in 1815, France assumed an identity as a sovereign nation state within the European balance of power. Germany joined that system in 1871 after its unification under Otto von Bismarck. The First World War challenged but did not destroy the identities of France, Germany, and other European states as externally sovereign. The collapse of the Versailles Settlement and the weakness of the League of Nations left nation states – including a resurgent Germany – the masters of European politics. The Second World War left France, Germany, and their neighbors again exhausted. However, French leaders were determined to rejoin the ranks of the great powers in a new international balance, and German leaders sought to win back the national sovereignty deprived them through defeat and occupation. An image of the state as sovereign, independent, and autonomous remained widespread during the immediate postwar years.

While external identity developed in roughly parallel fashion in both countries, internal identities diverged. In France, the revolutionary ideals of 1789 came to constitute a civic conception of national identity. Building the French nation involved forging a shared sense of identity around the Rights of Man and the idea of popular sovereignty – a largely successful, if continually contested, project. In Germany, efforts to forge a national identity around democratic ideals failed with the collapse of the 1848 revolution. A conception of identity in terms of shared culture, language, and ancestry prevailed and found its political expression in Bismarck's Reich. The French conception of national identity persisted through the collapse of the Third Republic in 1940, while the German variant persisted into the Weimar Republic before giving way to the racist ideology of the Third Reich in 1933. Both variants re-emerged after 1945. The constitution of the Fourth Republic reflected established civic conceptions of identity, while the Basic Law of 1949 established the Federal Republic as the legitimate political expression of Germans bound by culture and ancestry – including those in the Soviet-dominated German Democratic Republic (GDR). The differences between both conceptions of internal identity should not be overdrawn. French national identity traditionally contained cultural and ethnic, as well as civic, strands. And German national identity, particularly after 1945, contained a significant civic, democratic component. Nevertheless, differences of emphasis remained (Schnapper *et al.*, 1996; Brubaker, 1992; Dumont, 1991).

The post-1945 integration process posed a challenge for both sovereign identities, external and internal. Scholars have debated the extent to which transfers of sovereignty to supranational institutions, limited and incomplete, undermined the capacity of nation states to conduct independent foreign and domestic policies in practice (Milward, 1992). The creation of new institutions at the supranational level, however, certainly challenged the *identity* of nation states as sovereign actors abroad and at home. France, a victor in the Second World War, was to cede some of its newly regained external sovereignty and shift some authority away from the national institutions that embodied popular sovereignty. Germany, deprived of its sovereignty in defeat, was to renounce its full repossession and shift some authority away from the national institutions committed to the goal of national unity. From the outset, the integration process posed a challenge to established conceptions of national identity in both France and Germany.

Identity and EU legitimacy

What are the links between national identity, European integration, and EU legitimacy? This volume defines a legitimate polity as a broadly recognized framework for politics with representative institutions.[2] Identity relates primarily to the issue of legitimacy as recognition. To the extent that people identify with the political institutions or processes that affect their lives – that they recognize them as appropriate and consider them theirs – they endow them with legitimacy. Against this definitional backdrop, the onset of European integration raised a double legitimacy problem. On the one hand, it created new European institutions that were not an object of broad identification. On the other hand, it undermined sovereign national institutions that were an object of identification and possessed legitimacy. From the immediate postwar period onward, opponents of European integration could and often did highlight both aspects of the legitimacy problem. They inveighed against the creation of illegitimate institutions and the destruction of legitimate ones.

Each aspect of the legitimacy problem, the European and the national, pointed to a potential solution. In order to justify the transfer of sovereignty to EU institutions, pro-integration leaders could seek to construct an overarching European identity. They could construe Europe as a unified actor in world politics, or point to commonalities of history, culture, and political values linking Europeans with one another and with new European institutions. From the start, efforts in this direction ran up against three formidable obstacles: the relative weakness of European institutions; a diversity of historical experiences and cultures; and the resilience of existing national identities. Unlike the state-builders of an earlier era, the Europe-builders of the postwar decades did not have strong central institutions and instruments – political, financial, educational – at their disposal. They confronted greater ethnic, cultural, and linguistic diversity in the European than in the national context. And they ran up against established national identities defined in terms of sovereignty, internal and external.

This final obstacle pointed to the second aspect of the legitimacy problem – the challenges integration posed to established conceptions of national identity. Here, too, the contours of the problem suggested a possible solution: the redefinition of national identities in ways compatible with the integration process. Leaders could construe the nation state as part of an emergent supranational community – a new context for the realization of *national* history, culture, and political values.[3] They could, for example, describe transfers of national sovereignty as a logical and necessary outgrowth of two world wars, or as an effective way to safeguard national patterns of culture and politics amid new circumstances, especially international economic competition. Such efforts to address the legitimacy problem also ran up against the obstacle posed by traditional conceptions of national identity in terms of sovereignty. But they explicitly acknowledged the strength of national as opposed to European identity, and backed the transformation of the former, not its replacement by the latter.

New conceptions of national identity, it might be objected, have no direct bearing on the legitimacy of European institutions. Without a European identity, there is no EU legitimacy. However, if one conceives the EU not in terms of fixed institutions but as an ongoing, open-ended process, the objection loses its force. The necessarily contested and evolving character of the EU rules out any straightforward recognition of a stable set of institutions. At the same time, however, it does allow for the recognition of the EU as a process over time. Where Europeans acknowledge integration as an unprecedented process of cooperation which involves, but does not threaten, existing nation states, they endow the entire project with legitimacy. The construction of a European identity around European institutions would replicate the experience of nation states. But the reworking of existing national identities in ways compatible with integration, where successful, constitutes a legitimacy-building strategy better suited to the EU's character as a contested polity.

Analyzing the content of national identity

How can efforts to redefine national identity – and their success or failure – be studied in any particular case? Most efforts to gauge the content of national identity have relied on measures of public opinion across societal groups over time (Niedermayer and Sinnott, 1995; Reif, 1991). The approach set out here, and applied to the German and French cases in what follows, focuses on political discourse, partisan controversy, and critical historical junctures. This analytical focus requires some justification.

Political discourse refers to the way people talk and write about politics. Its analysis provides an important way to assess the content of national identity. Public opinion surveys can measure the intensity of national identity, but are less well suited to the determination of its content. They constitute a quantifiable but narrow form of discourse – responses to particular questions. The analysis of other forms of discourse (speeches, interviews, articles, etc.) provides a richer sense of how the nation is conceived in context – how it is situated externally and constituted internally. Such discourse typically has both descriptive and narrative elements. At a descriptive level, it depicts the nation's external affiliations and internal characteristics. And at a narrative level, it relates past historical episodes that situate the nation with respect to present situations and future projects (Fairclough, 1992; Polkinghorne, 1988).

As an object of study, political discourse is boundless. Here, the focus is on partisan discourse – the way in which political parties and their leaders approach the nation. The struggle for political control over national institutions – the business of parties – tends to give rise to contested conceptions of national identity. Those conceptions, articulated in different forums ranging from parliamentary debates to press conferences, both reflect and shape views of national identity espoused within society as a whole. Government and opposition leaders are the most important actors; their views of national identity ultimately have the greatest political and policy impact. Limiting the analysis to partisan discourse excludes other relevant kinds of political communication – that of interest groups and bureaucratic officials, for example. And unlike public opinion surveys, partisan discourse provides little insight into the views of national identity held by particular societal groups. But a focus on parties has two advantages. It makes the task of analysis manageable. And it rests on the plausible assumption that views of national identity espoused by democratic parties broadly reflect those held across society.[4]

A focus on critical historical junctures constitutes a final important analytical choice. Public opinion surveys provide a means to analyze gradual changes in national identity over time. However, they generate difficult problems of interpretation: the meanings of such key terms as "nation" and "Europe" can change over time. Moreover, their inattention to context obscures the particular content of national identity at any particular juncture. Discourse analysis, too, can be carried out over time. However, a focus on critical junctures – defined as those periods in the integration process when national identity is sharply contested – has a distinct advantage. Contending conceptions of national identity are most clearly defined at points of controversy. Lively debates within and across parties make it possible to pinpoint the content of views of national identity with greater accuracy. And careful comparisons across junctures can illuminate changes in the content of national identity over time.

The following two case studies examine the political discourse of the major French and German parties amid the ECSC and Maastricht ratification controversies. The choice of France and Germany is not arbitrary; from the outset, both countries have played a leading role in the process of European integration. The focus on major parties – Christian Democratic, Socialist, and Gaullist – corresponds to their leading role in the domestic politics and foreign policies of both countries. And the focus on ratification debates allows for a comparison of the content of national identity at two key junctures – the cold war and post-cold war periods. Given its limited scope, such an analysis cannot generate definitive conclusions about the relationship between national identity and EU legitimacy. However, a comparison of both cases does shed light on the contours of that relationship, its development over time, and some of its implications for the future of European integration.

The ECSC ratification controversy

The European Coal and Steel Community, proposed by French foreign minister Robert Schuman in May 1950, had complex postwar roots. The division of Germany and the onset of the cold war led to the creation of the Federal Republic in 1949 and subsequent efforts to anchor it within Western economic, political, and security institutions. The United States, the dominant power in Western Europe, was determined to harness German capabilities in the struggle against the Soviet Union, but also was sensitive to French concerns about German recovery. In this context, Schuman's plan to pool German and French coal and steel industries under a supranational authority represented a way to promote recovery in both countries and establish some supranational control over the Ruhr, the traditional basis of the German armaments industry. German chancellor Konrad Adenauer, like Schuman a Christian Democrat, was eager to integrate the Federal Republic within Western institutions. He greeted the plan with enthusiasm. After sometimes arduous negotiations, France, Germany, Italy, and the Benelux states signed the ECSC Treaty in Paris in April 1951 (Gillingham, 1991; Schwabe, 1988).

The subsequent ratification debates in Germany and France were the most important and the most heated. During the debates preceding the climactic votes in December 1951 and January 1952, Schuman, Adenauer, and other supporters of the ECSC in their governing coalitions, set out a variety of economic and security arguments for ratification. At the same time, confronted with principled nationalist opposition, they sought to redefine national identities, external and internal, in ways compatible with the project. Their efforts reflected national differences, but were also marked by certain parallels. Given the disastrous legacy of national suffering and violence, Schuman, Adenauer, and other ECSC backers argued, it made sense to conceive of the nation state not as completely independent and sovereign but as part of a future supranational Europe. The realization of deeper integration was also, they insisted, compatible with the internal dimension of national unity: with the democratic ideals enshrined in the French constitution and the unity pledge of the German Basic Law. Both sets of claims met fierce resistance, mainly from Gaullists, Communists, and Independents in France; and from Social Democrats and Communists in the Federal Republic (Müller-Roschach, 1977; Bjol, 1966; Muller and Hildebrand, 1997).

Schuman, Adenauer, and their supporters sought to recast received conceptions of the nation state as completely sovereign and independent in its external affairs (Schuman, 1960; Weidenfeld, 1976). This involved a particular narrative construction of history. In his original May 1950 initiative, Schuman portrayed integration as a compelling answer to decades of national conflict. "The coming together of the nations of Europe," he argued, "requires the elimination of the age-old opposition of France and Germany." Schuman suggested that it was not Western appeasement or German aggression alone which had made the Second World War possible, but also the balance of power system with its opposing national sovereignties. During the interwar period, he asserted, a "united Europe was not achieved and we had war" (Nelsen and Stubb, 1994: 11–12). For Schuman, the ECSC Treaty of April 1951 marked a new departure. During the crucial December 1951 ratification debate in the National Assembly, he construed the negotiations as a break with the national rivalries of the past. The ECSC was not simply "a compromise among divergent national interests, the result of continual bargaining." It was instead a "common construction to which each participant brought his personal contribution and the ardor of his faith."[5]

Adenauer, too, sought to change the established equation of national identity with full sovereignty in external affairs. He constructed a narrative in which international integration figured as the necessary consequence of national disaster – a catastrophe more complete than in the French case (Banchoff, 1996). In December 1951 in London, one month before ECSC ratification in the Bundestag, he argued that "the catastrophe brought the German people to the realization that an excessive nationalism had more than once destroyed peace." Germany's survival, and that of its neighbors, could "only be maintained within a community that transcends national borders."[6] While Adenauer echoed Schuman's view that national rivalries and the absence of integration had made war possible, he also mentioned a particular obligation of Germans to embrace Europe. "Do not we Germans have the obligation," he asked in a press conference on the occasion of Schuman's declaration, "after we – great numbers of us – assumed tremendous guilt through this war, to place all our spiritual, moral and economic powers in the service of this Europe, so that it becomes a force for peace in the world?" (Schwarz, 1975: 177).

The conception of external national identity set out by Schuman and Adenauer, and the historical narrative that underpinned it, was hotly contested in both France and Germany. Opposition leaders rejected the claim that the ECSC made good economic and security sense. But they also insisted on the continuing necessity of full national sovereignty – and related different narratives to back their claim. In the French case, General Adolphe Aumeran, an Independent who launched the most frontal assault on the Treaty in the National Assembly, insisted that full national sovereignty was necessary to meet the German threat. The cause of repeated wars, he charged, had not been national sovereignties and an unstable balance of power, but an aggressive and criminal Germany. An "egocentric nation" with a "will to power," Germany represented a marked contrast with France, a "nation of good faith and of good will." Those who believed that 1945 marked a sea change and that integration would prevent war were, he argued, living in a "fairy kingdom [*royaume des fées*]" (*Journal officiel*, 1952: 8876, 8881).

Other voices on the right, including Charles de Gaulle, were more moderate. The Gaullists, who represented the single largest parliamentary group in the National Assembly in December 1951, opposed the ECSC in the key ratification debate. But they were by no means committed anti-Europeans. Interestingly, de Gaulle and his followers articulated the federalist ideal during the immediate postwar years. However, their pro-European stance appeared premised upon a weak Western Germany, deprived of the Saar, and of autonomy in the Rhineland and the Ruhr. After the formation of the Federal Republic, which the Gaullists opposed, the party began to shift from a federal to a confederal direction. De Gaulle did initially express qualified support for Schuman's initiative. During the course of 1951, however, with the German rearmament debate in full swing, he grew increasingly wary of integration steps that might compromise French sovereignty. In justifying his party's anti-ECSC stance that December, de Gaulle made a plea in favor of a confederal, rather than a federal, Europe, one "with France standing tall."[7]

German opposition to Adenauer's view of national identity, and the view of the past and its implications upon which it rested, was somewhat more muted. The main opposition Social Democratic Party was not opposed to supranational integration in principle. Nevertheless, party chairman Kurt Schumacher rejected the Schuman Plan. He described it as an effort to undercut German sovereignty and make the FRG economically dependent on others. Moreover, unlike Adenauer, he did not construe 1945 as a sharp break in the underlying dynamics of international relations in Europe. He labeled the ECSC a French national project, "the solidarity of the victors over the vanquished" and an effort to "further French political and economic hegemony in Europe."[8] In view of this perceived continuity in national balance of power politics across the 1945 divide, Schumacher insisted that the Federal Republic should first regain its full external sovereignty and equality before considering steps toward supranational integration.

In both France and Germany, controversy also swirled around the implications of the ECSC for internal national identity. Alfred Coste-Floret, the Christian Democratic leader who presented the French government's case for ratification in the December 1951 Assembly debate, construed Europe as the culmination of the French revolution. He acknowledged that "for the first time in history, the French parliament is being asked to consent to abandon national sovereignty." But he sought to place that step within the revolutionary tradition. "We French," he argued, "have long been in the avant-garde of revolutions of this type, for the happiness of peoples and the prosperity of men" (*Journal officiel*, 1951: 8857). The ECSC, in this view, joined together the specific and universal dimensions of the French revolution; it furthered the goals of freedom, equality, and fraternity at the national and supranational levels. Along the same lines, Schuman insisted that the core ideas in his original May 1950 proposal were, as he put it, "French" ones (*Journal officiel*, 1951: 8894).

In the German context, the debate about the implications of integration for internal identity centered on the problem of national unity. Adenauer insisted that the Federal Republic's integration within the ECSC did not clash with its constitutional commitment to reunification. During the early 1950s, he set out a narrative linking German defeat and occupation; the gradual recovery of sovereignty within Western institutions; and the eventual achievement of national unity. German defeat and occupation, Adenauer argued, made it necessary first to regain the trust of the Western Allies. Integration within the ECSC and other Western institutions would further that trust and spur the recovery of sovereignty lost as a result of the war. And a strong and united West would force the Soviet Union to negotiate reunification on Western terms. As he put it in his December 1951 London address, one month before the final ECSC ratification debate, "We consider the integration of the Federal Republic within Europe a precondition for the realization of this unity by peaceful means, through the voluntary assent of all parts of the German people" (Schwarz, 1975: 236).

The opposition in Germany and France countered these efforts to render the integration process compatible with established internal national identities. Far-right deputies met Coste-Floret's invocation of the ideals of the French revolution with open derision, one even accusing Schuman of wanting "a national revolution in the same sense Petain did!" – in other words, one that sacrificed French independence (*Journal officiel*, 1951: 8863). Aumeran labelled the Schuman plan a "revolutionary act" in the negative sense, a "violation without precedent in the history of the Republic" and a "blow to French institutions" (*Journal officiel*, 1951: 8876). Here, as in the case of external identity, Gaullist objections were more nuanced. In the December debate, Léon Nöel expressed fewer concerns about the impact of the ECSC on French institutions, but did insist that any European construction should respect the powers of national parliaments. France should not place its democratic traditions at the disposal of a future "irresponsible technocracy" (*Journal officiel*, 1951: 8893).

In the German case, opposition leaders rejected Adenauer's claim that the ECSC furthered the constitutional imperative of national unity. Two weeks after Schuman's May 1950 initiative, Schumacher set out his priorities in a party conference speech: "We affirm this state in which we live as a starting point for a higher national unity, and we affirm this higher national unity as a starting point for an even higher international bond" (Albrecht, 1985: 751). Germans, Schumacher argued, should make reunification their top priority; they should conceive of national unity as a starting point, not the end result, of any supranational engagement. Herbert Wehner, another Social Democratic leader, also rejected Adenauer's narrative linking European integration and national unity. In the January 1952 ratification debate, he voiced concern that "inclusion in the so-called 'space of the community'" would make unification with those Germans "who must remain outside this space" difficult (*Verhandlungen*, 1952: 7762).

The juxtaposition of the French and German ECSC debates underscores the extent of the legitimacy problems facing leaders in both countries in the early 1950s. Schuman, Adenauer, and their allies argued that different aspects of national identity – sovereignty and independence, democracy and unity – were compatible with the integration project. In order to do so, they reconceptualized that identity and the narratives that underpinned it. Given the past legacy of nationalist conflict, they argued, sovereignty and independence should best be exercised within a supranational community. And given the legacy of the war and its aftermath, popular sovereignty and national unity – core dimensions of identity in France and Germany – could best be upheld within a broader European context. The resilience of established national identities, evident in the discourse of the main opposition parties, underlined the extent of the EU legitimacy problem in the early 1950s. Received conceptions of national identity in terms of sovereignty, internal and external, continued to resonate across the party spectrum. The final votes in favor of ratification – 377 to 233 in France and 232 to 143 in the FRG – revealed widespread concerns about the compatibility of integration with national identity. Two years later, in 1954, those concerns contributed to the failure in the National Assembly of the European Defense Community (EDC), an effort to extend integration to the security sphere.

The Maastricht ratification controversy

A detailed survey of shifts in national identity amid the European integration process would necessarily address subsequent important controversies: the Treaty of Rome in the late 1950s, the "Empty Chair" crisis of the 1960s, and the "1992" program. Here, the focus is the controversy surrounding Maastricht. While the ECSC marked the launching of the European integration process during the post-war years, the Maastricht Treaty signalled an ambitious attempt to extend it after the end of the cold war. Here, too, the initiative for deeper integration emerged against a shifting international backdrop. After the recessions of the 1970s and early 1980s, European leaders signed the Single European Act in 1986, committing themselves to the completion of a single market by 1992. They also revived the idea of European Monetary Union (EMU) and deeper political integration as subsequent goals to be pursued. The end of the cold war and reunification accelerated efforts in this direction. In an effort to bind the power of a united Germany, François Mitterrand pressed for EMU. And German chancellor Helmut Kohl, eager to embed the new Germany within a firm institutional context, concurred. The Maastricht Treaty of February 1992 committed European leaders to implement a single currency by the year 1999 and included further steps toward political union – a stronger parliament, the creation of a Common Foreign and Security Policy (CFSP), and a European citizenship (Sandholtz, 1993).

In their efforts to secure Maastricht's ratification during the course of 1992, Mitterrand and Kohl confronted complex political constellations. Mitterrand could count on strong support from his governing Socialist Party, the majority of the centrists around Valéry Giscard D'Estaing, and part of the Gaullist party of Jacques Chirac (Guérot, 1996). However, parliamentary debates surrounding necessary constitutional changes in May–July 1992 unleashed controversy, and the Maastricht Referendum held that September engendered a divisive debate. Kohl had the solid support of his Christian Democratic Party, of the Free Democrats, his coalition partner, and most of the opposition Social Democrats. But he also faced the difficult task of securing the support of the Bundesrat, or Federal Chamber, which voted on ratification in December 1992, the same month as the Bundestag. In seeking support for deeper integration, both Kohl and Mitterrand mixed appeals to interest and identity. They claimed that the proposed EMU and CFSP would deliver greater prosperity and security. At the same time, they countered the charge that a deeper European Union threatened national identity and therefore lacked legitimacy. Like Schuman and Adenauer, Mitterrand and Kohl set out narratives which reworked traditional views of national identity, external (states as sovereign abroad) and internal (states as sovereign at home). In rejecting these conceptions of national identity, Maastricht's opponents on both the far right and the far left questioned the legitimacy of the proposed new European construction.

Between the negotiation of the Maastricht Treaty in December 1991 and its ratification by referendum the following September, Mitterrand construed France as inextricably bound within an ever deeper Europe. A particular view of history and its lessons underpinned his stance. When asked on his return from Maastricht why the man on the street should support the Treaty, he recalled the horrendous toll of both world wars. Amid post-cold war uncertainty, he argued, failure to deepen integration risked a reversion to the destructive national rivalries of the past (*Politique étrangère*, December 1991: 151–52). Maastricht made sense not only to prevent a recurrence of the negative interwar pattern, but also to extend its positive postwar counterpart. In a major address in February 1992, Mitterrand argued that EU founders had "turned their history in a new direction" and made war in Western Europe unthinkable (*Politique étrangère*, February 1992: 164). At other points in the run-up to the referendum, he contended that deeper integration followed from French national experience; that France had "an eminent vocation to play a determinant role in Europe," and that "France is our fatherland, but Europe is our future" (*Politique étrangère*, January 1992: 38; June 1992: 122).

Like Mitterrand, Kohl invoked both pre- and postwar narratives in making the case for a European identity for the Federal Republic. "The united Germany wants no return to the Europe of yesterday," he insisted in a major January 1991 government declaration. "Old rivalries and nationalisms should not be allowed to revive" (*Bulletin*, 1991: 73). During the final ratification debate in December 1992, Kohl set out what he considered a crucial question – whether the Germans would "commit ourselves irremovably to economic and political union" or make possible "a reversion to earlier times" (*Verhandlungen*, 1992: 10824). Kohl also insisted on extending the success of postwar integration. He characterized Schuman, Adenauer, and their allies as "men and women who drew the consequences" from Europe's fratricidal wars and inaugurated a successful and ongoing supranational project. Unlike Mitterrand, Kohl did not envision a "determinant role" for his country. But he shared an insistence on the compatibility of national identity and deeper integration. "Germany is our fatherland," Kohl intoned more than once, "Europe our future" (*Bulletin*, 1991: 72).

French and German efforts to construe external identity and deeper integration as compatible met with less resistance than they had four decades earlier. The most articulate opponent of the Treaty in France, the Gaullist Philippe Séguin, rejected the claim that the alternative to deeper integration was a throwback to the instabilities of old.[9] But he also acknowledged the postwar success of integration in making war within Europe unthinkable. In a much-noted address to the National Assembly in May 1992 during a debate on the constitutional implications of Maastricht, Séguin attacked the "cult of federalism," but did not call for a return to the balance of power politics of the past. He expressed concern that deeper integration would abet, not constrain, German power. But he did not advocate an anti-German alliance. France, he reminded his listeners, remains "in solidarity" with the rest of Europe. In the spirit of de Gaulle, Séguin supported Europe, but with France "standing tall." Like de Gaulle, Séguin was averse to further sacrifices of national sovereignty. But he, too, did not advocate the abolition of European institutions already in place. For Maastricht's most influential critic, the reality of the EU constituted a starting point for French policy in Europe (*Journal officiel*, 1992: 863–78).

The German opposition perceived less of a tension between national external identity and European integration. SPD leaders fully embraced Kohl's description of the Federal Republic as an important part of an emerging supranational community. They also echoed Kohl's narrative account of the pre- and postwar periods and their implications for the present. During the debate that followed the Maastricht Summit, a leading party spokesperson, Ingrid Matthäus-Maier, portrayed the "unimaginability" of war in Western Europe as the "most important result of European unification" (*Verhandlungen*, 1991: 5803). And in a September 1992 Bundestag speech, then party chairman Bjorn Engholm argued that rejecting Maastricht risked "the collapse of the European Community as a whole and a reversion to the selfish rivalries with all their results that we know" (*Verhandlungen*, 1992: 9222). Like Kohl, Social Democratic leaders embraced a conception of the FRG not as fully sovereign or aspiring to sovereignty but instead – against the backdrop of its history – as an integral part of an emerging supranational community.

In the 1990s, as in the 1950s, deeper European integration also challenged established conceptions of internal identity – the view of states as sovereign in their internal affairs. In France, with its dominant civic conception of identity, both proponents and opponents of Maastricht considered national political institutions the legitimate expression of popular will. During the referendum campaign, however, Mitterrand insisted that French identity would not be jeopardized through further transfers of sovereignty away from those institutions. The ideals of the revolution, evident throughout the course of French history, would not be diluted within a supranational Europe. French patriotism, he insisted, should be "adapted to new conditions, which will make the country more beautiful and great tomorrow as part of a greater ensemble" (*Politique étrangère*, May 1992: 31). Foreign minister Roland Dumas made a similar point in a different way in the May 1992 National Assembly debate: "Who is going to convince us that a 2000-year-old nation is going to lose its soul through participation in a Europe which she helped to construct?" (*Journal officiel*, 1992: 843).

In the German case, reunification eliminated the tension between national identity and European integration that had existed in the 1950s. Kohl argued that Adenauer's narrative linking integration, Western strength, and the achievement of national unity had been realized (Banchoff, 1997). It was not self-evident, however, that the new Germany, having won its sovereignty from the Four Powers, should entrust a large portion of it to the EU. If the German nation, conceived in terms of shared culture and ancestry, had finally found one political roof, why should it eagerly dismantle it? In this context, Kohl articulated a new narrative linking German unity and European unity. While Adenauer had construed European integration as a means for German unity, Kohl portrayed reunification as an impulse for deeper integration. Upon his return from Maastricht, Kohl called the Treaty "proof that the united Germany actively assumes its responsibility in and for Europe and remains committed to what we have always said, namely that German unity and European unification are two sides of the same coin" (*Verhandlungen*, 1991: 5707).

As in the case of external identity, Mitterrand's efforts at redefinition and narrative reconstruction met with more opposition than Kohl's. In his May 1992 address, Séguin recalled the centrality of "the original pact" between the French state and its people which, "for more than two hundred years has been the foundation" of French politics. He argued that the proposed Europe "buries the principle of national sovereignty and the great principles of the Revolution: 1992 is literally anti-1789." The National Assembly, the expression of the French popular will, should not accept limits on its powers that would break this historical continuity. "Nation, State, and Republic," Séguin asserted, "are the means to construct a Europe compatible with the idea that France has always made of itself" (*Journal officiel*, 1992: 863, 865, 877). Séguin's views also resonated within the Communist Party. Its leader, André Lajoinie, warned in the National Assembly in April that "sovereignty belonged to the French people" and that Maastricht represented "a terrible menace" (*Journal officiel*, 1992: 391).

In the German case, Kohl's insistence that German unity and European unity represented "two sides of the same coin" did not encounter Social Democratic opposition. While some conservative intellectuals criticized the proposed transfers of sovereignty away from a newly unified Federal Republic, their views did not resonate among the major parties (Zitelmann *et al.*, 1993; Schwarz, 1994). What controversy there was swirled not around a threat to national political institutions, or around threats to new-found national sovereignty, but instead around Maastricht's implications for German federalism. The SPD-controlled Federal Chamber withheld ratification until assured a veto right over future transfers of sovereignty. Widespread concerns about states' rights did not, however, indicate a lack of identification with European institutions. With the exception of some outspoken state prime ministers, state leaders generally backed EMU and political union – on condition that the Länder be recognized as active participants in the process.[10]

Like Schuman and Adenauer in the 1950s, Mitterrand and Kohl reworked established national identities in ways compatible with deeper European integration. They argued that a further sharing of national sovereignty would preclude a reversion to interwar instability and extend the success of postwar integration. They also insisted that Maastricht represented not a break, but continuity with defining moments of the national past, the French revolution of 1789 and German reunification in 1990. Mitterrand's effort to legitimate the EU through the narrative reconstruction of French national identity met with considerable opposition. The resilience of traditional conceptions of national identity and established national narratives was evident in the hard-fought 1992 French referendum campaign, which culminated with a razor-thin majority for ratification. In the Federal Republic, by contrast, broad consensus around Kohl's conception of German identity facilitated Maastricht's approval with minimal opposition.[11]

Conclusion

A comparison of the ECSC and Maastricht ratification controversies in France and Germany suggests that the EU legitimacy problem has grown less, not more, pronounced over time. In both cases, efforts to rework national identities in ways compatible with the integration project met resistance. But that resistance was more pronounced in the 1950s, when the major opposition parties in both countries opposed ratification. This overall trend was particularly evident in the German case, where polarization between the major parties gave way to consensus. It was less clear in the case of France: while ECSC ratification was secured by a comfortable majority, Maastricht almost failed in a referendum. However, while party leaders were sharply divided in 1950, a broad pro-integration consensus had emerged four decades later. The 1992 referendum which almost sank the treaty was at least in part a referendum on Mitterrand's presidency. Séguin, Maastricht's most articulate and influential opponent, could not win over Gaullist leader Jacques Chirac. And even he did not call existing European institutions – and the postwar achievements of the integration process – into question.

A comparison of both historical junctures reveals a shift not just in the intensity but also in the nature of the legitimacy problem. During the early 1950s, opponents of integration underscored its incompatibility with the external dimension of national identity – sovereignty in international affairs. French opponents of the ECSC claimed that absolute sovereignty and independence were necessary to prevent a resurgence of aggressive German power, while German opponents warned that integration within the ECSC would advance French hegemony. By the 1990s, the experience of four decades of peace in Western Europe had altered received conceptions of national identity. Even those Gaullists, like Séguin, who opposed any further transfers of sovereignty to the EU, did not perceive – or pursue – a Europe of national sovereignties and rivalries akin to that of the interwar period. In both France and Germany, shifting views of national identity endowed the EU with broad legitimacy as a starting point for the exercise of state interests abroad.

A comparison of debates over internal identity reveals a different pattern. German concerns about tension between European unity and national unity were pronounced in the 1950s, but proved insignificant in the wake of reunification. In the case of France, however, Maastricht raised more internal identity concerns than had the ECSC. This is not surprising given Maastricht's more ambitious political and policy agenda, which included a European citizenship, more powers for the European Parliament, and Economic and Monetary Union. French national identity, and the dominant narratives which inform it, are inseparable from democratic political principles such as popular sovereignty and individual rights. As a result, French leaders may continue to have trouble shifting sovereignty away from national political institutions that remain a powerful locus of national identity. The legitimacy of the EU may hang on whether French leaders can construct a compelling narrative linking deeper integration with revolutionary democratic ideals conceived not simply as French, or as universal, but as European.

Over the postwar decades, French and German leaders have struggled to adjust – not to undo – the national identities forged over the previous century. Eager to integrate their economies for a variety of economic and security reasons, they have sought to redefine received conceptions of national identity in ways compatible with the integration process. This has involved not the recapitulation of nation state-building at the European level, but instead an effort to embed existing nation states within an ongoing and contested process of integration. Broad partisan consensus around the EU as a political fact of life, a starting point for policy in a growing number of areas, attests to the success of this strategy. With the exception of extremist parties on the right and the left, leading political forces in both Germany and France have increasingly come to view their nations as anchored within European institutions, and to recognize the EU as a legitimate framework for politics. The Europeanization of national identity, though still contested, constitutes an important and often overlooked source of EU legitimacy.

Notes

1 For a recent discussion of this external dimension under the label of "state identity," see Katzenstein, 1996.
2 On political legitimacy in general, see Connolly, 1984; Beetham, 1991.
3 On links between national historical narratives and national identity in general, see Renan, 1996; Zerubavel, 1995.
4 Recent empirical work supports this conclusion. See, for example, Wessels, 1995.
5 Ratification Debate of December 6–7, 1951, *Journal officiel*, 1951: 8894.
6 Adenauer address in London, December 6, 1951, Schwarz, 1973: 235. See also his address during the ratification debate of January 9, 1952, *Verhandlungen*, 1952: 7595–600.
7 Cited in Jouve, 1967: 181. De Gaulle used the term "federation" to circumscribe his view of Europe through September 1951, and switched to "confederation" thereafter. See Jouve, 1967: 177–78.
8 Cited in French National Assembly debate, *Journal officiel*, 1951: 8856. During the German ECSC ratification debate of January 9–10, 1952, a number of SPD speakers made this point with reference to the national, anti-German tone of much of the previous month's French debate. See, for example, Dr Henle, *Verhandlungen*, 1952: 7603.
9 On Séguin's views, see Garaud and Séguin, 1992. Other prominent critics included Philippe de Villiers, a centrist, and Jean-Pierre Chevènement, a Socialist. See de Villiers, 1992; Chevènement, 1992.
10 The chief skeptic was Edmund Stoiber of Bavaria. On the role of the Federal Chamber in the ratification process, see Gardner Feldman, 1994.
11 The government did manage a comfortable majority in the May 1992 Assembly vote on the constitutional changes required for ratification, a margin of 338 to 77, with 99 abstentions. The final German votes in the Bundestag and Bundesrat were almost unanimous.

Bibliography

Albrecht, W. (ed.) (1985) *Kurt Schumacher: Reden – Schriften – Korrespondenzen, 1945–52*, Berlin: Dietz.

Anderson, B. (1991) *Imagined Communities: Reflections on the Origin and Spread of Nationalism*, London: Verso.

Banchoff, T. (1996) "Historical Memory and German Foreign Policy: The Cases of Adenauer and Brandt," *German Politics and Society* 14: 36–53.

—— (1997) "German Policy towards the European Union: The Effects of Historical Memory," *German Politics* 6: 60–76.

Beetham, D. (1991) *The Legitimation of Power*, Atlantic Highlands, NJ: Humanities Press.

Bjol, E. (1966) *La France devant L'Europe: La Politique européenne de la IVe République*, Copenhagen: Munksgaard.

Brubaker, R. (1992) *Citizenship and Nationhood in France and Germany*, Cambridge, MA: Harvard University Press.

Bulletin des Presse- und Informationsamtes der Bundesregierung, Bonn.

Chevènement, J. P. (1992) *Une Certaine Idée de la France*, Paris: Albin Michel.

Connolly, W. (ed.) (1984) *Legitimacy and the State*, New York: New York University Press.

Dehio, L. (1962) *The Precarious Balance: Four Centuries of the European Power Struggle*, New York: Knopf.

de Villiers, P. (1992) *Notre Europe sans Maastricht*, Paris: Albin Michel.

Dumont, L. (1991) *L'Idéologie Allemande. France–Allemagne et Retour*, Paris: Gallimard.

Eley, G. and Suny, R. G. (eds) (1996) *Becoming National: A Reader*, New York: Oxford University Press.

Fairclough, N. (1992) *Discourse and Social Change*, Cambridge, MA: Polity Press.

Garaud, M.-F., and Séguin, P. (1992) *De L'Europe en général et de la France en particulier*, Paris: Le Pré aux Clercs.

Gardner Feldman, L. (1994) "Germany and the EC: Realism and Responsibility," *Annals of the American Academy of Political and Social Science* 531: 25–43.

Gillingham, J. (1991) *Coal, Steel and the Rebirth of Europe, 1945–1955: The Germans and the French from Ruhr Conflict to Economic Community*, Cambridge, UK: Cambridge University Press.

Greenfeld, L. (1992) *Nationalism: Five Roads to Modernity*, Cambridge, MA: Harvard University Press.

Guérot, U. (1996) *Die PS und Europa: Eine Untersuchung der europapolitischen Programmatik der französischen Sozialisten 1971–1995*, Bochum: Brockmeyer.

Hobsbawm, E. J. and Ranger, T. (eds) (1983) *The Invention of Tradition*, Cambridge, UK: Cambridge University Press.

Journal officiel de la République Française. Débats Parlementaires. Assemblée Nationale, Paris.

Jouve, E. (ed.) (1967) *Le Général de Gaulle et la Construction de L'Europe (1940–1966)*, Paris: R. Pichon et R. Durand-Auzias.

Katzenstein, P. J. (ed.) (1996) *The Culture of National Security: Norms and Identity in World Politics*, New York: Columbia University Press.

Kupchan, C. A. (ed.) (1995) *Nationalism and Nationalities in the New Europe*, Ithaca, NY: Cornell University Press.

Milward, A. S. (1992) *The European Rescue of the Nation-state*, London: Routledge.

Muller, H. and Hildebrand, K. (eds) (1997) *Die Bundesrepublik Deutschland und Frankreich: Dokumente 1949–1963*, Munich: Sauer.

Müller-Roschach, H. (1977) *Die deutsche Europapolitik 1949–1977: Eine politische Chronik*, Bonn: Europa Union Verlag.

Nelsen, B. F. and Stubb, A. C.-G. (eds) (1994) *The European Union: Readings on the Theory and Practice of European Integration*, Boulder, CO: Lynne Rienner.

Niedermayer, O. and Sinnott, R. (eds) (1995) *Public Opinion and Internationalized Governance*, Oxford, UK: Oxford University Press.

Obradovic, D. (1996) "Policy Legitimacy and the European Union," *Journal of Common Market Studies* 34: 191–221.

Politique étrangère de la France. Textes et Documents, Paris.

Polkinghorne, D. E. (1988) *Narrative Knowing and the Human Sciences*, Albany: State University of New York Press.

Reif, K. (ed.) (1991) *Eurobarometer: The Dynamics of European Public Opinion*, New York: St. Martin's Press.

Renan, E. (1996) "What is a Nation?" in G. Eley and R. G. Suny (eds) *Becoming National: A Reader*, New York: Oxford University Press.

Sandholtz, W. (1993) "Choosing Union: Monetary Politics and Maastricht," *International Organization* 47: 235–69.

Schnapper, D., Gosewinkel, D., Azoulay, F., Ferenczi, T. and Jurt, J. (1996) "Débat sur la Nation," *Commentaire* 19: 315–39.

Schuman, R. (1960) *Pour L'Europe*, Paris: Nagel.

Schwabe, K. (ed.) (1988) *Die Anfänge des Schuman-Plans 1950/51*, Baden-Baden: Nomos.

Schwarz, H.-P. (1994) *Die Zentralmacht Europas: Deutschlands Rückkehr auf die Weltbühne*, Berlin: Siedler.

—— (ed.) (1975) *Konrad Adenauer: Reden 1917–1967: Eine Auswahl*, Stuttgart: Deutsche Verlags–Anstalt.

Smith, A. D. (1992) "National Identity and the Idea of European Unity," *International Affairs* 68: 55–76.

Verhandlungen des deutschen Bundestages. Stenographischer Bericht, Bonn.

Weidenfeld, W. (1976) *Konrad Adenauer und Europa. Die geistigen Grundlagen der westeuropäischen Integrationspolitik des ersten Bonner Bundeskanzlers*, Bonn: Europa Union Verlag.

Wessels, B. (1995) "Support for Integration: Elite or Mass-driven?" in O. Niedermayer and R. Sinnott (eds) *Public Opinion and Internationalized Governance*, Oxford, UK: Oxford University Press.

Zerubavel, Y. (1995) *Recovered Roots: Collective Memory and the Making of Israeli National Tradition*, Chicago, IL: University of Chicago Press.

Zitelmann, R., Großheim, M. and Weissmann, K. (eds) (1993) *Westbindung: Chancen und Risiken für Deutschland*, Frankfurt: Ullstein.

10

POLITICAL RHETORIC AND THE LEGITIMATION OF THE EUROPEAN UNION

John Gaffney

This chapter will examine the role of discourse in the EU integration process, and in particular its function and importance as a political, not just rhetorical, resource for the provision of legitimacy. The aim is to establish that questions concerning the effectiveness and appropriateness of any European discourse or discourses are fundamental to the issue of political legitimacy in the European context, and that the legitimacy of the European Union depends upon the emergence of a European-level political discourse.

National discourses are embedded in national contexts. At the European level, that is, within the European framework of political exchange among elites and between elites and non-elites, the interactions of languages, histories, cultures, symbols, and myths are more fractured and less organized. Moreover, the absence of strong central institutions constrains the effective use of discourse by EU leaders. Anti-European discourse, with its roots in national political contexts, challenges and counters claims to European legitimacy. A European discourse, however, even though it lacks institutional grounding and strong mass allegiance, is not without rhetorical foundation; it therefore has potential as an agency for legitimation. It is the relationship of Europe to national discourses and their evolution, in conjunction with the development of its own institutional setting, which will inform the process of legitimation of European integration. In this connection, the developing trans-European party families, which are experiments in a shared and institutionally supported – and therefore politically oriented – European identity, are of particular significance.

This chapter will discuss some of the political problems surrounding the question of discourse and its links with the problem of legitimacy in the EU. However, two issues first need to be clarified: what we mean by discourse, and what it *does* in politics, both of these points being too often misunderstood or else ignored in the discipline of political studies.

Important in politics *per se*, particularly important in the European context, the study of discourse's political place is almost entirely unresearched.[1] The most essential theoretical point is that discourse is both autonomous and not autonomous from the institutions and practices surrounding it. That is, its enunciation is a moment of the political process, and depending upon its own internal structure and mode of delivery (its rhetoric) as well as its context, it will have the political effects of any political act; its context, however, frames it and will influence its use, non-use, and effectiveness. In terms of our study there are two formative contexts to discourse: first, the institutional framework of the EU and the political relationships within it, and, second, the politico-cultural framework in each of the member states and in Europe as a whole.

An analysis of the role of discourse raises questions of the first importance about the organizational and institutional constraints upon and opportunities for political initiative in the realm of discourse, especially in relation to popular legitimacy and leadership authority. We can take as the general framework of our study the political relationships within the EU as a polity, including national contexts, elite/electorate (citizen) relations, leadership/elite, leadership/electorate relations and, in the wider context, intergovernmental relations predominantly between national executives, and trans- or supranational relations across or beyond national borders. However, these relations, along with other structures, processes, and institutions are not standing structures and relationships, but evolving ones, irrigated – indeed, it could be argued, constituted and sustained – by the perpetual formal and informal flow and exchange of information, in a word, by the discourse within and between them, channeled, directed, and deflected by the institutional relationships within the European polity. This is true of electoral cycles, the role of the media, the "conjunctures" of processes with one another (e.g. the relationships of conservative and social democratic policies to one another at the European level as opposed to the national level), and, at the wider level, the Commission, Council of Ministers, and European Council, and European Parliament, the relationships of these to one another and, in turn, to national governments and electorates. Of course, it is important in this overall discursive framework to note that the most "legitimate" and intense political relationships and exchanges take place within the national contexts. Our analysis will focus upon what this means for the question of a wider political legitimation of European institutions and relations. We shall take political discourse to mean:

> the verbal equivalent of political action: the set of all political verbalisations, and expressible forms adopted by political organisations and political individuals. It generates response which may range from indifference, through hostility, to enthusiasm and which may or may not lead to political action. It is as complex in its inter-relations as political action is. The significance of any instance of political discourse will be affected by its overall relation to political action. And together discourse and action constitute political practice.
>
> (Gaffney 1989: 26)

Discourse and leadership

Leadership discourse offers an excellent illustration of, and is perhaps the most influential or consequential form of, political discourse.[2] This is so for two reasons. The first is that political leadership generally is in a nodal relation to political institutions: without them leadership is severely constrained because institutions legitimate leadership through ritual, sustain its authority and ability to act over time, and supply elite support. The second is that leadership in democratic regimes is in a particular relationship to popular legitimacy. And both of these sets of relationships – between leadership and institutions and between leadership and popular legitimacy – are discursive, that is, they involve organized linguistic exchanges. Given the nature of EU institutions, each of these reasons not only raises important novel questions about leadership, but also the question of the possibilities for a "voiced leadership" in the EU context. A first point to note is that EU institutions are not designed for the leadership purpose as it is understood in the national contexts, and that there is no centralizing institution in which or from which claims to sovereignty, legitimacy, and authority can be made. Second, in the EU the question of popular legitimacy is highly problematic. In terms of the two sets of political relationships necessary to create and sustain political leadership – executive authority, expressed through executive institutions, and popular legitimacy via the suffrage – European leadership is far from assured. A single institutionally supported leadership is at the present time inconceivable, a factor which complicates the problem of legitimacy.

The problem for the researcher when addressing the question of discourse and legitimacy is to assess the *compatibility* of competing and co-existing discourses, and the extent to which these provide a discursive framework for European-level political activity. It is not that there are not leaderships in Europe, but that there is no European-level leadership of the type associated with leadership at the national level. Because of leadership's relationship to political institutions and constituencies, which are themselves primarily national in the first instance, leadership *discourse* is also almost exclusively national in character. There may subsequently be intergovernmental, trans- or supranational manifestations of leadership, but they normally *proceed from* the national, are condoned and controlled by national sites of leadership and, for the reasons we have given, have much less "voice," virulence, and scope.

Such disparity of scale between the national and supranational is not, however, simply because politics is organized institutionally at state and sub-state levels. Magnifying the disparity is the fact that executive and legislative authorities in national states are bound into a popular legitimation that is more complex than simply institutionally derived. Their authority does not proceed from a chosen conferring of political authority which might also be conferred elsewhere; it is, in fact, difficult to conceive of it being conferred elsewhere, which has great significance for our approach to the study of European political legitimacy: national leaderships are enmeshed in a system of mythologies, symbols, and narratives which are themselves organized for the most part in the context of the nation state, and not only cannot be understood without reference to these, but also derive their *authority to act* from this context.[3] In the following section I examine the politico-cultural framework of national politics before going on to examine its implications for European discourse and its role in legitimation.

Discourse and national culture

Let us look briefly at two illustrative examples of national leadership rhetoric in order to illustrate the connections between discourse, legitimacy, and political culture in the national context. Let us turn first to Britain's most famous (and perhaps therefore most misunderstood) example of rousing, inspiring discourse:

> We shall go on to the end. We shall fight in France. We shall fight on the seas and oceans. We shall fight with growing confidence and growing strength in the air. We shall defend our island, whatever the cost may be. We shall fight on the beaches. We shall fight on the landing grounds. We shall fight in the fields. And in the streets. We shall fight in the hills. We shall never surrender.
>
> Winston Churchill, 1940

In what sense can we say that this is a representative example of British or English political discourse? In fact, I have chosen it precisely because, though lyrical and rich in images, it is not. We can identify cultural precursors in Macaulay and in Kipling, for example, but one of the reasons why the European dictators were so disdained by the British population throughout the 1930s and into the war itself was precisely their use of high, emotional rhetoric (newspaper cartoons of the period lampooning Hitler or Mussolini's rhetorical style are revealing here, as is, from the beginning of the war itself, radio comedy). Churchill's rhetoric is, in fact, different even in its sentence structure and intonation from other forms of British discourse. Why, then, was it so effective? For effective it was: from June to December 1940 Churchill's discourse arguably kept Britain as a state in the war, and kept the British as a nation in the war, and kept all other options off the table. How, then, can we argue that it is both exceptional and culture-specific? Within the limits imposed by a chapter of this length we cannot go into detail,[4] but can make one analytical point. In the speech, Churchill is in effect "inventing" our island (see first five sentences), cut off from France (where the encroaching combat was taking place), by the seas and the oceans. More importantly, however, what the speaker is actually offering to the island is not victory, but defeat (see sentences six to eleven): on the beaches of our island where the enemy comes ashore, we fall back to the fields surrounding our towns, then to the streets, then take to the hills. When cornered there, however, we shall not surrender: "We" are retreating. Churchill is in fact offering utter – but heroic – defeat as an imagined prelude to *listener dependency upon the speaker himself,* as the leader of the nation. We can say that the rhetorical power and *effective claim to legitimacy* of Churchill's speech lies in its relation to British political culture, that is, its *unusual* lyricism and *unusual* dramatization of Britain as an island on the eve of engulfment.

Let us briefly take another rhetorical fragment from another national European language, in order to see how different prevailing cultural conditions have different rhetorical and political effects upon claims to national legitimacy. The de Gaulle example we shall use is, of course, another classic example of leadership rhetoric, but here we shall concentrate on what it tells us about the cultural underpinnings of institutionally supported claims to legitimacy.

> Je vous ai compris [I have understood you].
> Charles de Gaulle, June 4, 1958

As the Algerian War drew the French Fourth Republic into political crisis in 1958 and the country to the brink of civil war, de Gaulle, the wartime resistance hero, re-entered the political scene in a very "stage-managed" way. He told the unhappy French that he understood them (it was to the Algiers crowd he spoke but his "real" audience was the French nation). Such communion, particularly at this time, was the essence of de Gaulle's political support. We could say much more here about the cultural significance of the "je/vous" relationship in de Gaulle's thought, what we might call the discursive intimacy between leaders and followers in French politics (to which de Gaulle gave an institutional framework by his 1962 reform of the constitution to elect the president by universal suffrage), and the French attraction to exemplary leaders. What we can say here is that this strongly personalized and romantic element is as integral to French political culture as it is normally inimical to British political culture.

What our brief reference to British and French examples demonstrates is that political discourse is in an intense and complex relationship to its national context. A secondary, though important, point which is implied by the examples we have considered is that national discourse is a rich political/rhetorical resource for highly personalized leadership, and that it is this resource, just as much as the screening out of central leadership institutions by the developing EU, which is missing at the European level.

Discourse and the problem of legitimacy at the European level

For an appraisal of *European* discourse we need, just as in the case of national discourse, to take into account the institutions themselves, the discourses allowed or encouraged by them, the personalities who might make discursive appeals, the constituencies to whom they make such appeals, the channels of such communication, the nature of the appeals, and the cultures or mythologies which underpin both the rhetoric used and the community or communities appealed to. Within the confines of an analysis of this length, we shall concentrate here on the discursive and cultural aspects of these issues.

At elite level, consensus is achieved because of the EU's commitment to its eleven official languages, and because of the elite's multilingualism. However, although the elites are multilingual, the people or peoples are not, and Europe *itself* since 1992 has become a *popular* issue, of both identity and communication *about* Europe *between* Europeans. The Maastricht Treaty and public reactions to it are the clearest manifestations of this. Anti-Europeanism often has been an effective domestic political stance in the member states, to the point where, by the mid-1990s, in several member states lack of popular awareness of the strategic issues involved had led to a bifurcation in which "elite discourse" and "popular discourse" had become the rhetorical representatives of pro- and anti-Europeanism respectively, the latter's main theme being the *illegitimacy* of the Union, in particular of its Commission and bureaucracy.

In fact, we can identify five established types of European-level discourse, each with a limited capacity to promote legitimacy: (1) the discourse of the European bureaucracy; (2) of European-level leadership; (3) of "Utopian" Europeanism; (4) of the elites; and (5) of national leaders about Europe. Let us look at each in turn, before examining the potential for a sixth, emergent discourse of transnational politics originating in European party families.

1 The discourse of the Brussels bureaucracy can be characterized as impersonal, necessarily humorless, and from a rhetorical point of view, dull. It is an administrative discourse.[5] Such a discourse might be "appropriate" to a particular institutional configuration and set of practices, particularly in situations where there are contested issues regarding executive authority. Its required tone is its political disadvantage; to legitimate the bureaucracy it gives voice to, it must restrict itself to the administrative register. Bureaucratic discourse does not inspire the pro-Europeans, and it is despised by the anti-Europeans. For the latter, it is the dull noise itself of the European machinery ticking over, working for the purpose of quietly stealing away the sovereignty of nations. Its deadpan tone is that of all the Union's legislation: its regulations, directives, decisions, recommendations, and opinions, and above all its treaties, especially the 61,000-word and astonishingly dull Maastricht Treaty on European Union. For some, the very dullness of this discourse is proof of its illegitimacy. For the antis, however, in a certain respect this dullness is also welcome. What the Euro-enthusiasts want and what the Euroskeptics do *not* want is the opposite: a rhetorical register that is inspiring, that makes you get up out of your seat; a "European" rhetoric that moves, or that stirs *something*, even if it is only attention, for it is such attention which provides one of the mainsprings of political legitimacy, particularly in phases of institution-building.

2 The limitations of bureaucratic discourse raise the question of the ambiguity surrounding the legitimacy of Europe's institutions, particularly the Commission as an executive, and therefore the dilemma of its discourse(s). The European

Commission could claim to be both a bureaucracy and an executive. It behaves like an executive in certain circumstances, but invariably it *talks* like a bureaucracy. After becoming President of the European Commission in 1985 Jacques Delors played greatly upon the ambivalence surrounding his legitimacy to act as an executive leader. It is arguable whether the President of the European Commission (appointed by the national governments) is an official or a leader. Delors, himself a pro-integrationist, saw his mission as leading the European nations to greater unity, and on a rising tide of integration began his presidency (1985–95) with the style, and discourse and imagery, of a supranational leader. Such comportment and a stream of rhetoric that was both pedagogical and transcendental facilitated the several outcomes of the Single European Act and the Maastricht Treaty. For several years Delors was treated internationally like a government leader or head of state. In the 1990s, however, the tide of pro-integration was dragged back by a relatively sudden undertow of "Euroskepticism." In interviews and speeches in the early and mid-1990s Delors's claims to leadership were dramatically tempered by a more wary defensive approach, more fitting of an administrative officer.[6] There is no doubt that in the future, it is the "earlier" Delors who will take on the status of the visionary pointing the way, but it is worth our noting that it was largely the use and abuse of these two discursive conventions within the Commission (of bureaucracy and of leadership) which allowed Jacques Delors to be such an innovative Commission President (Drake, 1995; Ross, 1995). The institutional norm here, however, is severely constraining of eloquence, and to date it has been only for brief shining moments of opportunity that the transcendental register has been struck with vigor by the Commission.

3 There is a higher pro-European register, as expressed by such organizations as the Federal Trust and the European Movement. These organizations have a certain missionary and Utopian aspect to them, yet are often rhetorically weak, and often suggest a political naivety, even though this is not necessarily justified given the expertise and knowledge of many of their adherents. Such an impression is partly due to their being based upon a world-view that is wary of the stirring rhetoric of the 1930s, partly due to their having no electoral constituency. Historically speaking, theirs is an interesting discourse as it is both transcendental and pan-European, but neither expansionist nor militaristic. Moreover, although it is largely (though not exclusively)[7] the domain of the elites, Utopian pan-Europeanism fits ill with leadership discourse itself, lacking the personalization and vigor characteristic of the latter. This discourse is often exclusive to the continent's political and especially social elites, drawing it even further away from the popular legitimacy of the discourse of nationalism.

4 Related to this "Utopian" discourse is that of the intellectual elites, the "serious" media of most European countries, the research centers, and universities throughout Europe, the think-tanks of most political parties, and the general attitudes and disposition of journalists and commentators. For the most part, this "enlightened" discourse is no less partisan in its underlying belief system: that "Europe" is a good thing, and international exchanges and a cosmopolitan

consensus which transcends national concerns are part of a European intellectual tradition several centuries old. It is extremely difficult to assess the political effect of this discursive disposition, given that it is not strictly related to political activity, but should be seen as an influential background, and the discursive social context of much writing and commentating on Europe. It is probably true to say that it has considerable indirect influence, while remaining thoughtful, intellectual, and restricted to a particular group.

5 An interesting exception to these restricted pro-European registers is the case of leading statespersons, François Mitterrand being the best recent example of this, who could speak "for" Europe with authority and persuasion. It should be remembered that the most recent "tide" of integration, though encouraged by Delors, was begun by national leaders, in particular by President Mitterrand of France and Chancellor Kohl of West Germany in the early 1980s. Moreover, a national leader like Mitterrand could use a higher rhetorical register than a "European" leader like Delors, in that, within the bounds of international protocol and national decorum, a Mitterrand had great rhetorical scope. Moreover, because of the relation of central national institutions to their international environments, what he said would be of great importance. Mitterrand's consistent pro-European appeals gave great strength to European integration in the decade from 1982 till 1992 (Drake, 1994). It should not, of course, be forgotten, however, that Mitterrand's authority to speak was drawn from his *national* legitimacy as an international statesperson.

This brief overview of the five types of discourse in the European arena generates two substantive arguments concerning legitimacy. The first is that, by and large, "European" or pro-European discourse is rhetorically weak and in only a tentative relation to the kind of political support which might sustain it vigorously and over time. The second point is related to this in that such effective supportive discourse as that offered by Jacques Delors and François Mitterrand is in a strong relation to chance and contingency, dependent as it is upon an alignment of individual action, domestic public policy, and international relations, an alignment more suggestive of astronomy than of politics! Is it, then, overall, the anti-Europeans and the nationalists who have the rhetoric – and the rhetorical high ground that goes with it – and the pro-Europeans who do not? This brings us to the question of transnational politics.

Transnational party families and EU legitimacy

Each of the styles and registers mentioned does have "correspondences," echoes in the cultures of each of the European states. Each of the national states has a bureaucratic style. Delors's style and mixing of discourse is not restricted to the French language or to France. The European Movement is similar in each of the member states. Intellectual exchange is cross-national, despite differences across countries. And national leaders resemble one another on a sliding scale running from businesslike and unceremonious to stately and grandiose. And it is not only in pro-European discourse that there are such overlaps. Anti-Europeanism exists in differing degrees in the European states, and there is, paradoxically, something of an "International" of hard-right nationalists. I have argued that these discrete traditions are fashioned according to the institutions and cultures in member states. However, there are also reservoirs of shared experience and perspective which allow Europeans to see themselves as sharing an inheritance.

This, of course, raises questions not only of legitimacy and European integration but of European identity: what, in fact, is being integrated? We can say that many of the shared elements of an identity as well as the shared themes and styles of a European discourse do exist, but are organized into political families: that is to say, that rather than search at the supranational (or subterranean) level for a shared culture (which is not to say that they do not exist at these levels also), we can best identify them in political clusters. At the level of the discursive expression of political ideas there are clusters of expression, sentiment, and allegiance which correspond relatively accurately to the transnational political families: Christian democracy, social democracy, liberalism, international communism, environmentalism, and the ultra-right. There are also other cleavages we can identify, for example a Northern European and Southern European divide, and state and sub-state conflicts of identity;[8] nevertheless, families of political cultures are clearly identifiable. Often membership of the same family stretches credibility to its limits; are the Spanish Socialists and the German Social Democrats really in the same family? Do not the parties from their own country share more with them than people and parties from the other side of the continent? This being said, it is possible that it is at this level that legitimacy within a European polity is to be found. Given the multi-level nature of the EU, movement toward a single identity as a means of legitimating the whole project is impossible. Party families, however, by bringing together affinities across national boundaries while simultaneously conferring value upon a European-level activity, could reinforce a European identity, alongside, rather than in place of, national identity, and thus serve to legitimate the integration project.

The litmus test for the plausibility of the families thesis as a way of imagining the political legitimation of European integration (and perhaps institutional reform) might be – leaving aside here the question of the actual languages involved, though it is a leaving aside which begs many fundamental questions – whether the families can forge a "discourse;" and within and between them are their discourses comprehensible to one another? Can each of the political families acquire a voice, and does the range of voices constitute a "background" or meta-language shared by each or recognized by each? And if we can call this situation one of discursive federalism, are there casualties in this process? The question of sub-state nationalism and of sub-state identity lie outside the scope of this chapter, but it should be mentioned here that there are arguments both for and against the view that European integration and European-level political organization run counter to the interests of regional identities.

In terms of political organization, very loose structures uniting the members of political families have existed for part or all of the twentieth century in the form of the Internationals (socialist, Christian democrat, liberal). More recently, these loose federations have been duplicated essentially, though not exclusively, at the European Parliament level by the creation of the transnational political parties whose aim is to group together and coordinate more effectively the parties within families. We shall not go into detail here on the structure and development of the transnational parties.[9] But in the realm of discourse there has been a considerable convergence within the party groups and families, largely due to their cooperation in the European Parliament, drafting legislation, and organizing joint positions. Such convergence, however, has been accompanied by a certain draining of rhetorical power. The joint political manifestos used at European Parliament elections are a good illustration of how tortuous has been the aligning of the parties' discourses. Over the three elections of 1984, 1989 and 1994 the Party of European Socialists which groups labor, socialist and social democratic parties, has toiled over a joint manifesto – moving from "opt outs" for some parties to a consensus blandness, to a recognition that relative freedom should be left to national parties when translating the manifestos for their respective countries. This has consumed a great deal of labor for documents which, to date, have been for the most part ignored by the national electorates during the European elections campaigns, and even by the national parties themselves.

Nevertheless, socialist, Christian democrat and other European-level discourses have emerged and continue to emerge, not least in the various party and inter-party exchanges with the new political parties of Eastern Europe. Such convergence has been further encouraged by the transnational parties through organized meetings of the leaders of national parties, whether in government or not, on the eve of European Council meetings and Intergovernmental Conferences in order to develop a European-level partisan voice, and one that would be politically effective in negotiations. It is perhaps ironic that the attempts by the parties to make themselves and their European-level activity more coherent have followed *national* models of political competition and cleavages which are clearly manifest at national levels. It is also not without significance that these convergences have taken place most forcefully within the Union's weakest institutions (the Parliament especially), where their political effects are contained and limited. Nevertheless, there is no doubt that a new form of political exchange has emerged in the last decade which is arguably the template for the legitimation of Europe as a political arena. It is also the case that because of their relation to national political parties, and to the question of democratic *representation* at the European level, the activity and discourse of the transnational families will remain significant.

Conclusion

I have argued that discourse is a fundamental element of the political process but that it is seriously under-researched in the discipline. One of the most important and misunderstood aspects of political discourse is that it does not simply enhance leadership, or reflect a political culture, or legitimate political authority; more importantly, it is a formative moment of politics, a *causal* element. Moreover, discourse in the modern period is framed essentially in national terms; this is not only because politics is institutionally organized at the nation-state level but because myths and symbols are deeply embedded in the culture of a nation, and inform the political process. Political actors who draw upon national mythologies and symbols as from a rhetorical resource can derive great tactical advantage in particular circumstances, given the richness of the resource.

It is arguable that in the post-1992 period, anti-European, national discourse, because of its relationship to national symbolism on the one hand and popular national legitimacy on the other, has enjoyed significant rhetorical advantage over pro-European rhetorical claims. Such anti-European developments, however, have sharpened the focus on the rhetorical justifications *for* European integration, just as developments such as German unification have become discursive "sites" informing and widening national debates. There has therefore been a degree of symbolic "spillover" in the area of rhetorical justifications of "Europe," the joining of an EU-wide debate about legitimacy or what would constitute the conditions of legitimacy.

I also identified a range of European-level discourses, politically the most interesting being those of Jacques Delors in the 1980s and 1990s. I have argued that discourse in certain circumstances can have significant political effects. Two points are critical in this regard. First, the EU's institutions and their relations to the media and to popular legitimacy do not lend themselves to what we might term "high" rhetoric such as is used in national polities, and creating the conditions for such use would involve institutional reform, although, as we saw in the case of Delors and of national leaders, "Europe" is not itself screened off entirely from such rhetoric. A second point to note is that, irrespective of institutional change or relationships, the higher rhetoric of national politics is also as it is because of the strength of myths and symbols underpinning national communities.[10] European-level discourse has access to perhaps fewer myths, or at least less powerful ones.

Nevertheless, based upon both the pragmatism and idealism of international cooperation – particularly in the largest political groupings, the socialist/social democrats and the Christian democrats, both of which also have a long tradition of international aspiration – a sustained and organized partisan-based discourse or discourses are emerging, and will continue to take hold if the institutions encourage them (e.g. by strengthening the European Parliament), and skill and imagination are used in the elaboration of transnational party rhetoric.

In terms of European integration, of course, the non-discursive is also determining: the continuing economic integration of the European landmass, and the question of appropriate political representation which such integration implies. It is, however, possible to *imagine* Europe today without recourse to Roman or Napoleonic models of empire. Such imaginings too are undergoing significant change since the post-1989 period. The new East–West dimension, or perhaps its fading salience, lies outside the scope of this chapter, but it is worth stressing how perceptions are changing, given that Eastern and Western Europe *each* regarded the

209

other side as a kind of historical extension of Nazism, and therefore themselves as the *sole* bastion of healthy Europeanism. This no longer is the case and will have profound effects upon how Europe will be perceived and articulated in the future, given that, as has been demonstrated in this chapter, legitimacy and identity are strongly linked to one another.

In terms of a European future, much depends upon what is perceived by the national communities as the European heritage and its representation in discourse. Much of the political heritage of course involves conflict: religious, civil, colonial, revolutionary, reformist, racist, genocidal, misogynist, feminist; it also involves and has involved conflicts and conquests concerning the rule of law, human rights, poverty, and social welfare. These in conjunction with different and conflictual national histories make the notion of a single shared identity difficult. Perhaps the answer, and an appropriate discourse too, lies not at the level of history but of culture. It may be the combination of shared and separate histories which makes a rich and diverse culture possible. It is perhaps discursive exchanges at this level of a common political purpose and future shared culture which will provide legitimacy for European political development.

Notes

1 While the study of discourse has an extensive literature, there is a gap in the analysis of the relation of discursive to political practice, that is, the "effects" of discourse on politics. The difficulty is compounded by the interdisciplinary nature of the relation. The most extensive research in this area has been done in the United States, particularly regarding the role of presidential rhetoric. See Atkinson, Calloway-Thomas and Lucaites, Decaumont, Drake, Gaffney (1989, 1991a), Jamieson, Kohrs Campbell and Jamieson, Wills, and Windt and Ingold in bibliography for representative examples of the study of discourse and its place in the political process.

2 See, for example, J. Gaffney (1993) "Language and Style in Politics," in Carol Sanders (ed.), *French Today*, Cambridge, UK: Cambridge University Press, pp. 185–98.

3 There is a wide range of literature on this area of political study which spans political anthropology, symbolic interaction theory, and leadership studies. There is little literature on this in terms of the EU (see Ross and Abélès in bibliography). For a recent case study on the symbolism of leadership, see L. Milne (1997) "The Myth of Leadership", in J. Gaffney and L. Milne, *French Presidentialism and the Election of 1995*, Aldershot, UK: Ashgate.

4 The author is currently researching for a study of leadership in this period where greater detail is given concerning the rhetoric of speeches and their effects; see also J. Gaffney (1992) "Churchill and 1940," Harvard University, Center for European Studies, November, and Gaffney (1995) Lunar Society Lecture, "The Politics of Language and European Integration," Birmingham, October.

5 It is true that within the bureaucracy there are many different "voices" (the Directorates General and the various levels within them). Publicly, however, one voice prevails.

6 For a detailed analysis of Delors's discourse and how it shifted from one register and leadership style to another, see Helen Drake, "Jacques Delors and the Discourse of Political Legitimacy," in Drake and Gaffney (1996).

7 Variations on this discourse include the discourse of leftist internationalism such as that of the Spanish Civil War, or the discourse of the various peace movements.

8 These differences also raise interesting questions such as whether "quietest" rhetoric is

more Northern European than Southern, and what sub-state variations come into play, and how.

9 See Simon Hix, "The Transnational Party Federations;" Robert Ladrech, "Political Parties in the European Parliament;" and Julie Smith, "How European are European Elections?" in Gaffney (1996).

10 For an arguably opposite view, that "national" myths are not necessarily as strong as is generally assumed, see C. Fieschi (1997) "The French Extreme-right: Filling the Ideological Vacuum", European Community Studies Association Conference, Seattle, WA.

Bibliography

Abélès, M. *et al.* (1993) *Approche Anthropologique de la Commission Européenne*, unpublished report.

Atkinson, M. (1984) *Our Masters' Voices*, London: Methuen.

Bréchon, P. (1994) *Le discours politique en France*, Paris: Documentation française.

Calloway-Thomas, C. and Lucaites, J. (1993) *Martin Luther King and the Sermonic Power of Discourse*, Tuscaloosa, AL: University of Alabama Press.

Chevalier, J. *et al.* (1994) *L'Identité politique*, Paris: PUF.

Decaumont, F. (ed.) (1991) *Le Discours de Bayeux*, Paris: Economica.

Delahaye, Y. (1979) *L'Europe sous les mots*, Paris: Payot.

Deloye, Y. *et al.* (1996) *Le Protocole ou la mise en forme de l'ordre politique*, Paris: L'Harmattan.

Dolan, F. and Dumm, T. (eds) (1993) *Rhetorical Republic*, Amherst, MA: University of Massachusetts.

Drake, H. (1994) "François Mitterrand, France and European Integration," in G. Raymond (ed.) *France during the Socialist Years*, Aldershot, UK: Dartmouth.

—— (1995) "Political Leadership and European Integration: The Case of Jacques Delors," *West European Politics* 18, 1: 140–60.

Drake, H. and Gaffney, J. (eds) (1996) *The Language of Leadership in Contemporary France*, Aldershot, UK: Dartmouth.

Gaffney, J. (1989) *The French Left and the Fifth Republic: The Discourses of Socialism and Communism*, London: Macmillan.

—— (1991a) *The Language of Political Leadership in Contemporary Britain*, London: Macmillan.

—— (1991b) "Labour Party Attitudes and Policy towards Europe," *Current Politics and Economics of Europe* 1, 3–4: 213–40.

—— (ed.) (1996) *Political Parties and the European Union*, London: Routledge.

Girardet, R. (1986) *Mythes et mythologies politiques*, Paris: Seuil.

Jamieson, K. H. (1988) *Eloquence in an Electronic Age*, Oxford, UK: Oxford University Press.

Kohrs Campbell, K. and Jamieson, K. H. (1990) *Deeds Done in Words*, Chicago: Chicago University Press.

Labbé, D. (1977) *Le Discours communiste*, Paris: PFNSP.

—— (1990) *Le Vocabulaire de François Mitterrand*, Paris: PFNSP.

Rivière, C. (1988) *Les Liturgies politiques*, Paris: PUF.

Ross, G. (1995) *Jacques Delors and European Integration*, New York: Oxford University Press.

Wills, G. (1992) *Lincoln at Gettysburg: The Words that Remade America*, New York: Simon and Schuster.

Windt, T. and Ingold, B. (1992) *Essays in Presidential Rhetoric*, Dubuque, IA: Kendall.

Wolton, D. (1993) *Naissance de l'Europe démocratique*, Paris: Flammarion.

11

CONCLUSION

Thomas Banchoff and Mitchell P. Smith

Many observers have expressed concern about the legitimacy of the European Union without considering what constitutes legitimacy in a polity that is not a conventional nation state. This volume has sought to address this shortcoming by defining a legitimate polity as a recognized framework for politics with representative institutions, and by underscoring the particular dynamics of recognition and representation in the multi-level EU.

The book's empirical chapters suggest three general conclusions about the sources of legitimacy in the European polity. First, a broad range of actors, including national political parties, trans-European business elites, organized labor, and officials of local and regional governments, increasingly articulate and pursue their interests through the European Union. Since the 1980s, these actors have come to recognize the EU as a starting point for politics across a growing range of policy areas. Second, the resulting political contestation takes place at an array of sites, within and around EU institutions, and engenders new patterns of political representation. Some of these patterns are evident at the national level, where parties are placing European issues on the political agenda; others cut across levels of governance, such as regional or national interest group mobilization in Brussels. Third, identification with the EU should not be conceptualized as a process of creating a unified European identity, especially not one that supplants existing national and regional counterparts. Identities which are contrasting but compatible are well suited to the complex and contested politics of the multi-level European polity.

Table 11.1 depicts the sources of EU legitimacy that emerge from the empirical analyses of policies, institutions, and identities in the individual chapters. As the table indicates, the legitimation of the European Union does not rely exclusively upon EU institutions, but also depends very substantially on the responses of *national* institutions to European integration. Any effort to conceptualize the dynamics of legitimacy in the EU must be attentive to the existence and interaction of multiple levels of governance within the European polity. There is no single European people that can collectively recognize the EU as a legitimate polity. And there are no strong central institutions capable of providing for direct, democratic representation of such a people at the European level. Instead, there exists a variety of peoples with multiple identities, in which the national component is

212

Table 11.1 Sources of legitimacy

Sources of legitimacy	Level of governance	
	National	*European*
Policies	Political actors, such as leaders of political parties, see integration as a means of achieving national projects (Marks and Wilson)	Contestation of economic and social policies mobilizes a range of actors to articulate and pursue their interests through EU institutions; focus on "European model" of society (Smith); cultural policy reinforces national and subnational identities and celebrates diversity (Pantel); CFSP process promotes value of reconciliation (Gardner Feldman)
Institutions	"Perceived irrelevance" of national political parties stemming from globalization processes renders the EU an attractive arena for practical problem-solving; national political parties, therefore, increasingly serve as representative links between European publics and the EU (Ladrech)	EU institutions becoming more open and responsive, particularly through informal channels (Banchoff and Smith); EP playing larger role in accountability and in interaction with European society (Wessels and Diedrichs)
Identities	National discourse (Gaffney); restructuring of national identities (Banchoff)	EU citizenship separates nationality from citizenship and sanctions multiple, compatible identities (Koslowski)

strongest, and a variety of interlocking representative institutions – European, national, and subnational – of which the European Parliament is only a part. Generalizing from the empirical chapters, the next two sections illustrate the dynamics of recognition and representation in the EU, and their implications for the problem of legitimacy within a multi-level polity.

Recognition: contestation and multiple identities

Since the relaunch of European integration in the 1980s, EU policies have created their own politics; governments, bureaucracies, parties, and interest groups increasingly have sought to shape policy and the allocation of collective goods at the European level. These actors are, of course, engaged in the pursuit of concrete interests; the legitimation of the EU is, in most cases, not among their priorities. However, in shifting political activity toward European institutions as a new – but not exclusive – framework for politics, interests that have become active at the European level legitimate European governance in practice. Both Mitchell Smith, in his study of debates over the "economic constitution" of the EU, and Lily Gardner Feldman, in her discussion of the Common Foreign and Security Policy (CFSP) as a forum for projecting EU values abroad, illustrate how this contestation gives substance to the European polity and promotes, rather than weakens, its legitimacy. Smith points out that both sides of industry have objections to the single market program: portions of the business sector complain about its dirigiste elements, while labor bemoans its laissez-faire character. Nevertheless, both business and labor increasingly recognize the EU as a venue for articulating and pursuing their interests. A similar pattern holds in the case of the CFSP. Gardner Feldman acknowledges the shortcomings of the CFSP, but establishes that Europeans recognize the positive legacy of postwar reconciliation upon which it rests. While member states continue to clash over the CFSP from case to case, they recognize the EU as an appropriate forum to contest foreign and security policy.

The link between contestation and legitimacy also is apparent in the activities of national political institutions. For example, national parties, faced with their own crisis of legitimacy at home, have become increasingly active at the European level, as Robert Ladrech demonstrates. In view of the growing salience of EU policy-making, they have sought to overcome an emerging sense of impotence through engagement in EU governance. National parties have placed European issues higher on national agendas, making the EU seem less alien and more relevant to their electorates. The self-interested pursuit of political objectives has spawned recognition of the EU as a framework for politics. Similarly, Gary Marks and Carole Wilson find that while the main political parties in West European countries continue to interpret the European integration project through the lens of national political objectives, their attitudes about the compatibility of national and EU objectives have changed. As a result, while parties are motivated by different national policy projects, members of most parties have developed a somewhat more favorable view toward European integration. This is especially true of social democratic parties, which increasingly view the EU as a vehicle for the pursuit of objectives that have become elusive at the national level since the 1980s.

Recognition of a political system by its citizens is not only a product of political activity; it is also a matter of identification. The peaceful coexistence of identities – subnational, national, and European – constitutes a form of recognition appropriate to a multi-level polity. The Maastricht ratification controversy saw an outburst of concern about threats to national identities as a consequence of deeper European integration. The far right seized upon the issue, insisting that any transfers of national sovereignty were illegitimate. And the proponents of deeper integration were compelled to acknowledge the absence of a European identity as intense as its national counterparts. However, as a number of the contributors to this volume maintain, in the context of European integration, a contested and open-ended process, it is not the supremacy of European identity but its compatibility with national and subnational identities that is most crucial for legitimacy.

214

In contrast to the conventional view that established national identities represent an obstacle to the legitimation of the EU, individual chapters suggest that their persistence – and conscious efforts to celebrate their diversity – may in fact enhance EU legitimacy. The debate over whether there is – or can be – a shared European culture and European identity is a divisive one. But, as Melissa Pantel points out, the Commission's approach to cultural policy, with its focus on unity-in-diversity, recognizes the irreducible existence of multiple identities in Europe. Acknowledgment of this diversity, she argues, represents the only workable starting point for any successful, broadly recognized EU cultural policy. Rey Koslowski makes a parallel argument for EU citizenship, which, unlike its state-level counterparts, does not coincide with an overarching nationality. EU citizenship incorporates a bundle of rights and duties that do not presuppose any underlying cultural unity. As such, this citizenship potentially constitutes a foundation for civic European identity that complements, rather than replaces, established national identities. Positive attitudes toward European citizenship suggest its potential as a source of EU legitimacy.

Furthermore, the substance of national identity can reinforce rather than erode EU legitimacy. Thomas Banchoff demonstrates this in his study of French and German debates about national identity. As Banchoff explains, leaders in both countries have sought less to foster a shared sense of European identity than to redefine national identities in ways compatible with the integration project. A comparison of political discourse in both countries in the 1950s and 1990s reveals the relative success of such efforts; the leaders of most major parties have come to reconceive the nation not as fully independent and autonomous, but as part of a cooperative integration project. In a similar fashion, John Gaffney does not dispute the widely observed claim that national rhetoric clearly remains more authoritative than European political discourse. Without much emotional resonance or institutional basis, European-level discourse is comparatively weak. However, Gaffney does propose that national discourses about Europe themselves point toward greater engagement in European-level policy-making and recognition of the EU as a starting point for politics in a number of areas. Both the Banchoff and Gaffney chapters suggest that national, not European, discourse is vital for the legitimation of the EU as an ongoing process in which states are implicated and transformed, but not subsumed.

Representation: informal patterns and multi-level institutions

The book also demonstrates the implications of emergent patterns of representation for the EU legitimacy problem. For most political theorists, as for most observers of and participants in EU politics, legitimacy is coterminous with democratic legitimacy. Democracy entails not only the consent but also the rule of the people. Political legitimacy in a democratic context requires representative links between government and the governed. The debate about a "democratic deficit" has attacked the underdevelopment of those links in the EU context. However, much of this criticism is based on conceptions of democratic representation with limited relevance for the EU. Within the context of a multi-level polity marked by the fusion of different policy-making instruments, the European Commission and Parliament cannot approximate the role of an executive and legislature on the national model. While these institutions perform important representative roles, their relations to citizens are not identical to those of executives and legislatures in the national context. An exclusive focus on European institutions, moreover, obscures ways in which democratic representation at other levels – and the national level in particular – *can* legitimate EU governance. A lack of transparency and the predominance of narrow functional interests still contribute to problems of democracy in the EU. But developments since the relaunching of European integration in the 1980s have spawned new, important forms of representation too often overlooked in the scholarly literature.

For example, the role of the European Parliament (EP) is not captured by either intergovernmentalist or federalist approaches, as Wolfgang Wessels and Udo Diedrichs convincingly argue. While it has increased its policy competences, the EP remains far removed from a traditional legislature on the national model. It still has to improve its links with European society, where it has considerable reserves of popular support. Here, the direct electoral connection is not unimportant. But due to diverse electoral systems and the tendency of national issues to shape EP campaigns, we are unlikely to see the emergence of a cohesive European party system in the foreseeable future. Increasingly, the EP's political importance derives from its more significant post-Maastricht role in the EU legislative process, and its growing links with national parties and interest groups mobilized around it. Ladrech's chapter demonstrates this latter dynamic clearly. In response to the growing importance of EU policy-making, national parties have also sought to join forces with like-minded parties from other states. The European-level party cooperation that results – alongside party groups already organized within the EP – provides an additional representative link between European institutions and citizens.

The Commission, too, has an important representative role not captured by traditional conceptions of the executive. Smith shows how recognition of the EU as a framework for the contestation of the social dimension of the single European market has sparked the mobilization of diverse societal interests. As part of a reaction to the liberalization wrought by the single market and the intensification of regulation by the EU, representatives of business and labor interests increasingly have sought to articulate their concerns, and those of their constituents, at the EU level. This mobilization has taken place alongside – and not in place of – existing patterns at the national level. As Smith argues, the Commission is not only an actor, but also a site of contestation. Moreover, the Commission has extended its efforts to expand links with interest groups.

Pantel and Koslowski illustrate how this dynamic has emerged in other contexts. Pantel notes that through its encouragement of unity-in-diversity in cultural policy, the Commission has increased its links with national and subnational groups and encouraged the articulation of their interests at the European level. And Koslowski shows how the Commission's initiatives on citizenship policy, in particular efforts to extend voting rights to EU nationals living abroad, have expanded political participation.

In addition to these informal roles of EU institutions, the national level of governance also contributes to legitimation of the European construct. As states become embedded within a multi-level polity, their representative institutions can serve to legitimate the EU as a whole. In this regard, the emergence of European issues in national politics is particularly important. By placing the EU on the national agenda, party leaders have made national political processes, from elections to legislation, occasions for European citizens to influence the integration process. The major parties across the EU increasingly have portrayed European issues in terms of familiar cleavages, making integration seem less foreign. Furthermore, most have insisted that the European Union does not pose a threat to existing national identities.

Marks and Wilson demonstrate that the greater salience of European policy-making since the 1980s has not led to a negative reaction at the domestic political level. Anti-Europe parties have emerged, but the main party families – social democratic, liberal, Christian democratic, and conservative – continue to support the integration process. Political contestation around Europe has shifted from a nationalist–European axis to a left–right axis pitting a social democratic against a neoliberal vision. As European issues move up the national agenda, national party competition increasingly provides a means for European voters to shape the integration process. These new patterns of contestation around the EU at the national level do not necessarily presage the emergence of a cohesive European party system. John Gaffney notes that differences in national political culture and discourse are obstacles to coherent European parties. National parties possess both traditions and institutional bases that their European counterparts do not. However, to the extent that national parties come to see themselves, and their states, as bound up within the integration process, they may be able to increase cooperation further with like-minded parties in other member states. In this scenario, European publics will not only be voting more on European issues in national elections; they will simultaneously, if indirectly, come to exert influence on the politics of the EU.

Banchoff's focus on national identities in France and Germany demonstrates an additional way in which national politics can legitimate European governance. National ratification debates at critical junctures like Maastricht not only revolve around interests, they also reveal changing and contested conceptions of national identity. Banchoff shows how French and German party leaders have been able to portray their countries as inextricably bound within the integration process, fending off the attacks of nationalists in the process. National debates about identity have important implications for legitimacy. Where national identity is redefined in European terms, for example, it is less difficult to incorporate EU citizenship provisions into national law, a process that Koslowski analyzes. And where nationalist

217

objections to transfers of sovereignty are defused, domestic political debates about Europe can shift from the nationalist–European to the left–right axis, a process that Marks and Wilson document. Within a multi-level polity, political processes at both European and national levels have important implications for the problem of legitimacy.

Conclusion: legitimacy in a contested polity

The patterns of recognition and representation outlined in this book underscore the dual nature of the EU as a contested polity. On the one hand, the EU is emerging as an increasingly salient framework for political conflict. More and more political actors are engaged at the European level. On the other hand, the EU's institutional make-up is complex, evolving, and itself contested. While contestation has spawned recognition of the EU as a framework for politics, the contested, evolving character of the EU has generated new forms of representation. Approaching the EU neither as an international organization nor as a European super-state in the making, but as a multi-level, contested polity, casts its legitimacy problem in a new light. This analytical step suggests different approaches to both dimensions of legitimacy – recognition and representation – and their possible future evolution.

That future evolution is far from clear. Ultimately policy contestation can erode rather than bolster legitimacy if it begins to undermine the perception shared by political actors that the EU is a productive route to pursuing their interests. In this connection, many observers have pointed to the emergence and persistence of far-right parties and movements opposed to the EU as a threat to this perception. However, the initial successes of these parties after Maastricht did not rupture the pro-Europe consensus among most major parties in Europe. Still, the EU's two major projects at the turn of the century – monetary union and expansion eastward – have the potential to spark a nationalist backlash against EU governance. National currencies have symbolic resonance; their loss could mobilize nationalist opponents. So too could economic or social problems that might accompany the introduction of the euro. Similarly, the costs of enlargement to East and Central Europe could provoke bitter national debates about EU membership. The contributions to this volume suggest that both outcomes are less likely than critics propose. The years since the Maastricht ratification crisis indicate a broadening of recognition of the EU as a framework for politics. The increasingly shared perception that the benefits of interest articulation at the European level exceed the costs will not quickly be reversed. A wide range of actors now perceives opportunities to realize their interests at the European level that they believe have diminished at home.

There is also a point at which the contested nature of EU institutions can undermine the legitimacy of the European construct. Given the complexity of the EU institutional set-up, stable forms of democratic representation are difficult to generate and sustain. The absence of familiar central mechanisms – and of overall transparency – will continue to raise questions about legitimacy. Answers to these questions will depend in part on how parties and interest groups combine their activities on the national and European levels. Perceptions of EU legitimacy also will depend on European institutions themselves; whether they can work together in ways that secure interest articulation and political participation from below. Here, too, the challenges of monetary union and enlargement are complicating factors. A single currency may lead to an even greater role for the EU in economic policy, and may place tremendous power in the hands of an appointed board of the European Central Bank, refocusing attention on the issue of democratic representation. And expanded EU membership has the potential to make existing forms of representation – in and outside the EP – unwieldy and inadequate. Therefore, the critical question confronting the EU will be whether the integration process can continue to broaden patterns of democratic representation in the face of these challenges.

The end to the "permissive consensus" in the 1990s placed the legitimacy issue at the center of EU politics. It awoke many Europeans to the fact that more and more decisions affecting their lives were being made at the EU level. Political controversy underscored the seriousness of the legitimacy problem, but ultimately revealed the reserves of legitimacy that the EU possesses. European policies and institutions increasingly are the object of popular dissatisfaction and critical public scrutiny. Such critical examination has not, however, threatened the overall stability of the EU. Instead, it has made EU policies and institutions the object of greater recognition and a target of more intense mobilization, which in turn has spawned new forms of representation. Like the nation states that comprise it, the European Union will continue to struggle with the problem of political legitimacy. But it will do so in ways that reflect its character as a contested, multi-level polity.

INDEX